Fruteros

The publisher and the University of California Press Foundation gratefully acknowledge the generous support of the Lisa See Endowment Fund in Southern California History and Culture.

Fruteros

STREET VENDING, ILLEGALITY, AND
ETHNIC COMMUNITY IN LOS ANGELES

Rocío Rosales

UNIVERSITY OF CALIFORNIA PRESS

University of California Press
Oakland, California

© 2020 by Rocío Rosales

Library of Congress Cataloging-in-Publication Data

Names: Rosales, Rocío, 1983– author.
Title: Fruteros : street vending, illegality, and ethnic community in
    Los Angeles / Rocío Rosales.
Description: Oakland, California : University of California Press, 2020. |
    Includes bibliographical references and index.
Identifiers: LCCN 2019052050 (print) | LCCN 2019052051 (ebook) |
    ISBN 9780520319844 (cloth) | ISBN 9780520319851 (paperback) |
    ISBN 9780520974166 (epub)
Subjects: LCSH: Street vendors—California—Los Angeles. | Ethnic
    neighborhoods—California—Los Angeles. | Immigrants—California—
    Los Angeles—Social conditions. | Hispanic Americans—Social
    conditions. | Latin America—Emigration and immigration.
Classification: LCC HF5459.U6 R67 2020 (print) | LCC HF5459.U6
    (ebook) | DDC 381/.180979494—dc23
LC record available at https://lccn.loc.gov/2019052050
LC ebook record available at https://lccn.loc.gov/2019052051

Manufactured in the United States of America

28 27 26 25 24 23 22 21 20
10 9 8 7 6 5 4 3 2 1

Para mis padres, Gloria y Jesús.

A mi mamá que me enseñó como observar.

A mi papá que me enseñó como contar una buena historia.

Contents

Illustrations

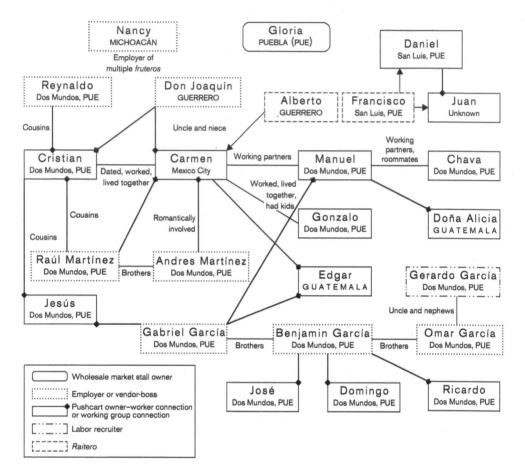

Figure 1. Fruit vendor *paisano* network.

1 Introduction

Jesús was the first *frutero* I visited regularly and befriended.[1] He was one of the thousands of street vendors who, on a daily basis, fanned out across the city of Los Angeles and became part of the urban landscape (see figure 1). Fruit vendors (*fruteros*) in the city are distinctive.[2] They work behind large pushcarts weighed down by many pounds of produce and ice under rainbow-colored umbrellas (see figure 2). On their street corners, *fruteros* prepare and sell made-to-order fruit salads.

Jesús was clearly perplexed at my presence in the beginning; I asked too many questions, and I stood too close to him because his infrequent and soft-spoken responses were barely audible above the constant din of street traffic. At five feet six, he was two inches taller than me, but he never stood straight, so we were mostly at eye level. He was twenty-one years old when I met him in 2006. He was slender and dark skinned with a wispy mustache and goatee. His standard uniform included dark wash, loose-fitting jeans with arabesque tan stitching over the back pockets and an equally loose-fitting black hoodie. Jesús never looked directly at me. He always kept his eyes directed down at the waist-level tray table where he prepared fruit. Oftentimes while talking, he would wipe a wet rag across the cutting board and tray table to busy his hands and give

Figure 2. A *frutero* working in central Los Angeles.

his downward gaze a purpose. Jesús sold made-to-order fruit salads on Pico Boulevard.

Pico Boulevard runs from downtown Los Angeles all the way to the coastal city of Santa Monica. Standing along it, one is visible to thousands of passing motorists and pedestrians. Fruit vendors work out of large and heavy pushcarts; through the Plexiglas tops of these pushcarts, customers can see and pick which fruits and vegetables they want to include in their prepared-on-site fruit salads. Service is always quick: less than three minutes after making a selection, customers have a clear plastic bag or cylindrical plastic container of chopped fruits and vegetables in hand, garnished with salt and chili powder, with a plastic fork sticking out and inviting the customer to dig in.

One day, after two weeks of almost daily visits, I was late leaving campus and arrived at the vending site after the 3 p.m. school pickup rush. When I approached, I saw that his pushcart was nearly empty. "I almost thought you weren't coming today," he told me. "I don't have any good fruit left."[3] My favorite items were also the most popular: watermelon, cantaloupe, pineapple, and mango. He offered to prepare a bigger-than-usual fruit salad with the less popular leftover items: cucumber, coconut, papaya, and on this occasion, oranges. I agreed. I came for the conversation, not for the fruit.

"Do you work every day?" I asked.

"I keep bank hours," he replied and then laughed at my puzzled face. With his knife he gestured toward the bank he was standing in front of and said that he worked six days a week, with reduced hours on Saturdays, and was closed on Sundays.

"Are the bank customers your customers?"

"Some of them. I can give them smaller bills after they visit the [ATM] machine. But I get school kids and people who ride the bus and people going to work." With his chin he motioned to a passing bus behind me. A westbound bus making local stops brought a steady stream of people every twenty to thirty minutes during off-peak hours. I rode the bus to get to Jesús's corner as well. The Big Blue Bus, a bus system based out of the city of Santa Monica, would leave me half a block past the bank where he worked, so I often saw him through the large bus windows tending to customers as I arrived.

Throughout the following weeks, I varied my arrival times to get a sense of Jesús's workday. Some days, I arrived late and helped him put things away; other days I arrived early and watched him set up. The days were routine and mundane, and when Jesús did not have customers, he texted friends and family on his phone. He talked about getting bored often and explained that he was trying to learn how to nap while standing up. Figuring out successful leans to achieve this became part of an ongoing conversation.

It took many visits before I felt comfortable talking about issues related to immigration status. The topic eventually came up when Jesús asked me, "Do you have legal status papers?" I explained that I was born in Texas to Mexican immigrant parents. Jesús was from a small, rural town in the Mexican state of Puebla and had arrived in the United States only a few months before I met him. Though he had entered into the country without authorization, he knew he had a job waiting for him as a fruit vendor. A former neighbor in Puebla who now lived in Los Angeles had promised him the job. Jesús had a wife and two young children in Puebla. He intended on returning to them just as soon as he made enough money to pay for his wife's medical bills. During each of my visits, I would learn something new and interesting about Jesús and his job.

One midweek day after a couple of months of visits, the bus I was riding passed the bank, but there was no sign of Jesús. I thought I might stay aboard to visit other vendors further along the boulevard but decided to walk to his corner and ask the parking lot attendant if he knew anything about Jesús's absence. Along the curb next to the sidewalk where Jesús usually parked his pushcart, I saw a melting pile of crushed ice.

Had I just missed him? Why would he leave so early in the day? It was the Salvadoran parking lot attendant who answered all of my pressing questions. The health department had done a "sweep." They had dumped Jesús's produce into large trash bags and, before taking the pushcart, had asked him to dump out all of the remaining ice onto the sidewalk.

"Did they arrest him?" I asked, thinking immediately that it could be related to Immigration and Customs Enforcement. I was told Jesús had been given a ticket and was picked up by some of his friends right after the incident.

"I don't understand," I said, trying to make sense of all the details.

The attendant shrugged and said bluntly, "It is illegal to be a street vendor."

At that point, I had no sense of how crackdowns worked or how often they occurred. I was immediately full of questions: If vending was illegal, how did street vendors reconcile their occupation's public and conspicuous presence with an illicit activity's need to remain private and hidden? Was the money that vendors made sufficient to counterbalance the loss of income from a crackdown? Could the items confiscated be recovered? The questions I had that day only scratched the surface of the complicated relationship street vendors have with the city. This was further complicated when other actors—like business improvement districts, neighborhood associations, and street gangs—became involved. What proved even more interesting was the *paisano* network that helped fruit vendors withstand this and other assaults on their economic and social wellbeing. Though a *frutero* works on a street corner alone, he is often part of a large network of *fruteros* who are also his *paisanos* (hometown associates).[4] In this way, he is not alone.[5] It was the complicated web of relations within that *paisano* network that captured my sociological imagination.

While *fruteros* are ubiquitous in the city, few know much—if anything—about them. This is an account of their lives as migrants, as workers, and as members of an ethnic community.[6] This is a story about immigrant adaptation among entrepreneurial newcomers in a hostile context of reception. The presence of *fruteros* on street corners throughout the city represents a confluence of larger social and economic forces. *Fruteros* are labor migrants who have crossed international borders in search of improved economic opportunities. Because most of them are undocumented, they confront obstacles that prevent them from legally participating in the formal economy. However, they are socially networked into the informal fruit vending occupation through strong hometown ties. These hometown, or *paisano,* ties come to define their work and personal lives in the United States in powerful and meaningful ways.

Migration scholars have long documented how newcomers lean on their community of *paisanos* for assistance on arrival. Immigrant social networks and the social capital that they provide to their members are important sources of support in the lives of newcomers.[7] Yet the experiences of *fruteros* reveal that immigrant social networks are not only sources of support overflowing with social capital that benefits all members equally. They can also be overwhelmed by the economic poverty of their members and by the hostile context of reception in which they exist. In addition to being a source of support, these networks can also facilitate exploitation. To capture this complexity, these pages include stories of stability and insecurity, of settlement and return migration, of ethnic solidarity and exploitation. They demonstrate that *paisanaje* (compatriotism) functions as much more than a social safety net. In this book, I argue that it is more useful to think of *paisanaje* among immigrants in the United States as an ethnic cage. This concept is the theoretical contribution of this study. The context of reception gives the ethnic cage its form; the individuals within give it its function.

THE ETHNIC CAGE

A popular *ranchera* song by the *norteño* group Los Tigres del Norte is called "La Jaula de Oro" (The Golden Cage). The song is narrated from the perspective of an undocumented immigrant who is painfully aware of the freedom that he has lost in coming to the United States. "Of what use is money," he sings, "if I am a prisoner in this golden cage?" The ethnic cage concept presented in this book is meant to echo this song's sentiments.[8] It speaks to the struggle found in the dual nature of something and provides a useful way of understanding the harmony and conflict found in the ethnic community of *fruteros*. For some, the ethnic cage is large, invisible, and functions to corral community while keeping threats at bay. For others, the ethnic cage is small, visible, and functions to confine the individual when that same community does harm. Yet as I show throughout this book, the ethnic cage can serve different functions at different times for the same individual because personal, social, and work relationships are dynamic.

The powerful symbol of the cage is a familiar concept to ethnographers. Carol B. Stack began her classic study *All Our Kin* (1974) with an excerpt from Maya Angelou's *I Know Why the Caged Bird Sings*. The excerpt, and the study that followed, conveyed the richness of giving and receiving in the context of desperate need. Like Stack, I examine the relationship between reciprocity and poverty. She looks at this relationship among black families who are internal migrants, moving from the rural American South to the industrial Midwest, whereas I focus on Latinos who are international migrants, moving from rural Mexico to an urban American West. Stack finds cooperation and mutual aid among kin; I find this to be true among *paisanos* as well, but I also find suspicion and exploitation. This community of *fruteros* presents a case in which both cooperation and mutual aid exist alongside exploitation. Like others before me who stumbled on unsavory aspects of immigrant life, this is not the story I set out to record.[9] Fieldwork over several years revealed how structural hardship inspired ingenuity among *fruteros*, but this ingenuity often helped *and* harmed fellow *paisanos*. In the years I spent among *fruteros*, I saw both the promise and the pain of community.

Social networks matter. They can structure how the poor survive economic destitution and how newcomers integrate into a new country. Indeed, precariousness is a condition for which social networks can provide assistance in the form of resources. Social networks, however, are developed and utilized within structural contexts. W. E. B. Du Bois (1899) was among the first American sociologists to identify the use and benefits of robust social (e.g., mutual aid organizations) and kin networks among Philadelphia's Seventh Ward residents. Du Bois maintained his focus on the social conditions that created the economic precariousness of the Seventh Ward residents. Similarly, Cecilia Menjívar's (2000) work on Salvadoran immigrant networks focuses on the hostile immigration policies, limited economic opportunities, and resource-poor community that make the rendering of aid conditional and uneven. She found that for Salvadoran immigrants in the Mission District of San Francisco, it was the hostile context and the limited resources that prevented networks' members from helping each other.

For *fruteros* in Los Angeles, structure matters—these informal workers must continuously navigate a hostile context of reception. As undocumented immigrants working in the informal economy, these street vendors confront laws that prohibit their presence *and* their work. In many ways, this context contributes to their economic precariousness. Yet where the Salvadoran immigrants in Menjívar's study failed to open doors to newcomers because there was no help to be given, the Mexican immigrants in my study opened doors to newcomers both to offer help and to exploit. This is the ethnic cage. Newcomers are not turned away. Their *paisanaje* grants them entry, but it does not guarantee benevolence.

WHY FRUIT VENDORS?

"Working on the street, like this, is starting at the bottom," Cristian, one of my main respondents, originally from the small town of Dos Mundos in the Mexican state of Puebla, explained on one of the many days we sat and waited for customers while watching people and cars go by.[10] Throughout my time in the field, it was not uncommon to hear of vendors working on street corners as *fruteros* just days after arriving in the country. At the end of the workday, as I rode through town in a pickup truck with Cristian and his girlfriend, Carmen, originally from Mexico City, hauling their pushcarts to the storage warehouse commissary (known by vendors as the *comisaria*), they would honk and nod to their fellow *fruteros* working on the street corners we passed. Carmen always followed each encounter with a quick description of the person for me: "That guy works for Raúl, he's been here for a few weeks"; "That one doesn't know how to hold the knife yet 'cause he's new"; or most often, "He just got here, he's from Dos

Mundos too." Although I did not select this population of workers knowing they would be such recent arrivals and be working in an occupation
dominated by *paisano* connections, these characteristics proved to be
important when scrutinizing the impact of social networks.[11]

To be sure, street vending has a long history among recently arrived
immigrants. The Library of Congress has thousands of images of street
peddlers in turn-of-the-century New York City, and among the top subject
headings for the photographs in this visual repository is the term "ethnic
neighborhoods." Looking through these black-and-white images of peddlers in the Syrian Quarter, Little Italy, and Little Jerusalem continuously
reinforces the connection between immigrants and street vending. The
overrepresentation of immigrants among street vendors is observable in
the modern-day vendor membership of New York City's Street Vendor
Project, a nonprofit organization providing legal representation and advocacy to street vendors. In Los Angeles, another major metropolis that, like
New York City, serves as an immigrant gateway, street vendors are also
representative of the many recent arrivals to the country. Yet while New
York has an estimated twenty thousand street vendors selling food, flowers, books, art, and other products, in Los Angeles there are an estimated
fifty thousand street vendors, ten thousand of whom sell food products.[12]
These significant numbers should not obscure an important characteristic
that made Los Angeles distinct from New York City. Throughout my time
in the field, Los Angeles was the largest American city that prohibited
street vending.[13] This prohibition often resulted in the confiscation of
products and pushcarts, the issuing of fines and citations, and at times,
arrests. It was the risk associated with this informal occupation that made
the use and abuse of ethnic networks so widespread and meaningful. And
it was this prohibition—whose impact I saw almost immediately—that
solidified my interest in understanding the social world of *fruteros*.

CRIMINALIZING IMMIGRANT STREET
VENDORS IN LOS ANGELES

Many laws structure fruit vendors' presence on street corners, and these
laws in turn structure the social and economic relationships vendors have

with others and with each other. Citywide crackdowns on street vendors conducted primarily by the health department—known by vendors as *salubridad*—contribute to the marginalization of the vendors, and fear of crackdowns structures vendors' relationships. I conducted fieldwork among fruit vendors from 2006 to 2012. Throughout that time, there was an overarching law in the Municipal County Code that prohibited vending on sidewalks within the city of Los Angeles. More broadly, street vendors were subject to scrutiny, citation, and arrest based on laws and regulations from various city, county, and state agencies.[14]

Enforcement within the city was carried out by three agencies: the Los Angeles Police Department (LAPD), the Los Angeles Department of Public Works (Bureau of Street Services), and the Los Angeles County Department of Public Health (LACDPH). Prior to 2014, vendors could receive citations from and be arrested by Los Angeles Police Department officers for nuisance or littering violations in addition to illegal vending citations. In 2014, the Attorney Administrative Citation Enforcement (ACE) program was implemented, which provided a noncriminal enforcement approach to nuisance abatement. The ACE program issued administrative citations in place of criminal citations or arrests for quality-of-life offences, which included illegal vending. The administrative citations issued by ACE could be resolved through the payment of a fine, with no resulting criminal record, probation, or threat of jail, but it did not entirely remove the threat of arrest.[15] Because fruit vendors sell food products, they are also subject to California Health Code regulations, which are enforced by the LACDPH. Health inspectors could confiscate pushcarts and products during their crackdowns. Street Services investigators from the Department of Public Works also carried out enforcement of sidewalk vending violations. These strict antivending ordinances and the corresponding crackdowns were a perpetual risk to vendors, whose livelihoods and public presence are continuously contested.

In addition to being bound by local and state-level policies, those fruit vendors who were undocumented were also subject to federal immigration laws that prohibited their presence in the country. Los Angeles has long been considered a "sanctuary city" for undocumented immigrants due to policies like LAPD's Special Order 40. This police mandate was implemented in 1979 and prevents LAPD officers from questioning individuals for the sole purpose of determining an immigration status—a measure meant to establish trust between officers and the city's various immigrant communities. While there is no clear definition of a sanctuary city, cities that define themselves as such tend to follow certain practices that protect resident undocumented immigrants. The term generally refers to cities that do not allow municipal funds and resources to be used to enforce federal immigration laws. Of course, there is no true sanctuary for immigrants residing in the United States without legal permission.

Cities are neither wholly inclusionary nor exclusionary. Even in cities that vow to protect immigrants, there are limits to the protections that they can provide.[16] The tension between inclusion and exclusion is the defining feature of immigrant "illegality" in the United States. The strict binary between "legality" and "illegality" misrepresents the reality of immigrants' lived experiences (Kubal 2013; Menjívar 2006) and ambiguities within the law itself (Chauvin and Garcés-Mascareñas 2012). Thus, scholars use terms like "legal ambiguity" (Coutin 2003), "semi-legality" (Kubal 2013), "liminal legality" (Menjívar 2006), and "illegal citizenship" (Chauvin and Garcés-Mascareñas 2012) to capture the complexity surrounding unauthorized immigrants' formal exclusion under federal immigration law and their partial inclusion as residents entitled to certain legal rights and protections.

It is important to note that local policies, not just federal laws, can be used to police and displace immigrant populations.[17] Within Los Angeles, sociologist Ivan Light has documented how local government has disrupted unwanted immigration by enforcing antipoverty legislation. Enforcement targets activities that include "sweatshops where low-paid work violates wages, health, and safety regulations and slums that violate municipal housing ordinances" (Light 2006, 10). Although Light focuses on immigrant workers operating in the wage economy, the local quality-of-life policies and enforcement activities he investigates also heavily target street-based workers like *fruteros*. These enforcement activities include crackdowns carried out by the LACDPH and the LAPD, which target vendors operating in violation of city and county ordinances that regulate sidewalk activity and public health and safety. Light argues that this local political intolerance of immigrant poverty prompted crackdowns that, in turn, contributed to the deflection of immigrants to other U.S. cities.

There are, of course, many undocumented immigrants living in Los Angeles who did not leave, and many others have continued to arrive as enforcement and surveillance increased. This book focuses on one such group of workers and how they persisted in the midst of this federal and local government assault. While Ivan Light argues that poverty intolerance provoked crackdowns, I argue that the crackdowns themselves contributed to and perpetuated poverty and marginalization among *fruteros*. It was this hostile local context of reception that helped give the ethnic cage its form. Among the survival strategies vendors employed to counteract the hostile context was a heavy reliance on the *paisano* network. Yet the *paisano* network could both provide help and exacerbate harm—this is the dual nature of the ethnic cage.

TIES THAT BUILD, TIES THAT BIND

The positive functions of social networks, especially among newly arrived immigrants, have received much scholarly attention. Within studies of international migration—between Mexico and the United States in particular—social networks are routinely found to ease entry into the new country and reduce the short-term costs of settlement (Browning and Rodriguez 1985), facilitate job acquisition (Bailey and Waldinger 1991), perpetuate migration patterns (Massey and Espinosa 1997), and promote remittance practices (J. H. Cohen 2005). The fruit vendors' hometown social network offers some benefits: it directs migrants to Los Angeles— an immigrant metropolis—and once they arrive, it steers them to work in the street-based fruit vending business. The role of migrant social networks in that process is not novel. Previous studies examine how Mexican immigrants use social networks to acquire jobs in particular industries and create immigrant labor markets (Fitzgerald 2004; Mines and Montoya 1982). However, this book moves beyond how immigrants get jobs using their immigrant social networks and instead focuses on how those social networks both build and bind the *paisano* community.

It is important to recognize that a focus on only the positive functions of immigrant social networks can be problematic for several reasons. First, this flattens complex narratives. Relationships between people are complicated and dynamic. It is unrealistic to assume that ties between individuals offer only benefits, especially when vulnerabilities related to context of reception, immigration status, class, and gender are present. In this book, I unpack immigrant social networks and understand them outside of a context in which they only promote or ease immigrant incorporation. *Paisano* social networks are constantly changing. They offer different individuals within the network uneven benefits, and they can be simultaneously helpful and exploitative. The ethnic cage concept is meant to capture this complexity. Although cages evoke a negative connotation, it is important to remember how, in a hostile context, such a cage can serve as a protective barrier. A diver in a shark cage can feel the protection of her enclosure even as it confines her movement.

To be sure, scholars have addressed the negative functions of ethnic social networks (see, for example, Gold 1994; Kim 1999; Mahler 1995; Smith 1996). Yet whereas scholars such as Cecilia Menjívar (2000) and Carol Stack (1974) explain the negative effects of social networks as a consequence of the dissolution of these networks or their inability to render aid—something generally attributed to a lack of resources or information as a result of a hostile context of reception—I argue that these negative effects can also be a result of the actual constitution of the networks. For fruit vendors, *paisano* networks do not dissolve due to a lack of resources; rather, they are structured to both render aid *and* facilitate exploitation. Among fruit vendors, individuals are not alienated or denied assistance; instead, migrants are invited or even recruited to come to Los Angeles, and they work with the expectation that they can, at least initially, be made to do so for little to no pay.[18]

The concept of the ethnic cage also complicates the ethnic enclave model. According to sociologist Alejandro Portes, the ethnic enclave consists of "immigrant groups [that] concentrate in a distinct spatial location and organize a variety of enterprises serving their own ethnic market and/ or the general population" (1981, 291). Fruit vending is an informal immigrant business that operates within a larger Latino ethnic enclave.[19] The purpose of the ethnic enclave model is to explain how immigrant and ethnic groups thrive on the basis of socially embedded, small entrepreneurship and avoid a secondary labor market characterized by low-paying, low-skill jobs with high turnover rates that lack opportunities for promotion. The ethnic enclave model captures how immigrants create and promote industry within their communities, even when facing racist or xenophobic hostility, and attributes it to ethnic solidarity. Ethnic solidarity manifests itself through immigrant social networks (Portes and Bach 1985). This solidarity in hostile contexts of reception allows coethnics to come together and associate, create ethnic markets, and then form ethnic enclaves in which ethnic businesses "organize themselves to trade exclusively or primarily within the enclave" (Zhou 1992, 4).[20]

However, because the ethnic enclave model is meant to explain immigrant attainment, it obscures the exploitative undercurrents that may also constitute it. In attributing the formation of the ethnic enclave to ethnic solidarity, the model ignores the self-interest and opportunism that may guide certain actors and glosses over the exploitation that limits other network members' aspirations to upward mobility. In a critical review of the ethnic enclave model, Jimy M. Sanders and Victor Nee note the need for "detailed analysis of the actual pattern of exchange between bosses and workers within immigrant enclaves . . . before generalizations can be made about ethnic solidarity's effect on the socioeconomic mobility of workers" (1987, 765). This study responds to that call and examines the power dynamics that underpin the underresearched occupation of street vendor labor in the predominantly Latino community of Los Angeles. It highlights the experiences of immigrants upon which enclave businesses are built and presents a case in which exploitation by fellow *paisanos* contributes to downward mobility and return migration. Here workers are forced to recognize their low status not only in the new destination country but also within a newly constituted hierarchy of hometown associates.

Through the case of the *fruteros,* this book complicates our understanding of social networks by looking at what they provide and to whom. Expanding on the scholarship of others, I focus on the impact of undocumented status (N. Rodriguez 2004; Saucedo 2006), gender (Hagan 1998), power differentials between workers and bosses (Cranford 2005), and the structure of opportunities in the receiving context (Menjívar 1997). Local policy can contribute to creating a hostile context of reception for recent immigrants, which has a domino effect that impacts opportunity, network relations, and immigrant integration. The law, at both the federal and the local level, entangles immigrant vendors so that webs of social relations must continuously contend with it. In the chapters that follow, I show how social networks simultaneously benefit and exploit—how they help integrate newcomers and fuel return migration. My aim is not to refute the benefits of immigrant social networks—they are perhaps the most important factor in the successful integration of recently arrived newcomers. Instead, I provide a multifaceted account of immigrant network use across time and within a tightly knit community of *paisanos* to show how it becomes an ethnic cage. Within this ethnic cage, members can become trapped by both the benefits and the mistreatment through a dynamic that enables and constrains them.

RESEARCH STRATEGY

I gained entrée into the fruit vendors' social world slowly by visiting individual vendors working in distinct neighborhoods throughout the city. I had awkward initial interactions and extended conversations with many vendors in much the same way that I did with Jesús. In the beginning, I spent time hanging out on corners with individual *fruteros*. I varied my arrival times to see different parts of their day. Within weeks, I was helping various *fruteros* pack up at the end of the workday and accepting rides to bus stops. These rides helped me meet vendors who worked together and gradually expanded my snowball samples.

The majority of fruit vendors that I approached were young, Spanish-speaking, Latino men because this demographic was overrepresented among *fruteros*. They were also primarily from one small town in the Mexican state of Puebla that I call Dos Mundos.[21] A few vendors were from Guatemala, but there was much more turnover among those young men. Although I am fluent in Spanish, my accent and diction are from the U.S.-Mexico borderlands; this contrasted with vendors' southern Mexico accent and diction. I would often ask for clarification on the meaning of certain words or expressions, and this allowed the vendors to embody a mentorship role. Other aspects of my biography helped as well. As a first-year graduate student at UCLA at the time of my research, I was new to the city and did not have a car; as a result, the vendors often took me under their wing to ensure that I did not get lost.[22] All of this made me realize how much being a stranger in a strange land resonated with them and allowed me to inadvertently tap into their charitable side.

When approaching young Latino men in the field, it helped more than hindered me to be a young Latina. I was nonthreatening, though sometimes vendors would jokingly ask if I was a covert health inspector. It helped that I had an abundance of enthusiasm and displayed interest in their lives; the job itself also had a fair amount of downtime in which to talk. Occasionally, I would have to shut down flirtatious talk, though I never pretended to have a significant other to curtail it. I did not want these interactions to circle around a lie. However, despite the many connections I made with male fruit vendors in a male-dominated field, it was a young woman, Carmen, who became my greatest resource and ally. She was one of three key informants who functioned as a social network hub, introducing me to various other vendors and giving my presence more credence.[23]

Carmen was nineteen years old when I met her in 2006. She had been in the country for three years at that point. She was high-spirited, with a soft, sweet way of talking that made conversation easy. Yet she was no one's fool and used barbed language to cut down belligerent customers and territorial business owners just as easily. She was from Mexico City but was dating Cristian, a vendor from Dos Mundos, and was well connected to his *paisanos*. Carmen introduced me to other vendors and was the first to entrust me with her pushcart and to invite me to her apartment for dinner, where I met her roommates, who were also vendors. She routinely recruited vendors for me to interview and, after years in the field, would refer to me as her cousin (*prima*) to any outsider who inquired about my presence.[24] Throughout the six years I spent in the field, she dated three fruit vendors from Dos Mundos, and I was able to spend time with them in social settings—as a third wheel.

I took notes while hanging out, and after about a year I began carrying and using a small digital recorder. After spending some time with vendors, I began to ask for formal interviews outside of work hours; I provided financial compensation for these sessions because they typically took over an hour and required meeting up late in the evening.[25] Over half of these interviews were with vendors from Dos Mundos or from the surrounding vicinity (but who considered themselves Dos Mundos *paisanos*). I may have oversampled Poblanos (people from the state of Puebla), but all the information I gathered pointed to their overrepresentation in the fruit vending business in the areas of town that I was visiting.[26]

I spent most of my time following a smaller group of these vendors and seeing the rest in social settings, like the summer celebration of the patron saint of Dos Mundos. During two summers, I worked alongside vendors, beginning the day in the predawn hours at the wholesale fruit market and ending it at the vendors' homes in the late evening.[27] Sometimes vendors would let me work the pushcart on my own while they ran errands, and on one occasion I found myself in the middle of a health department crackdown. I also spent time before and after normal working hours in the private residences of two fruit vendors. These residential locations were often used to host birthday celebrations, hometown association festivities, and other social gatherings.[28]

Throughout my six years in the field, I also interviewed other individuals who touched the lives of vendors. I interviewed the owner of the wholesale fruit market where the vendors shopped. I tracked down former community organizers associated with a street vending association that had been active in the 1980s. I spoke to organizers associated with a more recent street vending legalization campaign that began in 2009 and spent time attending rallies, town halls, and City Council meetings related to this movement. When hot dog vendors in the Fashion District were experiencing a crackdown-related crisis, I collected their testimonies for the Coalition for Humane Immigrant Rights of Los Angeles (CHIRLA), an immigrant rights organization that helped vendors with their police encounters. I visited Mexico City and Dos Mundos in 2011 and 2017 to meet vendors' families. I asked fruit vendors in Los Angeles for family referrals and made interview requests prior to my visits. In Mexico, I conducted fifteen interviews with former vendors as well as wives, grandmothers, aunts, mothers, and fathers of current fruit vendors. These visits to Mexico gave me a sense of what vendors in Los Angeles had left behind, what they were trying to build with their remittances, and how successful they had been at building it. This multisite fieldwork carried out in migrants' place of origin and destination can reveal the full scope of the migration experience and, according to sociologist David Fitzgerald, "offers advantages for gaining access to members of multi-sited networks and explaining the effects of place on a variety of outcomes" (2006, 2).

Despite having gained entrée into the world of these *fruteros,* I was always an outsider. When I would arrive with Carmen, Cristian, or Manuel at the warehouse where vendors stored their pushcarts, other fruit vendors would stare at me and ask who I was. This was not only because I looked and dressed differently but also because I was not a *paisana.* Many of the vendors had grown up together or were related to each other, and I could not be seen as one of them. There was a high turnover among fruit vendors in the warehouse space—with vendors leaving the space when they could no longer afford to pay the rent or moving in when they could— and so I was always new to someone who had just arrived. On the street and in social settings with vendors, I was continuously reminded of the privilege that I had and was accorded. I spoke English, was a U.S. citizen, and had a decent education. Instead of minimizing my privilege with vendors, I would use it to help them when they needed someone to translate, someone who had Internet access, or someone with a valid driver's license to drive or visit a precinct jail. Vendors shared so much of their lives with me that using my privilege to help solve problems that arose for them became one way of repaying them. It also allowed me to enter into the web of reciprocal obligations that characterized many of their social relationships.

ORGANIZATION OF THE BOOK

How did migrants from a small, rural town in the Mexican state of Puebla become so dominant as *fruteros* on the streets of an American metropolis nearly two thousand miles away? In chapter 2, I explore how the vending business emerged, how it is structured, and how Dos Mundos *paisanos* enter the business. Many well-developed social networks funnel prospective migrants into the job, with fellow *paisano* employers often funding the passage across the international border and providing housing to workers on arrival. The chapter follows the migration and occupational trajectories of four Dos Mundos migrants and Carmen, from Mexico City, and the ways in which their first vendor bosses both helped and exploited them as new arrivals, a process that gives the ethnic cage its various functions. The chapter also looks at how some immigrant vendor bosses, also from Dos Mundos, landed at the top of the occupational hierarchy by benefiting from instrumental advantages in their personal biographies.

Chapter 3 explores the challenges and risks that *fruteros* face on the streets of Los Angeles while working. While the perils that *fruteros* confront are visible to passersby primarily during health department crackdowns, vendors must constantly manage various risks posed by their positioning in public space. These risks are met with distinct survival strategies developed by *fruteros* both to minimize risk and to maximize profit. On their street corners, *fruteros* must forge alliances, engender sympathy or solidarity, and establish and maintain trust with their customer base. Throughout, vendors must forge ties that bind, ties through which resources flow, obligations accumulate, and exploitation is facilitated.

In chapter 4, we see the reach of ethnic community, which exists and carries on beyond the work sphere. For *paisano* vendors, the personal and professional often mix; romantic entanglements often affect work arrangements, and financial entanglements rely on intimate knowledge of fellow associates. While different types of connections between vendors— as employers, roommates, romantic partners, and business associates— can help make the *paisano* network more vibrant, they can also wreak havoc if relationships and partnerships sour. The chapter focuses on the devastating consequences when trust fails and things fall apart.

Chapter 5 focuses on Manuel and a fateful evening when a three-block drive to a local barbershop resulted in his arrest. When word spread about his possible deportation, the community response—in words and in actions—revealed the fragility of *paisanaje* when confronted with the power of the state. Ultimately, the *paisano* community of fruit vendors distanced itself from Manuel in a way that gave its members economic and psychological cover but that devastated Manuel financially and emotionally. When one group of Dos Mundos *paisanos* banished Manuel, he moved closer to a group of more marginalized *paisanos*. Manuel's crisis broadcast a key feature of the ethnic cage: *paisanaje* grants entry but does not guarantee benevolence.

What was gained by these young vendors' international migration and what was lost? In chapter 6, the families left behind in Puebla provide a partial answer rooted in remittance-driven material gain. The social fractures and reverberating emotional pain triggered by loss provide another answer. While *fruteros* in Los Angeles were trapped in an ethnic cage of restructured *paisanaje,* their family and friends in Mexico were living in a community being transformed by departures and the migration industry that profited from and enabled them. As a result, this migration industry monetized social relationships between town residents and created greater fissures between the haves and have-nots.

The concluding chapter revisits the concept of the ethnic cage and asks: How long does the ethnic cage endure? And more broadly, in what ways does international migration change *paisanaje?* Time and distance undoubtedly bring about change, and change can sometimes weaken and fracture ethnic community. Indeed, change did occur within the Dos Mundos hometown association in Los Angeles when the group splintered after a contentious election. I explain how *paisanaje* endured despite this fracture and how the ethnic cage concept can help us better understand immigrant adaptation.

2 Becoming a *Frutero*

"I never imagined I'd be selling fruit on the street." Almost every fruit vendor I spent time with told me this at one point or another. Yet this statement seemed incongruous with many of the vendors' migration histories. Many of them had left their hometown of Dos Mundos knowing they had this job waiting for them. In some instances, even the journey across the border was financially subsidized by fellow *paisanos* who later became their employers in Los Angeles.[1] Why, then, did these young migrants assess their trajectories in this puzzling manner? While many young men leaving Dos Mundos assumed that fruit vending would be a good entry point into the U.S. labor market, few of them thought that it would be the only job they would hold. Fruit vending is a socially networked occupation that is easy for Dos Mundos *paisanos* to enter and, because of the well-developed system of support and reciprocity as well as the exploitative tactics employed by some bosses, difficult for them to leave. In this chapter, I examine how the business is structured, how these migrants come to work as *fruteros*, and how those at the top of the occupational hierarchy come to inhabit that role.

Vendors themselves attribute the origins of fruit vending to a single migrant who was a fruit vendor in Puebla before working as a fruit vendor in Los Angeles. According to several accounts, this entrepreneur immigrated to the United States sometime in the 1980s.[2] Although he employed only his family in the business, his fellow *paisanos* emulated the business model. In the hands of these *paisanos*, fruit vending became an "immigrant niche" occupation filled largely by other Poblanos.[3] The same kinship and *paisano* networks that facilitated entry also created "social closure," contributing to a more concentrated immigrant niche.[4] Fruit vending, as it is practiced, did not exist previously. Therefore, this flow of immigrants did not displace any other ethnic or native populations—as is the case in some other industries—when Poblanos arrived.[5] The Mexican immigrant enclave economy found in the Los Angeles wholesale produce market also helped bolster this fruit vending immigrant niche (Alvarez 1990).

Through the years, fruit vendors' collective experience led to improved business tactics, which contributed to the proliferation of vending. I estimate that over a thousand fruit vendors operate within Los Angeles County.[6] *Fruteros* operate in a space created by economic restructuring and globalization effects (Massey, Durand, and Malone 2002; Sassen 1990; Sassen 1993), ethnic entrepreneurship (Light and Rosenstein 1995; Zhou 2004), and immigrant strategies imported from sending countries (Hamilton and Chinchilla 2001). Economic restructuring reconfigured income distribution in the United States so that an increasing population of low-income consumers began seeking cheaper goods from the informal sector (Hamilton and Chinchilla 2001; Sassen 1990). Fruit vendors were able to provide a cheap product by decreasing the distance between wholesale retailers and customers and by minimizing overhead costs. Because the product (fruit salads) had widespread appeal and because fruit vendors were easily accessible on public sidewalks, the customer base quickly expanded beyond the initial "captive market" found in the low-income, immigrant community (Rath and Kloosterman 2000, 660). Even without this expanded customer base, "immigrant replenishment" might have provided ample customers for fruit vendors (Jimenez 2008, 1533). As anthropologist Robert Alvarez Jr. noted, "the continuing growth of the Mexican population [increases] . . . the 'built-in' market for Mexican commodities" (1990, 107).

HOW THE BUSINESS WORKS

Most migrants enter fruit vending as workers employed by established bosses who own multiple pushcarts (see figure 3). Pushcarts cost between $800 and $1,200; recent migrants with little economic capital or information about where to purchase one neither easily nor quickly acquire pushcarts.[7] As a result, bosses become an important resource for recent migrants. Bosses pay vendors a daily wage (between $40 and $60) in return for earnings made from daily sales. The sales a fruit vendor makes can vary on a daily basis, ranging from $80 to $300.

In most instances, pushcart owners are responsible for buying fruit at the wholesale market every morning (which costs between $80 and $120); paying the monthly rent at the commissary warehouse where pushcarts are stored or providing storage in their own homes, usually in backyards; and transporting workers and their pushcarts to their respective street corners to vend. Because pushcarts are heavily weighed down by significant loads of fruit and ice, vendors remain on their street corner for the day and are not ambulatory.

Some bosses also work as vendors in addition to owning other pushcarts that they employ workers to operate. These "vendor-bosses" have multiple responsibilities and face different types of threats due to their dual roles. In some cases, vendor-bosses amass several pushcarts and stop vending themselves to focus on the logistics associated with vending. When they cease to work as vendors, they become pushcart-owning employers. Employers will sometimes take on a supervisory role and "patrol" the streets for ongoing crackdowns in an effort to protect their pushcart investments.

On the street, the risks that workers and pushcart owners face are different. Vendor workers and vendor-bosses are exposed on the street corner: they receive citations; can be harassed by the LAPD, customers, neighborhood business owners, and gang members; and can be subject to arrest for vending. If their pushcarts are confiscated, they may be unemployed for some time before a new pushcart can be acquired. Pushcart owners lose their investment when crackdowns result in the confiscation of their products, utensils, and/or pushcarts. Pushcart owners may also see themselves as responsible for posting bail for their vendor-workers;

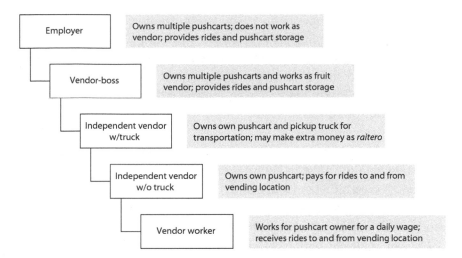

Figure 3. Fruit vendor occupational hierarchy.

however, this financial commitment varies based on the type of relationship that exists between workers and the pushcart owners.

Under favorable conditions, workers are able to save money to buy their own pushcarts and become independent vendors. When this happens, they may continue to rely on their former bosses for rides and pay weekly fees for fuel expenses. Depending on their relationship with the boss and the number of pushcarts the latter has available, a newly independent vendor may need to find a new street corner to work. A street corner "belongs" to the vendor who discovered it or the boss who has worked a pushcart (as a vendor or a vendor-boss) there. Pushcart owners who have multiple pushcarts and a vehicle to transport them will often give preference to their workers over other independent vendors seeking transportation. In these cases, independent fruit vendors will look for another vendor with space in their pickup truck to transport them. Fruit vendors typically work in groups of two to four and will change groups depending on space in pickup trucks, work relations, and personal disputes or conflicts. As I show later, workers who would get mistreated by a boss they worked with could, and often did, move on to work for a different boss.

In ideal circumstances, a fruit vendor may be able to save enough money to buy both a pushcart and a used pickup truck to transport it. At this point, the vendor may be able to make extra money by providing rides (as a *raitero*) to other independent vendors. Because arguments or disagreements within working groups occurred with some regularity, it was almost always possible to pick up an independent vendor and form a new arrangement. While there was little movement to jobs outside of the *frutero* world, there was a lot of turnover within these smaller working group arrangements.

Ultimately, if they could save enough money, these independent vendors were able to invest in additional pushcarts and employ their own workers. The resulting economic mobility hierarchy, from low to high, is: vendor worker, independent vendor without a pickup truck, independent vendor with a pickup truck, vendor-boss, employer.

Due to multiple variables—such as daily sales, varying prices at the wholesale market, inclement weather, and ongoing crackdowns—the income that could be generated was unstable. Throughout my time in the field, I saw vendor workers save money for months and become independent vendors only to have their pushcarts confiscated by the health department and become vendor workers for a boss once again. Others saved enough to buy pushcarts and pickup trucks only to lose them due to crackdowns, because of limited consistent income, or for driving without a license. It was very difficult for vendors to save enough money to make an investment in pushcarts and vehicles, but it was even more difficult to *maintain* those investments once they had been acquired.

The majority of vendor workers and independent vendors I followed faced persistent economic instability. Yet they had few prospects for finding work elsewhere with comparable or better pay. The *paisano* network they had access to as *fruteros*—which included *paisano* connections at the wholesale market that sometimes allowed them to purchase fruit on credit during hard times—was also difficult to walk away from. Their reliance on the *paisano* network also bound them to it, and this helped give the ethnic cage its function. Some did think of alternative occupations, but they feared losing the assistance their work structure and peers provided as well as the system of loans and rotating credit associations (*tandas*) that had been established within this community.[8]

THE WORKERS

Dos Mundos *paisanos* find their way to fruit vending through their social networks. Some travel directly from Dos Mundos to work as *fruteros,* while others initially travel to other cities in the United States before reaching out to *paisanos* in Los Angeles for jobs in fruit vending. All the vendors I got to know had used their hometown connections to get the jobs, but they all encountered different work arrangements even when they worked with the same boss. As stated previously, social networks do not treat all members equally, and some workers fared better than others. The migration and occupational narratives of five vendors—Carmen, Cristian, Manuel, Jesús, and Gonzalo—showcase this inconsistency in network use. Both Cristian and Manuel had landed in different cities—Fresno and Salt Lake City, respectively—before deciding that coming to Los Angeles would offer them more social and/or material benefits. Manuel had hoped to escape the doldrums of life working in the fields on farms in Fresno, while Cristian had been looking for steady work and pay. Jesús and Gonzalo had traveled directly from Dos Mundos to Los Angeles knowing they had a job waiting for them. Both had used financial resources provided by their future employers—the García brothers—to make the journey. While the two men arrived only a year apart, Gonzalo, who arrived later, fared much better. Gonzalo benefited from a solid premigration relationship with his future employer and arrived at a time when the García brothers were not experiencing health department crackdown losses. Carmen, a vendor originally from Mexico City, who tapped into the Dos Mundos network through a romantic relationship, came to the United States with the most street vending experience. She also had her own familial connections to the fruit vending business. Yet she had not expected to be selling fruit on the street when she arrived. Carmen's story, unlike those of the Dos Mundos men, shows how gendered expectations of obedience from familial networks pushed her into a Dos Mundos network dominated instead by reciprocal obligations. The stories of these young migrants are told in sequential order according to the year they arrived in Los Angeles.

Carmen

Carmen was sixteen years old when she arrived in Los Angeles from Mexico. However, it was not the first time she had been to the city. Years earlier, as a five-year-old, she had accompanied her father to Los Angeles for a six-month stint. During those months, her father held multiple jobs—working in a garment factory, fumigating restaurants, and cleaning carpets. Carmen, meanwhile, was enrolled in primary school.

Carmen was incredibly close to both her parents, and as a child she had been her father's shadow. She had helped him vend in the street markets of some of Mexico City's toughest neighborhoods. When I met her parents in Mexico City in 2011, it was clear her father was incredibly proud of her. Don Martín, Carmen's father, explained how she came to be his helper at such an early age:

> She was two years old when she started coming to sell with me in the *tianguis* [street markets]. We'd sell what we call here in Mexico City *chácharas* [bric-a-brac]—different appliances, tools, everything. This was a way of surviving. From the day she was born, she was always by my side. When she turned two, I started taking her with me. We would leave at 6:00 in the morning and return at 7:00 p.m. We would spend all day in the *tianguis*. When she turned five years old, she and I went to the United States. We arrived in Los Angeles in 1993 and stayed there for almost six months, and then we came back and continued working in the *tianguis*.
>
> When we returned, we started selling *fayuca* [contraband] in Tepito [a neighborhood close to the historic center known for its black market]. In the beginning, I went to Tepito to buy a used iron, blender, radio, recorder, and then we sold those things and then kept buying more to sell. Carmen would help me arrange the items on the floor for customers to see as they passed. She helped arrange the stand and then would help take down the stand.

Years later, when Carmen's mother began selling food and fresh-pressed juice from a stand in front of their home, Carmen helped out as well. All of Carmen's childhood and early teen years were spent helping her parents with their street vending businesses. "Did Carmen like working at such an early age?" I asked Carmen's father.

> Look, she was always very attentive to what you told her, and it is not that I have not been hard with them [his children]. But I think it was useful for them. I wanted them to learn to work so they could do things fast and with-

out saying: "I can't or don't want to do that." No. They [Carmen and her older brother] had to do it. She never grumbled about doing things. I would tell them it was for their own good because when they grew up they could survive and fit in anywhere, they would be received because they were helpful persons. She was a good worker. She would say, "I can do this, and you do that." But she was still a girl and had no thought of saying, "Now we're going to do it this way." She did what you told her to, she was helpful. Then she grew up, she went to elementary school and high school and finished well. She was a good role model for her two younger brothers.

When Carmen was in primary school, her older brother left to work in the United States. He was fifteen years old when he left the household. Growing up, she heard stories of her brother in the United States, and she came to have dreams of following him. When she turned sixteen, she gathered the courage and told her parents she wanted to go to Los Angeles to continue her studies. "Carmen left July of 2004," Carmen's mother explained when I ask about her daughter's departure.

Carmen had been invited to come to Los Angeles by some friends and family members she had in the city. Her older brother was already well established there. When she discussed the idea of migrating with a neighbor, they agreed to travel together. However, when the time came, the neighbor reneged, and Carmen traveled with distant relatives from her mother's side.

"What did you think about that?" I ask Carmen's parents.

"Well, I did not agree," Don Martín replied. "It was as if something was taken away from me. And with pain and everything, she had to go far away from us." Carmen's father had issues with her migrating as a young woman. "I knew the experiences people have to live in order to arrive in the United States, and because of that it was difficult to let her go. I thought many things, because I knew what happened in order to arrive to the other side. First she had to think about money to leave, second about passing through, third about getting there. How was she going to live? Even when you arrive with family, it's not the same as being with your parents. All that gave me pause."

"Did you tell her not to leave?" I asked.

"Uh huh. But she said, 'Nothing will happen to me, I am going with some people that will help me cross.' She was trusting known *coyotes*. But she did suffer trying to cross," he explained.

"She suffered a lot," Carmen's mom emphasized.

"It was very painful for me," Don Martín added.

Carmen's older brother had gone to the United States without seeking his parents' *bendición* (blessing), and they feared Carmen would do the same if they refused to let her go. For this reason, they did not stand in her way when she told them she was leaving.

"I thought, 'I do not know if I am doing right or doing wrong letting her go,'" Don Martín explained. "But I also thought, 'If she leaves without my permission maybe she will go another way, and it is better that God guides her.' So we chose to let her go. But we also suffered when we found out she could not cross [the border]. It took her weeks. It was something very unbearable, the lack of communication [during that process]."

Carmen made three different attempts before she finally got into the country safely. Her first two attempts, through the Arizona desert, resulted in her being apprehended by U.S. Border Patrol agents. During the second failed attempt, the group walked for four days, and Carmen carried a single gallon of water. She was told not to drink but to merely wet her lips with the water.

After that attempt, Carmen's aunt in Los Angeles intervened and hired another *coyote* to cross her in a smaller group and by a less dangerous path. Carmen's aunt and uncle on her mother's side paid for the journey north, which cost $2,100.

Carmen's aunt and uncle both worked in the fruit vending business. Her uncle, Don Joaquín, owned several pushcarts and worked as a vendor himself. Carmen had plans to live with them when she arrived and to attend school. When Carmen left Mexico City, she told her parents she was going to the United States to study, not to work.

"Did you not have the hope that she would work and send you money?" I asked her parents.

"No, no, no," Carmen's father said.

"In the beginning we thought she was really going to study and to work for her own expenses," Carmen's mother stated.

Don Martín then added, "But there *was* a moment when I told her, 'Look, if there's a way for you to work, [you should,] because your uncle and aunt are not going to support you, and we do not have the means to send you money for whatever you are going to study. If you can find a good job and try to study and work, then do that. If you can't, I'm sorry, but you will have to work.'"

Carmen enrolled in classes to learn English, and she attempted to make a go of it, but she struggled. Her uncle also told her that if she was going to live under his roof, she needed to contribute to the household. About seven months after arriving, she dropped out of her classes and began working full time as a waitress in a small restaurant. After a month, the restaurant closed, and she lost her job. She then started working at a jewelry shop in downtown Los Angeles, but it paid too little. Still, she worked at the shop for about eleven months.

Later, after Carmen had started working as a *frutera* on the corner, she would tell me stories about how unhappy she had been working at that jewelry shop. "They didn't know how to value a person," she explained about the job. The owners were strict with her, patting her down in her underwear and bra area every time she asked to go to the restroom during work hours. She preferred the autonomy of working on a street corner by herself without anyone watching her every move. But she did proudly note that she learned how to count in Farsi during her time at the store because the owners were Iranian.

After quitting that job, Carmen asked to work for her uncle, Don Joaquín, who owned multiple fruit pushcarts. He lent her a pushcart and paid her a daily wage just like any of his workers. Don Joaquín taught her how the business worked. Later, he gave her the pushcart to work on her own.

When I asked about why she decided to leave Mexico, Carmen admitted that she felt her parents were too strict with her. In Los Angeles, she found her uncle and aunt were also too strict with her. They kept her on a very strict curfew, and she felt like she could not explore the city the way she wanted. As soon as she could, she moved out of their home in Los Angeles. The easiest way to transition out of the house was through her romantic relationship with Cristian, which she had begun when he started working with her uncle.

Together, Cristian and Carmen rented a bedroom in a two-bedroom apartment and split the $520 monthly rent. When Cristian left the work arrangement with Carmen's uncle, he began working more closely with his Dos Mundos *paisanos,* and Carmen was quickly integrated into that community. Carmen enjoyed much more autonomy in the Dos Mundos *paisano* network than she had with her own familial network. While she would occasionally ask her uncle for advice or small favors, she remained much more integrated with the Dos Mundos *paisanos* she met through Cristian. She participated in their social celebrations and rotating credit associations known as *tandas,* and helped with Dos Mundos hometown association issues.

Cristian

Cristian left Dos Mundos when he was twenty years old and traveled initially to Salt Lake City. Cristian was always quick with a smile and had a sharp mind. He had an aquiline nose that seemed more pronounced because of a dark mole near it on one of his cheeks. He was the oldest child and only son in a family with four children. Cristian's primary reason for migrating was not to remit to his parents; in fact, his parents were well established in a three-bedroom home and had discouraged him from migrating. Instead, Cristian sought adventure north of the border. His reasons for leaving Dos Mundos were rooted in a sense of curiosity.

"I just wanted to know the world. I didn't want others to tell me what the United States was like, I wanted to know for myself," Cristian explained when I asked him why he decided to leave Dos Mundos.

Cristian's departure, like those of others before and after him, was hurried. One day, Cristian went to the town store in Dos Mundos to pay a bill and saw a neighbor who told him he was leaving for the United States later in the week. Cristian returned home and told his mother he was going to go too. She cried and begged him to stay, and his father did not approve of his plans. Because it was sudden, Cristian sought out the local moneylender for a loan to make the trip.

Four days later, Cristian set out on his adventure with neighbors and cousins. Their journey was riddled with difficulties. Cristian had traveling companions but had not done much by way of planning. In Mexico, he had worked in construction with his father. Cristian would typically spend his days helping his father, who had a bad back, by pushing a wheelbarrow around; he didn't do much actual construction. Despite this, he believed construction was one potential avenue for employment in the United States. When Cristian left Dos Mundos, he had no job waiting for him on the other side of the border and no clear destination.

Cristian later came to believe that his border crossing experience was an event that came to define him. Throughout the years, he often wanted to talk to me about it, and in every retelling, the details in the narrative were as concrete and vivid as if they had occurred the day before. It was the experience and the decisions he made as a result of that crossing that defined his occupational trajectory in the United States.

It took Cristian and his companions fifteen days to cross into the United States. Border Patrol agents apprehended them twice. The third time, the *coyotes* took them through a different town in the Mexican state of Sonora. He crossed in a small group of nine people, all from Dos Mundos. Cristian knew some of the nine better than others. They began walking at nightfall on a Wednesday and stopped around 6:00 a.m. to rest. Although they were told the walk would take three to four hours, it lasted three days. On Friday, they arrived at a pickup location in the mountains and waited until the next day. As Cristian recalled:

We waited there until Saturday night. During the day, no lie, many different groups arrived. Some groups had ten, or fifteen, or twenty people. [In the end,] there were like three hundred people just waiting to be picked up in the mountains. Then [pickup] trucks began to arrive, they would yell out names, and people would get in. We got in the back of a pickup truck and sat down, but the driver yelled at us to stand up; this wasn't a "special ride," he said. Thirty of us got on, all standing up and holding on to each other. There were eight trucks each carrying between twenty-five and thirty people. The trucks took off in the dark with the lights off and had advanced some two hundred meters when someone started shouting, "The fly, the fly [*el mosco, el mosco*]!" We just asked ourselves, "What's *el mosco?*" The driver turned off the truck, turned everything off, and we waited. Then we felt the rumbling of the helicopter. It hit the caravan of trucks with bright lights. Because we were already all stacked on top of each other, everyone fell on top of each other trying to run away.

Everyone ran, and I did too, but I didn't go far. I went maybe twenty meters from the truck and hid in a bush. Immigration agents descended. Four other guys and me were hiding in the bushes when the agents saw us. One agent grabbed me by the backpack, and I took it off and ran. . . . I hid not far away. Vans came and took everyone. I could see the people being loaded up into the vans from my hiding spot. It took them about two hours, and they left. They tore the trucks to pieces, destroyed the radiator, the tires. After they left, I just sat still for half an hour. You couldn't hear anything, just silence. Even the animals were silent. That's when I got scared. I was alone.

I started walking to the trucks, but it was dark, and I couldn't see. The moon wasn't out. I sat down, and then I wanted to run after the agents in the vans so they would take me too, but they weren't there anymore. I started yelling the names of my *paisanos*, but no one would answer. I started to cry. I couldn't hear anyone anymore. I thought, "I'm the only one left." I stayed by the trucks thinking someone would come. This was the route they always took, and someone would come.

About an hour later, I heard some people talking, and I hid. They were talking and talking, and I recognized the voice of one, a guy from over here [Dos Mundos]. I yelled his name, and he recognized me. Then there were two, then four of us. Of the nine of us who came together in the group, only four remained. The sun was starting to rise, and we were hungry and thirsty. One of the guys who had made the passage before said, "The trucks must have something, at least water." We went to the truck and found bread [*pan* Bimbo] and some gallons of water, and some ham, but not much. We got it and split it four ways.

Then we started to hear some yelling. The sun was rising, and more people were starting to arrive. They saw us standing there and they would run to us. One of the four guys said, "Let's go, because they're going to beat us [to take our food]. They are all hungry, they are all thirsty." So the four of us took what we could and hid. More people arrived, and we saw them beat each other for the food and water they found in the truck. Around noon some trucks came to pick us up again, some were already carrying people. Six trucks arrived, but no one wanted to give us a ride because they didn't know the person [*coyote*] who was crossing us. The last truck asked us who had led us. We said, "Our guide was Freddy," and they asked how many of us there were. We said four, and they took us along with twenty-five or thirty other people.

It was a four-hour car drive. They dropped us off near a highway, and they said someone else would pick us up that night. They dropped us off at 5:00 p.m., and a truck picked us up at 10:00 or 11:00 p.m. and took us to a house in Phoenix. Once there, we started [phone] calling our relatives, the people who were going to pick us up, so they could pay. They told us the charge was $1,500. One of the guys who was with us [in the group of four] told them OK [about the price]. He asked his brother for money. His brother was in Utah. They told us that to drop us off in Utah they would charge $2,000 per person, and it was three of us going. He [the guy with the brother] said no, that he was going to call his brother to come pick us up. And he came to pick us up in Phoenix. But that guy, he ended up charging us the same, $2,000. That [debt] was a little bit difficult to carry.

Cristian went to Utah with this *paisano* acquaintance because they had survived an ordeal together and because he was the only one with a destination in mind where there were family members waiting. The brother of the acquaintance paid the *coyotes* $1,500 to cover Cristian's crossing and then charged Cristian $2,000 for the drive to Utah. Cristian arrived with a $3,500 debt to that man, and it proved difficult to repay because he could not find work in Salt Lake City. After three weeks, he had only worked a handful of days in construction despite continuously seeking out work as a day laborer. When he did work, the pay was low in comparison to his peers because he did not have a construction background. Cristian learned everything he needed to know on the job. "They [the construction bosses] wanted us to work as if we had five years of experience. But we didn't. We barely knew how to use a measuring tape," he explained.

Cristian eventually found more steady work on a project renovating homes, but after a few weeks, work slowed due to the winter months. It was then that he reached out to *paisanos* in Los Angeles, and they told him to come work as a fruit vendor. In late 2004, three months after arriving in Utah, Cristian dutifully left for Los Angeles. His cousins, the Martínez brothers, lent him the money to make the journey, and so Cristian would again arrive in a new city carrying a debt. He was planning to work with his *paisano* Reynaldo. But by the time Cristian got to Los Angeles, the pushcart he was meant to work had been confiscated by the Los Angeles County Department of Public Health. Cristian and his cousins were left unemployed again. When Reynaldo finally acquired a pushcart, he employed Cristian without pay, stating that he was still making payments for the cart:

> He [Reynaldo] would feed us and let us live in his house, and in two weeks he bought two carts, and we began to work. But he didn't pay us. Because he was just starting up his business, he said he didn't have money to pay us. Told us to give him a chance. Since he'd bought the carts, he said he wasn't going to pay us [right away] but that we should help him and he would just let us live with him and feed us, but he didn't pay us. Just gave us food and a roof to sleep under. So we worked with him like this for about two months. And he wouldn't pay us.
>
> I mean, we would work, and we would have good sales at the spots where he took us to sell. It's just that he had this other guy who managed the money

for him, and I don't know whether he took the money for himself or didn't keep the books straight. Because we had good sales, we would sell a lot, and we *were* putting out enough money to pay for the carts. I think that in about two weeks, the carts paid for themselves. We put out enough money. But he said he didn't have any money, that he wouldn't pay us, that the fruit was expensive. So we told him, if he wasn't going to pay us we would go. And he said, "Whatever suits you. If you guys want to leave, then leave. But I don't have money to pay you. But if you're leaving, I need you to pay me for the meals you've eaten and the months you've lived with me." Well, then we told him, "We don't have money to pay you because you haven't paid us! If you want us to pay you, you'll have to pay us!" So he says, "Well, let's add up how much you guys owe me and how much I owe you." When we arrived [in Los Angeles], he said he was going to pay us $50 a day. But during that argument, he said he would pay us only $40 a day. But we added up the amount for two months—the month and a half we worked for him at $40, and he subtracted the meals—breakfast, lunch, dinner—and the months of rent. He charged us $6 per meal, almost $20 a day for food. He subtracted rent at $150 a month, plus electricity and gas. He owed us about $1,600 or $2,000, and after he subtracted everything, he owed us $700. But [even after that] he never paid us!

"Who is this guy? Have you seen him since you stopped working for him?" I asked. We were talking in 2006, and by this time Cristian owned his own pushcart.

"[That guy] is my cousin!" Cristian told me. "I see him all the time. He still hasn't paid us. It's been years since that argument."

By working without pay for months, Cristian had helped subsidize Reynaldo's business as well as his household expenses. The issue eventually resulted in a major fight.

"When we fell out with my cousin [Reynaldo], we got kicked out of his house and had no place to live or work. And these other guys got us a place to live. With one of my relatives, I guess, but very distant. They got us a place to live and gave my cousins work, but they didn't give *me* work [as a *frutero*]. They didn't have work for me, [they told me] that I should look on my own."

"Why didn't they give you work? Did they not have enough pushcarts?" I asked.

"Well, also because they didn't like me very much. They took me to work with this other man," he replied.

Cristian had led the charge against Reynaldo for the lost wages, and this history followed him to these new bosses, who were wary of his potential to protest exploitative work arrangements. Fearing a similar issue if they did not pay him, they opted not to hire him as a worker. Although Cristian did not work with this group, he did live with them. As he explained, while they might not have liked him, they did like and need his rent money.

Cristian began working with another boss, Don Joaquín, who was from the Mexican state of Guerrero. This man worked with mostly his own family members, including his father-in-law and his niece. Eventually, Cristian's uncle from Dos Mundos began working with the group as well. Don Joaquín paid Cristian $40 a day. When sales were low or when rain prevented him from working, Cristian was paid only $20 a day, which meant he struggled to pay for food. Cristian worked for Don Joaquín for nine months. He eventually started dating his employer's niece, Carmen. After a few months, they moved in together. Carmen left her uncle's house, where she had been strictly supervised, and split the rent on a bedroom with Cristian in a Highland Park apartment.

After leaving the employment of Carmen's uncle, Cristian went to work for his cousins, Raúl and Andres Martínez. They offered to pay him $60 a day, plus food delivered to him during the lunch hour or extra money for lunch. Cristian ended up working with them for about a year. The pay and meal arrangement helped him save money, and when he left he was able to purchase his own pushcart. The Martínez brothers continued giving him *raites* [rides] to his street corner, for which he paid $30 a day. The money he made as an independent vendor ranged from $80 on a slow day to $250 on a good day. Cristian enjoyed working independently:

> The difference [between working for someone and working on your own] is that you don't have anyone telling you what to do [when you work for yourself]. You work when you want to work, and when you don't, you don't. Nobody's yelling at you about whether you had good sales or not. Because when you work for someone, if you don't make the amount you're supposed to, they yell at you, or they subtract from what they pay you. [As an independent vendor,] no one tells you what to do, no one gets on your case, you just work, and at whatever hour we want to go home, we go home.

When Cristian had worked for an employer or a vendor-boss, he had worked seven days a week. On his own, he would work four or five days a week. Later, when Carmen and Cristian lived together, they were able to pool their money and create a bit more financial stability for themselves. However, Cristian did not untangle himself completely from the Martínez brothers or his *paisanos*. When Cristian wanted to purchase a pickup truck, he asked Raúl, who had U.S. citizenship, if he could buy it in his name.[9] Raúl agreed, and several months later Cristian was the proud owner of a used white Chevy pickup truck. Both Carmen and Cristian also participated in the Dos Mundos *tanda* and relied on it to make big payments toward the truck. These *tandas* among fruit vendors involve a number of participants making regular contributions to a fund that is given in whole or in part to each contributor on a rotating basis (for more on *tandas*, see chapter 4).

Jesús

Jesús left Dos Mundos in 2006, when he was twenty-one years old, knowing he would be a fruit vendor in Los Angeles. Financial need drove him to the job. In 2005, his wife had become sick after giving birth to their first child, and the illness was complicated further during her second pregnancy, when she started suffering from convulsions. His family was financially strained by the costs that the illness provoked. The family quickly found themselves in serious debt due to expensive medical procedures. It was decided that Jesús would go work in the United States to make money quickly and repay the debt. But of course the journey required getting into more debt.

Jesús was the oldest son in his family and the only one to migrate to the United States. He migrated unwillingly and knew he would return to his wife and children as soon as he could. It was Jesús's *concuño* (his sister-in-law's husband) who invited him to Los Angeles to work as a vendor. Jesús went to the local Dos Mundos moneylender to finance the trip and received a loan with a 15 percent interest rate. The journey was difficult; he was apprehended several times by Border Patrol agents, and it took him a month to get to Los Angeles.

His difficult time entering into the country perhaps foreshadowed the difficulty he would experience during his time in the United States. Jesús crossed the border with the niece of his *concuño*, and it was that *concuño* who also helped him get a job as a fruit vendor. As Jesús explained, "He

[Gerardo García, uncle to Benjamín and Gabriel García] helped me cross into the United States. He told me that I was going to work in fruit. He passed me over [the border] so that I could come work with him in the fruit business. Well, he also invited me to come over here because one of his nieces wanted to come and she didn't have someone to accompany her."

For Jesús and a few others, Gerardo García functioned as a kind of *coyote*. He did not physically take migrants across the border, but he facilitated the process and paid any necessary fees upfront. Jesús himself referred to Gerardo as his *coyote*. Gerardo García had the contacts to make the passage across the border as safe as possible for Dos Mundos migrants and knew others who could transport them into the Los Angeles area, past checkpoints several miles from the border. Once in Los Angeles, Gerardo García delivered the new workers to his nephews, Benjamín and Gabriel García, who owned and operated fruit pushcarts. In this way, Gerardo García was an informal labor recruiter, supplying his nephews with workers and profiting off the costs associated with moving the workers from Dos Mundos to Los Angeles. Gerardo was related by marriage to Jesús, but Jesús did not consider him family. "He's just someone I know from Dos Mundos," Jesús said. Many people in Dos Mundos are related by blood or marriage, which is common in small towns, and so a familial relationship is not always a good indicator of a strong network connection.

Informal labor recruiters have existed alongside most mass migrations of people and have received important scholarly attention. Historian Gunther Peck studied labor recruiters among immigrant workers in the late nineteenth and early twentieth centuries. He focused on the role of *padrones*, immigrant bosses who enslaved compatriots by acting as professional middlemen, and argued that *padrones* were modern entrepreneurs who used corporations and labor contracts to create coercive networks. As a middleman, a *padrone* was able to "traverse legal, lingual, class, and racial boundaries that separated new immigrants from North Americans" (Peck 2000, 2).

While the actions of *padrones* are similar to the actions of Gerardo and his nephews, the labor recruitment of the Garcías differs in that none of the Garcías would be considered middlemen who can traverse boundaries. In fact, the Garcías—though immigrant bosses—shared certain vulnerabilities with their workers. Like the Dos Mundos migrants they brought to the city to work, the Garcías were undocumented, not fluent in English, and had similar ethnic/racial backgrounds. For Jesús, those similarities in background made the subsequent verbal abuse and stolen wages intolerable. As he explained, "You come to the United States expecting abuse from Anglos [*Americanos*], not from your own *paisanos*."

Working conditions were less than ideal for several reasons. Street vending in Los Angeles can be heavily policed, and Jesús got caught up in health department crackdowns within weeks of starting the job. When Jesús arrived, he began working for Gabriel García, who would pay him $50 a day to work his pushcart. But Gabriel did not always have his workers' best interests in mind. He was also difficult to work with because he had a terrible temper and berated Jesús daily. This deeply unsettled Jesús and contributed to his decision to return to Mexico as soon as he could:

> [Gabriel's bad temper,] that's what I didn't like. Sometimes you had everything ready, and [he'd still yell at you]. He had his girlfriend, and sometimes on Saturdays or Fridays he'd go out dancing and . . . the next day, because he knew the man who sold fruit, he would just make the [wholesale fruit] order on the phone and it would be delivered, and we had to have the carts ready to go out at 8:30 a.m. There were days when he would stay asleep and ask for the fruit, and the fruit would get there at 8:30 or 8:00 a.m., and then he would get up with his bad attitude and [yell at us]. Everything bothered him, and if I answered back, well [*shakes head*]. You would try to explain that the fruit had just arrived and that you didn't have anything to prepare, and he didn't care. . . . [It takes an hour or an hour and a half to get the carts ready,] so we wouldn't have enough time. He'd come out all angry, yelling, "Hurry up!" And sometimes—since that's just the way we got along—sometimes cursing.

Jesús maintained a sojourner mentality and kept working for the Garcías for many months, though it was often unbearable. It took him five months of work to repay the moneylender in Dos Mundos. The money remitted by Jesús went directly to his wife, who made payments on their medical bills, and to the moneylender.

After a year, Jesús was finally presented with an opportunity to leave his job with the Garcías. During a large crackdown, the health department confiscated eight pushcarts belonging to the García brothers. Using this as an excuse, Jesús went to work with his cousin Cristian. He was so eager to leave the Garcías that he worked out an arrangement where he would share a pushcart with Cristian and work only a few days out of the week.

Despite having had a job waiting for him in Los Angeles, Jesús was a victim of limited job prospects and underdeveloped social networks. The fact that he came from Dos Mundos affected the opportunities available to him. Had his town been larger, more urban or metropolitan, and with a more diverse stream of migrants, his social network would have included more "weak" and "strong" ties to migrants working in different types of occupations (Granovetter 1973). Jesús might have had different job prospects in the United States. However, what and whom he knew was limited because of where he came from, and he ended up in a job working with an abusive *paisano*. Jesús did not have much personal incentive to find a better job because he expected to return to Mexico as soon as he had saved enough money to pay for his ailing wife's medical treatment.

Jesús did not have many options when he came to the United States— he had been offered and accepted the job working as a fruit vendor even before he arrived in Los Angeles. While this long-distance recruitment and job acquisition does reveal a positive side of social network use, Jesús was unhappy working for this *paisano* boss but felt that he could not quit based on this unhappiness alone. Jesús had only had a passing acquaintanceship with Gabriel in Dos Mundos before he started working for him in Los Angeles, and he did not know and was not told that Gabriel was a bad boss. Jesús was trapped in this job for several reasons, including an obligation to pay for his wife's medical bills. He regularly sent money to his wife even when he did not have enough to cover his own living expenses. He stayed in touch with his family, diverting funds to buy calling cards and a cell phone. Jesús was constantly homesick and dealt with this by calling his family as much as possible, which further depleted his income.

Manuel

Like Cristian, Manuel had also landed in another city before arriving in Los Angeles. Manuel was seventeen years old when he left Dos Mundos in 2005. Manuel initially left Dos Mundos to work in the fields of Fresno.

Manuel went north with Margarita, a neighbor and his grandmother's *comadre* (a fictive kin relationship based on a godparent role to each other's children), who was visiting Dos Mundos for a few months before returning to California, where she was a farmworker and field manager. Manuel had plenty of experience working in the fields of Dos Mundos, and Margarita knew him to be a hard worker. She had no problems recommending him to her boss for the job. Manuel left with Margarita on a Thursday, was on the other side of the border by Sunday, and was working in the Fresno fields on Monday morning.

Manuel found the work in the Fresno fields to be difficult and fast-paced, but the pay was good, especially when compared to the pay in Mexico.[10] Initially, he did not spend much of his downtime doing anything that would require spending money, so he was able to remit much of his checks back to his grandmother, Doña Julieta, who would make payments to the local moneylender who had financed his journey north. Manuel had left Dos Mundos because he wanted to earn more money and help his family live a better life. According to Manuel, if he had not ventured north to the United States, he would have left Dos Mundos anyway, seeking a job in construction in a neighboring Mexican city like his uncles had done. His steady remittances to Doña Julieta indicated to his uncles that there was good work to be had if they ventured north. About a year after Manuel left, two of his uncles joined him in Fresno. They worked long hours and were able to save money, but they thought life in Fresno was dull. Together, Manuel and his uncles decided to go to Los Angeles.

Manuel and his uncles had distant cousins—the García brothers, Benjamín and Gabriel—who owned fruit pushcarts and offered them jobs. Once they arrived in Los Angeles, Manuel and his uncles took jobs as fruit vendors and began living with these cousins. Like Jesús, Manuel was not treated well by the García brothers. They would often not pay Manuel and would berate him on the job. While working for them in the Hollywood area, he was arrested for vending on two different occasions and had a pushcart confiscated. The García brothers began seeing Manuel as a liability and told him to work with another group. He did, and in the process he moved out of their house. For the next year, Manuel jumped between three different vending groups, including the Martínez brothers' group, trying to find a stable situation.

Manuel's problems with citations, arrests, and confiscations followed him, mostly because the Hollywood area was heavily policed and all the bosses he worked for had street corners in that part of Los Angeles. Despite all the jumps between bosses and households, Manuel eventually saved enough money to buy an $800 *carro pirate* from the wholesale fruit merchant. These cheaply made pushcarts lack a proper drainage system and cannot be certified due to their shoddy construction, and they are often confiscated by the health department during crackdowns. Manuel connected with his *paisano* Chava, who was known for being a bit of a curmudgeon and antisocial when it came to *paisano* social events, and moved into an extra bedroom in the South Central Los Angeles home that Chava rented with another man.

Initially, Chava was Manuel's *raitero*—dropping him off mornings and picking him up. The rent in their shared home was low enough that Manuel was eventually able to purchase a used pickup truck from another vendor. Afterward, Chava and Manuel saw less of each other. Chava worked alone and enjoyed the solitude; he owned his own pushcart and a pickup truck. He came and went but rarely spent much time in the house they shared. At one point, they had a large pool table in the dining room. Carmen and I would hang out with Manuel in his home playing pool after work. Often, Chava would come home and lock himself in his bedroom as opposed to joining us in the dining room. Carmen and Manuel laughed off Chava's antisocial tendencies. Chava and Manuel, and later also Carmen, stored their pushcarts in the home's backyard under a white-tented tarp.

Manuel struggled financially as a *frutero* in Los Angeles; he often wore the same clothes and would wear down his tennis shoes before buying a new pair. Other vendors often talked about him as if he were a bad luck charm, and Carmen struggled to understand why he was doing so poorly relative to the rest of them. Manuel also had a string of run-ins with the health department and the police department that added to his financial vulnerabilities. If Manuel's story had ended with a working life in Fresno, he might have been more financially stable. His premigration level of need had been high, but he had not left Dos Mundos with desperate urgency. Manuel's reasoning before departing Dos Mundos was sound; he had known what he could gain from international migration and had adequate contacts with a Dos Mundos network that had provided him work on arrival. In Fresno, he had been embedded in a community of Dos Mundos *paisanos* that had helped him settle into his new job and life. He had housing, provided by Margarita and her family, and he had community.

For Manuel, leaving Fresno for a job as a street vendor in Los Angeles was a larger turning point with bigger risks than leaving Dos Mundos for Fresno. When Manuel decided to work for the García brothers, he traded in his good *paisano* network in Fresno, rooted in a long *comadre* relationship between Doña Julieta and Margarita, for a less sound *paisano* network rooted in distant kinship ties in Los Angeles. Importantly, Manuel left to work for the García brothers, whom he knew were employers to other *paisanos*. However, crucial information about their treatment of workers had been left unspoken. When Manuel arrived in Los Angeles, he found himself enjoying the pleasures that city life afforded but struggling with his new employers. The *paisano* community was different in the Fresno and Los Angeles contexts. The *paisanos* in Fresno were older and had families, whereas those in Los Angeles were young, unmarried, and without children, which suited Manuel's lifestyle better. And even though the treatment and pay were worse in Los Angeles, after a few months Manuel could not see himself returning to Fresno.

Gonzalo

Gonzalo was the last of this group of five to arrive in Los Angeles. In 2007, just as Cristian was returning to Dos Mundos to visit his parents, Gonzalo was leaving Dos Mundos. He was seventeen years old at the time. Gonzalo went directly to Los Angeles, where he had lined up a job as a fruit vendor. He migrated to work for the García brothers, and when he got to the city they had a pushcart ready for him. Less than a month after arriving, Gonzalo sent his family in Dos Mundos his first remittance.

Gonzalo left Dos Mundos with a cousin who was two years older; neither of them had migrated before. A neighbor, who was in his forties and who had migrated north several times before, took them. Gonzalo explained that he had left because he wanted to experience something different, he wanted adventure, and he knew that his small town could not offer that. He said that he was struck with courage when he heard of his cousin and neighbor's plan to go north, and he knew he had to act quickly.

Gonzalo was very close to his family, and he believed that if he thought about his plan to leave for too long he would lose his courage and the opportunity.

The fairly stable life Gonzalo led in Los Angeles came after a difficult passage north. Gonzalo struggled to enter the United States. The group he was with got lost and wandered through the desert. The small backpack he was carrying with all of his possessions had to be discarded along the way. "When I was trying to cross over, we got lost," he later told me. "We were walking around for days. We didn't have any water left. One morning after all that walking, I thought we might all die in the heat. But then we walked into a small area with livestock, and that livestock was standing in some muddy water. I remember being so thirsty that I drank from that water that had cow shit in it. It was horrible, horrible. I didn't even feel human."

When Gonzalo was finally picked up and taken to Los Angeles, he stayed with the García brothers, who had promised him a job and housing. As soon as he arrived, they took him to buy new clothes and shoes. By that time, the García brothers, who were originally from Dos Mundos, were well established in Los Angeles and in the fruit vending business. They owned several pushcarts and gave Gonzalo a cart to work. The brothers paid for Gonzalo's *coyote* and helped him adjust to life in the country. Like everyone else, Gonzalo had gotten a loan from the local Dos Mundos moneylender before leaving. His decision to leave was abrupt, and his family had not saved any money for the journey. However, unlike others, Gonzalo was able to pay off the loan relatively quickly because he started working as soon as he arrived.

Unlike Jesús and Manuel, Gonzalo had a strong and healthy relationship with the García brothers. He had been friendly with the García family in Dos Mundos. His parents were also good friends with the parents of the García brothers. This proved to be important to his quick adjustment and recovery from debt. The other major difference was the stability of the García brothers' business when Gonzalo arrived. At that time, they had evaded major health department crackdowns and had several pushcarts working the streets. Unlike Cristian, who had to wait without employment while the Martínez brothers recovered from a health department crackdown, Gonzalo began work immediately.

Gonzalo benefited from the prosperity and goodwill of the García brothers. This helped him land at the top of the hierarchical vending world. The money and stability provided by the García brothers helped Gonzalo establish himself rapidly after arriving. He was able to repay his debt to the García brothers, and the interest they charged was not financially crippling. He was quickly able to save money and purchase his own pushcart. Years later, he became involved in a romantic relationship with Carmen, which helped both of them financially because they split the cost of housing, food, and transportation. While the García brothers were willing to help Gonzalo establish himself as an independent vendor, they were less receptive to their other workers' wishes to do the same.

THE BOSSES

Two sets of brothers from Dos Mundos figured prominently among the fruit vendors that I followed. The García and the Martínez brothers were often the reason international migration occurred. They helped facilitate migration by funding it or encouraging it by promising *paisanos* a job on arrival. These two sets of brothers employed many recent arrivals. Throughout my time in the field, these sets of brothers were consistently able to maintain their pushcart investments and quickly replace pushcarts after a crackdown.[11]

Gabriel, Benjamín, and Omar from the García family and Raúl and Andres from the Martínez family often had the most employees working for them. The García and the Martínez brothers were all in their late twenties and early thirties. The García brothers had much more economic capital than other Dos Mundos migrants when they arrived in Los Angeles because their father owned the two corn mills in Dos Mundos. The entire town of Dos Mundos depended on the mills to produce their dietary staple of corn tortillas, and therefore the García family had name recognition, financial stability, and status within the community. The García brothers had a high socioeconomic status in Dos Mundos and transplanted this standing to Los Angeles within the Dos Mundos *paisano* community when they became pushcart owners and bosses. The uncle of the García brothers, Gerardo García, also facilitated the movement of Dos Mundos migrants across the international border and into Los Angeles so that they could work for his nephews. The García family was very secretive about its operations, and given how many workers told me the García brothers were behind their international migration, it is likely that the family expanded their business ventures into the migration industry. The migration industry is composed of the entrepreneurs, businesses, and service providers that develop, profit from, facilitate, and sustain movement across international borders (Hernández-León 2005).

The Martínez brothers had much less economic capital than the García brothers, but unlike every other Dos Mundos migrant I spoke with, Raúl Martínez had U.S. citizenship (he had been born in the United States, although he was raised in Dos Mundos and did not speak English). As a result of his citizenship, Raúl was able to apply for benefits to which others did not have access, could drive his pickup truck with a state-issued driver's license, and was able to purchase pushcarts and vehicles in his name as opposed to finding and paying a relative or close acquaintance with citizenship or legal residency to carry the responsibility of official title ownership. His citizenship decreased his vulnerability as a vendor and increased his autonomy as an employer. Despite the fact that Raúl operated in the informal sector and in a prohibited venture, his citizenship diminished the "legal violence" to which he was exposed.[12] Meanwhile, Andres Martínez benefited from his brother's citizenship by purchasing vehicles and certifying pushcarts in Raúl's name.

To save enough money to purchase pushcarts, the Martínez brothers sometimes employed unsavory tactics and had a reputation for not paying their vendor workers even when no crackdowns had occurred. Vendor workers often accused the Martínez brothers of "living beyond their means" and using vendors' salaries to pay the rent on what was perceived as a big house in East Los Angeles. The García brothers, on the other hand, had a reputation for being verbally abusive and duplicitous in their relations with workers. They too had periods of time when they did not pay their vendor workers despite seemingly high sales profits. Most of the vendor workers with whom I spent my time who at one point or another had worked under one of the García brothers speculated that the lack of pay was due to the brothers buying plots of land in Dos Mundos.

One evening in 2007 as I was waiting with José for Benjamín García to pick him up at the end of the workday, he said, "I called home [to Dos Mundos], and my family told me they [the García brothers] had paid for plots of land. I bet you that's my pay right there." The García brothers had not paid José for over two months at that point. José lived in a house with the brothers, and they justified the lack of pay by postponing his rent due date and purchasing the groceries for the house occupants (who included other vendor workers). The groceries that José consumed were, of course, added to the tab that he owed the García brothers. The irony of this situation was not lost on José.

Eventually, José became romantically involved with a Mexican-American woman and moved in with her after only a few months to escape the García brothers' system of nonpayment coupled with debt creation. When I visited Dos Mundos in 2011, I saw that the García family had four houses on a hill in the center of town. Three of those homes were under construction; each of them was two stories high and had architectural features of American homes (slanted roofs, pillars, car garage). One house belonged to the García brothers' parents, and each of the García brothers owned one of the remaining three houses, those under construction. While it was speculation that the Garcías were buying land in Mexico with vendors' wages, on the ground in Dos Mundos it was certainly clear that the García family had made a large investment in both land and construction.

The social and structural advantages of the García brothers and the Martínez brothers mitigated the hostile context of reception toward street vendors in Los Angeles. If the structure of opportunities conditions how help is given and received, then these two sets of brothers were ideally positioned both to *be* employers and to help each other *maintain* that status. Meanwhile, antivending ordinances and the resulting income instability pushed these employers to exploitative practices in an effort to secure a foothold in an unrelenting informal venture. On their part, vendor workers were willing to take jobs with no pay and/or to incur debt because of the limited opportunities found in Dos Mundos and the potential of greater exploitation in other Los Angeles industries where they did not have *paisano* connections. This exploitation at the hands of compatriots and the vendors' willingness to endure it in the absence of opportunity elsewhere is not a new phenomenon.[13] The García and the Martínez brothers and their exploitative practices were not exceptional but rather a product of their context.

Both the García and the Martínez brothers provided or created enough benefits (loans to facilitate migration, employment, housing, community, etc.) for workers to see some good in the midst of all of the bad. Of course, the vendors who received better benefits had more reasons to look beyond the exploitative work-for-no-pay situation. Domingo, one of the few vendors who was both over thirty-five years old and a cyclical migrant, depended on the García brothers to pay for his *coyote,* a guide who took him across the border clandestinely. The García brothers would pay about $2,000 for this service, and in exchange Domingo would work without pay for a few months. Domingo was also one of the few *fruteros* who worked seven days a week (others worked six days a week).

One rainy night, I was running errands with Carmen, who was by that time firmly embedded in the Dos Mundos network owing to her relationship with Cristian. I had asked Carmen if all the *fruteros* were young men, and this prompted her to call Domingo, a long-time *frutero* and one of the few older vendors in their circle, to ask if I could interview him. On rainy days, vendors across the city did not work. When the rain lasted several days, there was an abundance of downtime. Carmen and I picked Domingo up from the García house, and when he emerged, he explained that he was thankful to leave it.

"Thank you for picking me up, I was getting fed up with being in that house," he said as he got into Carmen's car. Domingo explained that he lived in a back part of the house with several other workers, while the Garcías lived in the front part of the house.

"What were you all doing tonight?" I asked.

"They were playing cards, but I don't like to gamble. My money is for saving, not for giving away [*no para regalar*]. Besides, I have to buy my son a gift for his birthday." He asked Carmen whether she might be able to give him a ride to the store the following day, and they arranged a pickup time.

"What did your son ask for?" Carmen asked, looking back at him from the passenger seat.[14]

"He wants an aluminum baseball bat," he said.

"Can't they find baseball bats in Puebla?" I asked.

"You know how they are, they think just because it comes from the north [the United States] that it's better. Even though it's probably made in Mexico!" We chuckled, and he settled into the backseat, looking out the window at the rain-soaked streets.

Domingo started migrating to Los Angeles in 2000, when he was thirty-seven years old. In Puebla, he had worked as a butcher, and his wife had worked at a tortilla factory. They both earned very little money and were living in a small rented room. He had three children at the time, and that life was not sustainable, so he migrated to improve their conditions. Specifically, he wanted to be able to build a house for his family. The first time he came to Los Angeles, he stayed for only three months before returning home because he missed his family. But life was not much improved for them. He steeled himself and returned to the United States for a three-year stretch, and in that time he was able to remit enough money to buy a plot of land and start building a home. After those three years, Domingo became a cyclical migrant. He would stay in Dos Mundos for three months and work in Los Angeles nine months. When I interviewed him, he and his wife had four children and a newly constructed home a few minutes outside of Dos Mundos.

Domingo and I spoke for over three hours in Carmen's bedroom while she prepared food in the kitchen, and he asked if he could linger afterward because he did not want to return to the García house so soon.

"It gets hard sometimes, to live like this [in a house with so many occupants], and with them. . . . Here I can exhale"—he breathed out loudly—"but over there I only sigh."

Domingo did not own a car. When it rained and he did not work, he was stuck indoors with the other vendors and bosses all day and all night. Although he was free to leave the house, the lack of pay resulting from his indebtedness meant that he had little money to spend and no method of transportation with which to move around. His employment with the García brothers had long-reaching effects that included Domingo feeling trapped and unable to breathe. Domingo talked continuously about returning to Dos Mundos, and the thought of home made his "bad times" in Los Angeles bearable. However, this sojourner mentality played a role in inhibiting him from developing more diverse networks that could move him out of fruit vending and into a more economically valuable and viable line of work. Domingo also felt a sense of obligation to the García brothers because they had been funding his trips to the United States for years as a cyclical migrant.

"I'm grateful for what they [García brothers] have done for me, don't get me wrong," Domingo continuously interjected when he spoke harshly of the García brothers. "Who else would pay for me to come year after year?"

After we dropped him off, Carmen told me that Domingo was a very hard worker. He never skimmed money off the top when he turned in his daily sales—a practice that was common among vendor workers. The García brothers valued Domingo, which is why they would pay for him to return year after year.

"The Garcías aren't idiots [*no son pendejos*]. They wouldn't pay for *any* worker to come and go like Domingo," Carmen said, bemoaning the fact that Domingo did not see his own worth.

CONCLUSION

Coethnic exploitation, specifically regarding nonpayment for work completed, within ethnic enclaves has been understood among academics as purposive and beneficial. According to sociologists Alejandro Portes and Robert L. Bach (1985), ethnic ties create a sense of collective purpose and entail reciprocal obligation; employers profit from the willing self-exploitation of fellow immigrants but are also obliged to provide them with supervisory positions and training and to support their move into self-employment.[15] It is ethnic solidarity that creates this sense of purpose and reciprocal obligation. Yet the treatment of vendor workers under different sets of bosses contradicts the "beneficial" exploitation rooted in ethnic solidarity observed in the ethnic enclaves.

In assessing the limits of ethnic solidarity in the enclave economy, Jimy M. Sanders and Victor Nee (1987) make a distinction between immigrant workers and immigrant bosses—a distinction premised on capital differentials. They find that entrepreneurs in ethnic enclaves receive earning returns to human capital comparable to those immigrants in the primary labor market, but the same is not true for employees. Sanders and Nee stipulate a need to revise the enclave-economy hypothesis to include this distinction yet note that such a revision diminishes the claim that the ethnic enclave is a protected sector of the U.S. economy where immigrants can avoid discrimination and achieve upward mobility. It is in this void that the concept of the ethnic cage fits. With this conceptual intervention, we can understand the protection *and* harm produced within a tightly networked ethnic, or *paisano*, community.

Fruit vendor employers were exploitative in a way that was interpreted by workers as self-serving. When employers suffered losses following a crackdown, workers tolerated periods of nonpayment. However, nonpayment by employers without a corresponding crackdown contributed to workers feeling that they would never be able to save enough money to buy their own pushcarts and establish independent businesses or survive a crackdown and the subsequent loss of employment. This exploitative treatment by vendor employers, combined with the punitive regulatory environment in which they worked, led some workers to speak of return migration as the only suitable solution to their financial problems.

There are limits to ethnic solidarity. Among *fruteros*, employers faced different realities than their workers. Employers had the possibility of recovering after a crackdown by leaning heavily on their workers and exploiting their labor. Some employers showed no signs of supporting workers' movement into self-employment and would often shift workers to another vending group instead of helping them establish themselves as independent vendors. Employers did not view workers' movement into self-employment positively. When a former employee wanted to keep their street corner due to a customer base that expected to see them there, for example, they were met with indifference or disdain. The unwillingness of employers to help vendor workers establish their own pushcart businesses might have been due to the fact that former workers would one day compete with them in a city with a limited number of viable street corners (those that had good pedestrian traffic and were close to the wholesale fruit market and where vendors stored their pushcarts). Vendor workers consequently had restrained aspirations.

Among most bosses and employers, self-interest and a desire for self-preservation amid continuous crackdowns broke down any semblance of "ethnic solidarity." Yet a major problem with this concept is that in its absence, one cannot blame its opposite, namely "ethnic enmity." The indebtedness and downward mobility of newcomers was not rooted in the desire of some compatriots to see other compatriots suffer but in the power and status some *paisanos* possessed and sought to maintain. Fruit vendor workers, meanwhile, were continuously forced to recognize their low status in a newly constituted hierarchy of hometown associates.

Bosses who paid for workers' passage across international borders, provided them with housing and employment on arrival, and later exploited them for their labor were both providing assistance to integrate newcomers and setting roadblocks in their path to upward economic mobility. They were simultaneously helping and harming their fellow *paisanos*. The structure of the work—operating in an unpredictable informal sector—and the role of the immigrant bosses—exploiting highly vulnerable recent arrivals—are part and parcel of the ethnic cage. After all, the ethnic cage is forged in the fire of a hostile context of reception. In the following chapter, I explore the further risks *fruteros* confronted on the job and in the streets.

3 Managing Risk on the Street

The Pico-Union neighborhood of Los Angeles is always bustling with traffic and pedestrians moving between various transportation nodes and shopping centers catering to Latino customers. It is a working-class neighborhood and one of several locations where I spent my time doing fieldwork. In this area, it is not uncommon to hear low-flying police helicopters hovering above, the thundering sound mixing with the honks of cars moving through the streets. The frenzied activity of the day is countered by a slowdown in the evening. Once the sun begins to set and the temperature drops, dozens of Latino families descend from their homes and apartments to stroll the neighborhood. Parents walk about with children in tow. Pico-Union is a lively area, and these types of neighborhoods, with an abundance of pedestrians and traffic, often attract street vendors, who profit from the bustle of activity. It was in this Pico-Union neighborhood, about a year after beginning my fieldwork among street vendors, that I witnessed my first joint police and health department crackdown. Despite working out in the open, street vendors are often truly seen by others who move in the same space only during these crackdowns. In these moments, the precarity of their social position is made highly visible.

During this time, Carmen and Cristian owned two pushcarts. However, Jesús's falling-out with the García brothers had led him to make an arrangement with Carmen and Cristian to use one of their pushcarts a few times out of the week. On the days that Jesús worked Carmen's pushcart on her corner, Cristian and Carmen would work together at the Pico-Union location, though Cristian would often run errands in his pickup truck throughout the day. The day of the crackdown, I spent the morning helping Carmen work at the location that Cristian typically worked. It was a corner in front of a gas station that had three other fruit vendors lining the perimeter. That is how lively the neighborhood was—one commercial space could host four street vendors selling the same item. It was late morning, and Cristian brought us lunch from a nearby restaurant. When Cristian arrived and parked in the gas station lot, he showed us the plastic bag with our Styrofoam containers of food. Carmen told me to eat in the truck with Cristian while she continued to attend customers, then we could switch places.

Cristian and I were sitting in the truck, listening to the radio and eating, when Cristian looked up and let out an extended curse, "*Chiiiiinga tu madre* [Motherfucker]." I followed his gaze and saw two police cars, an unmarked van, and a garbage truck surrounding all four vendors. The police officers divided up and walked briskly to each vendor—two selling on the northern edge of the sidewalk, and two selling on the eastern edge. I instinctively opened the truck door to walk over, but Cristian grabbed my shoulder and told me to wait. He did not want the police officers to come over to the truck and start asking him questions. He did not have a driver's license, and the truck was in another person's name. The scene unfolded before us as spectators.

We strained to hear the conversation through the rolled-down windows. We could see the health inspectors asking the vendors if their pushcarts had permits. Carmen handed them some paperwork, which they looked at and then gave back. The inspectors then took out large black bags and dumped into them all of the peeled and unpeeled fruit sitting on top of ice inside the pushcarts. The colorful umbrellas were taken down and hauled off along with the milk crates, cutting boards, knives—everything that was not thrown into the garbage truck was confiscated. The remaining ice was dumped out onto the sidewalk, and one pushcart without a permit was hauled away. Tickets were given to the vendors, and most of them reached for their phones to make calls.

Some passersby moved around the activity, but several stopped and stared. A few heckled the cops, yelling in Spanish, "Why don't you leave these people alone?"; "You should be arresting drug dealers!"; or "Is it a crime to work?" Within minutes, it was over, and the police cruisers, unmarked van, and garbage truck raced off to the next location and away from the growing discontent. Cristian was already on his phone calling other vendors in the area, telling them to hide their pushcarts and giving them the direction that *salubridad* (the health department) had taken.

Cristian and I stepped out of the pickup truck and walked toward Carmen. Cristian assessed the damage; he owned the cart that Carmen had been working, which had not been hauled away. The other vendors worked for different bosses, and they were all on their cell phones calling people. I offered condolences. A few passersby lingered and asked the vendors what they were going to do; others complained about the injustice of the crackdown. The gathered crowd eventually receded into the background as people hurried on to their destinations.

Carmen looked at Cristian and asked, "What now?"

Cristian looked around and then down at his phone to check the time. "Wait here, I'll go get you new things." He left to make the rounds. Later, I would accompany vendors on similar treks, heading to the commissary or a vendor's backyard to pull boxes of extra produce, to Chinatown to buy new umbrellas, cutting boards, utensils, and containers, and then to the market for bags of ice. That day, though, I remained behind with Carmen while Cristian gathered a fresh batch of supplies.

"Is this how it always is?" I asked, referring to the health department crackdowns.

"I'm sorry it happened, but I'm glad you got to see it. Do you see how they treat us? Like garbage! *Pinches viejos, hijos de su puta madre* [Fucking men, sons of bitches]!" Carmen replied, her anger surfacing in a tirade of expletives. She started cleaning up her area, continuing to curse under her breath, and I gave her space while helping her sweep. Cristian returned, and within a couple of hours Carmen was selling again, though with a more limited supply of produce. The mood was somber for the rest of the day, and they decided to pack up earlier than usual to put the day's events behind them.

Fruit vendors engage in an informal occupation that, as practiced, was forbidden at the time in Los Angeles by city, county, and state laws. Pushcarts could be certified by the Los Angeles Health Department as mobile food facilities in a somewhat complicated bureaucratic process that required the vendor to have a special pushcart with drainage, push-cart blueprints, a detailed vending location and route sheets (if the cart was nonstationary), proof of commissary warehouse pushcart storage, clearly labeled containers showing the contents of food dispensed and the packaging date, and a permission slip from a local business allowing vendors access to a restroom. Each of these requirements created a business opportunity for other Latinos. For example, some made the pushcarts, and others made blueprints for those pushcarts. A vendor could buy a sheet of adhesive labels to put on their food containers from some entrepreneurial person with a computer and a box of Avery brand address labels.[1] In addition to supplying all of these documents, vendors had to pay a fee of over $400.

This certification was contingent on the vendor selling only prepackaged food that was prepared in a licensed warehouse commissary. But, as any fruit vendor will explain, customers never want prepackaged fruit salads. The appeal of fruit vendors lies partly in their ability to make made-to-order fruit salads. It is precisely that action, preparing food on the street, that health department inspectors regulated most severely. The Los Angeles Health Department, in conjunction with the LAPD, periodically monitored the streets of Los Angeles to enforce those food safety laws, resulting in crackdowns.

Crackdowns that resulted in the confiscation of goods, the issuing of citations, displacement, and even arrest could be financially and emotionally devastating for fruit vendors. A crackdown is one of the worst-case scenarios for a street vendor. Although the individual crackdowns can be unexpected, the fact that they will occur is a routine part of being a fruit vendor. It is in that moment of intense activity that regular customers and passersby become aware of the risk that *fruteros* face by vending on the street. For a fleeting moment, bystanders can turn into supporters of street vendors in a show of solidarity. These crackdowns function as flashpoints, moments in time when street vendors become truly visible to passersby. But working on a street corner involves many different types of risks, most of which are unseen by those same passersby. This chapter focuses on the ways in which *fruteros* manage those risks and the survival strategies they employ in their day-to-day working lives. These survival strategies are meant to decrease risk and increase sales but are often short-term solutions that do not resolve larger issues rooted in the regulatory structure of the Los Angeles local government.

Risks vary, ranging from informal street gang shakedowns to restaurant owners or office building cafeteria managers who see *fruteros* as customer-stealing competition. Throughout the day, vendors must manage unruly customers to avoid being seen as a source of conflict and maintain regular customers to make a profit. Vendors must forge alliances with fellow street workers to keep their pushcarts safe; they must engender sympathy or create trust with nearby business owners or managers to get access to restroom facilities; they must present themselves as professional and hygienic to customers even when these markers (such as apron use) make them more visible to health inspectors during crackdowns; and they must understand that a friendly and cooperative relationship with police officers cannot protect them from arrest. *Fruteros* must harness the resources available to them, both from their network of *paisanos* and from the street corners where they work. They must forge robust ties that bind; ties through which resources flow and obligations accumulate.

CLAIMING SPACE AND BUILDING ALLIANCES

The positioning of fruit vendors throughout Los Angeles County is anything but random. Vendors seek sidewalk spaces that offer access to customers, protection, a useful infrastructure, and potential allies. Often, geographical location is a trade-off, as safer locations are less profitable than high-risk locations. For example, high-density neighborhoods with plenty of Latino, working-class pedestrians can be profitable locations for vending. These neighborhoods tend to attract multiple street vendors who want to profit from the environment. Yet more street vendors make the area more attractive for health department crackdowns. Health department officials can be more effective when they conduct crackdowns in locations where they can cite, confiscate, and arrest multiple vending prohibition violators. A location farther west of downtown Los Angeles may have fewer pedestrians and be less profitable than a dense neighborhood in a central area, but it is also less likely to attract a health department crackdown. The distance from a more profitable area with a high concentration of street vendors also creates more time for street patrols and alerts from fellow *paisanos* to be effective. Crackdowns typically begin in areas with high concentrations of street vendors. *Fruteros* must know how to carefully balance these risks and benefits when deciding where to vend.

The first criterion when scouting a new location is the presence or even abundance of Latinos. While hitching a ride from Daniel, a vendor whose brother-in-law owned pushcarts and was always on the hunt for new opportunities, I was asked about Westwood Village, the neighborhood in West Los Angeles where my university was located. Were there vendors working in the area? Were there Latinos in the area? Although new to the area at the time, I had noticed plenty of Latinos—most often working in the service-oriented businesses of the neighborhood. A few weeks later, Daniel's brother-in-law dropped one of his workers near the southern part of campus to test the Westwood Village location; the vendor was soon cited by police and told to move. Daniel explained to me that a "Latino area" to him was measured more by the number of Latino residents.[2]

When discussing this issue with Carmen and Cristian, they explained that Latino neighborhoods provided a sense of security because they contained a known population. Cristian further explained that to his knowledge, Latinos had more "experience" buying from street vendors. Though fruit vending caters to a wide range of people and thrives in areas not considered to have high concentrations of Latino residents, some pushcart owners, like Daniel's brother-in-law, use the Latino population of an area as a preliminary test to measure a neighborhood's tolerance of their presence and to roughly calculate the potential for sales. This process is representative of immigrant entrepreneurship, where businesses cater to a captive market of coethnics before catering to a broader clientele (Rath and Kloosterman 2000).

The first set of vendors I met was well established in the neighborhoods of West Los Angeles. For these vendors, the farther west they ventured—into neighborhoods that were less Latino dominated and more affluent—the less severe police officers were, the scarcer gang members became, and the less frequently health inspectors appeared. Some of these characteristics might seem unexpected, but one reason vendors in these areas are not as severely regulated is that there are fewer of them. Areas like the Fashion District and MacArthur Park, which are closer to downtown Los Angeles, have many more street vendors. As a result, they experience stricter regulation, since crackdowns initiated by the health department have the capacity to be more successful if they focus on areas with many clusters of potential offenders. But while vending farther west carries less risk, it can also be less profitable. West Los Angeles vendors see fewer pedestrians than their downtown counterparts. Vendors must make a choice between less risk and lower sales or high risk and higher sales.

In an effort to seek pedestrians in a city dominated by a car culture, vendors will gravitate toward businesses that generate pedestrians. Banks, grocery stores, hand car wash lots, gas stations, and public transportation nodes are popular locations. The most popular location is near or in front of a bank. Vendor transactions are in cash, and ATMs provide would-be customers with a ready supply of it. Among the vendors I visited and interviewed, all were working or had worked in front of a bank.

Banks also often employ street-based service workers, like parking attendants, with whom fruit vendors can create an alliance. These attendants may not be able to help when police or health inspectors arrive, but they can help to hide a vendor, convince a bank manager that a vendor does not pose a threat to the business, act as mediators when disputes between fruit vendors and customers arise, and relay information to cart owners if and when a vendor is arrested. All the vendors who worked in front of banks that had parking attendants befriended them as soon as they could. Often, this was done by giving away free fruit. In the months that I worked with Carmen, we saw four different parking lot attendants cycle in and out of the location, and she made a special attempt to befriend each of them. Beyond the strategic aspects of these friendships, parking lot attendants were often coethnics who spoke Spanish and could help vendors pass the time on slow days.

Edgar, one of the few Central American *fruteros* in the group, worked in the parking lot of a large chain grocery store and befriended the Latino store manager by offering him free fruit. Conversations between the two often revealed very useful information for Edgar. The parking lot where Edgar worked also functioned as an informal mechanic's shop. When the mechanic's customers were dissatisfied with the service they received, they would sometimes complain to the grocery store manager. The manager, angry about their misplaced complaints, would often call the police on the mechanic. The police would do nothing, claiming that it was private not public property and that fixing cars was not a crime. The manager gave this information to Edgar.

Edgar explained, "I sometimes ask the manager of the grocery store, 'Hey, and what if the cops come?' And he tells me not to worry about it and says, 'He [the cop] has no reason to bother you 'cause when I call him they tell me they can't do anything because it's private property.' And so we [fruit vendors] don't have to leave. The manager calls the cops on [the mechanic], but the cops don't do anything 'cause 'it's private property.'"

While the information given to Edgar by the store manager was not entirely accurate—vendors, even when they operate on private property, are in violation of ordinances that could prompt police officers to issue a citation or arrest—it nevertheless showcased the alliance between the two men. The store manager felt comfortable enough to share his job-related frustrations with the vendor, who felt safer on the street corner as a result of this friendship.

Where vendors decide to set up shop and the alliances they create at those locations do not completely eliminate the risk of crackdowns. However, they do much to set a fruit vendor's mind at ease and might even help with evasion tactics down the line. A carefully vetted street corner location can significantly reduce the level of stress a fruit vendor feels while on the job. And the stress of the job was a recurring motif in all my conversations with vendors. Vendors who feel safer in their locations are likely to be more efficient workers and therefore more profitable and less likely to lean on their social networks for resources. It is for this reason that street corners with positive geographic and alliance-building qualities are guarded ferociously by the vendors who work them and not easily ceded to other vendors (within or outside their *paisano* networks).

Information about which street corners are taken is well known, and vendors who know a street corner is taken will try not to violate this tenancy when no fruit vendor is present. However, occasional altercations about street corner tenancies did occur.

After a year of visiting Carmen, I showed up one day to her spot in a Mid-City, affluent neighborhood only to find another young woman vending fruit from a pushcart a few feet away—but close enough that they both shared the shade of the same large tree. They were both working in front of a bank and catering to bank customers. As I approached Carmen, I gave her a look that said, "What is going on?" Carmen responded by cocking her head, pursing her lips, and crossing her arms over her chest. I walked past the unknown vendor and immediately asked Carmen if she knew the girl.

"No! That idiot [*esa pendeja*] was here this morning when I got here. But this is my corner. I'm not leaving. Fucking bitch [*Pinche vieja*]." She said angrily and loud enough for the girl to hear, though she pretended not to.

The girl working the other pushcart was thin and wore tight black jeans and a small tank top that exposed her midriff. She was shorter than the tall pushcart she worked, and so she had to climb onto a milk crate and lean over to reach the area where her fruit was resting over ice, exposing her behind as she did so. Throughout the day, as the girl attended to clients and leaned into her cart, Carmen would scoff and say, "She looks like a fucking prostitute, that's why all her customers are men!" However, I did not notice a higher number of male customers throughout the day, and in fact the customers were evenly distributed between men and women.

Carmen waged "war" by talking loudly about the girl whenever there were no customers around and sweeping the leaves and dust in her area over to the girl's side. Carmen never thought of being violent. She knew any type of altercation like that—in that affluent area and in front of the bank, with its security guards—could compromise her vending spot and her faithful clientele. When Carmen's regular customers came by—and most often when they were other women—they would partake in criticism of the new girl with Carmen. Day after day, the new girl kept showing up. Eventually, Carmen's regular customers and bank employees started confronting the girl and telling her she had to leave because Carmen had been working that location for as long as they had known, so it belonged to her.

It was the community that Carmen had nurtured in her years at that corner that ultimately provided the support and backing she needed to fend off this competition. After a couple of weeks, the girl stopped showing up. The years of time and effort Carmen had put into building up her alliances on that corner had paid off.

PAISANO STREET PATROLS AND ALERTS

Fruit vendors rely on one another for help. Their *paisano* networks facilitate entry into the business, provide loans to buy pushcarts, create distribution channels between the wholesale fruit market and preparation sites, allow for collective drop-offs and pickups, and provide money to bail vendors out of jail, pay citation fines, or fund reentry to the country after deportation. It is often a fellow *paisano* who provides recently arrived immigrant vendors a job and pushcart. And it is likely a fellow *paisano* who will be called in the event of a citation or arrest. Therefore, *paisanos* often have a financial interest in keeping each other working safely.

During a lull in conversation with Daniel on the street corner, as I munched on jicama, someone in a black pickup truck drove by and whistled to get his attention. Often, repeat customers would signal their arrival with a honk or whistle so that Daniel could begin preparing their usual order. Such customers would treat Daniel, and other fruit vendors, like a pseudo drive-through business. In these cases, I was often tasked with running the prepared fruit salad up to the car and receiving the cash payment. This time, however, the pickup truck did not stop. The driver, who was headed east, made eye contact with Daniel and motioned with his hand— pointing upward with his index finger and making a circular movement.

"Quick, help me pick up!" Daniel said.

"Are you leaving?" I asked, surprised by the urgency in his voice.

Daniel did not respond. He shoved his cardboard box of trash under his pushcart storage area, took down his umbrella, and instructed me to follow him. I offered to carry the umbrella. He walked fast down the block away from Venice Boulevard, pushing his half-full cart. I followed, fumbling to fold up the large rainbow umbrella while holding my plastic bag of jicama. Daniel tucked the pushcart into an alley behind an office

building and placed the umbrella on top. Then, leaving the pushcart unattended, we walked back to the corner and started walking west along
Venice. We crossed a street half a block away, and Daniel motioned to a
bus bench.

"What's happening?" I asked.

"Let's sit," he said.

Daniel explained that the man in the pickup truck was his brother-in-
law and the owner of the pushcart he was working. His brother-in-law
owned several pushcarts and routinely spent the day "patrolling" the
streets. When health department crackdowns were ongoing, vendors
would communicate important information via cell phones about the
routes inspectors were taking. Sometimes, Daniel's brother-in-law would
attempt to follow the inspectors' vehicles at a distance and warn anyone
along the route or in the general vicinity via cell phone.

Later, while vendors were unloading carts at the commissary, they
admitted that the inspectors were aware of being followed.

"Are your street patrols effective with *salubridad* [the health depart-
ment]?" I asked.

"No way! [*No manches!*] Sometimes two or three pickup trucks follow
them, you think they don't know what's going on? They [the inspectors]
even run red lights to lose their tails!" Cristian chuckled as he told me this,
and other vendors within earshot laughed and nodded.

That afternoon with Daniel, however, the whistle and hand gesture signaled that the area was "hot" and that Daniel should hide the pushcart.
His brother-in-law was racing to the "scene," trying to find the caravan of
health inspectors; they often traveled behind a police car in a van followed
by a garbage truck—and, if the vendors were to be believed, tailed by a
group of Latino men driving pickup trucks. Luckily for Daniel, that day
was uneventful. After several minutes, the black pickup truck returned,
and the driver signaled that all was clear, so we walked back to pull the
pushcart out from its hiding spot.

Daniel was well known along that busy Venice Boulevard corridor lined
with businesses. Office workers from the building he stood in front of routinely bought fruit. A nearby medical center also provided a steady stream
of regulars. High visibility on the boulevard combined with the small side
street where ample parking was available allowed passing blue-collar

workers to stop by for a bag of fruit. Gardeners and cable installation men would stop by during the workday for fruit and sometimes also a quick chat. When Daniel left his pushcart unattended in the alley, he knew no harm would come to it. It was a safe Westside neighborhood, he was known by workers of the area's businesses, and the pushcart was far too heavy and cumbersome for a passing opportunist to steal. That was the safety that was provided by all of Daniel's ties in the neighborhood. But only his *paisanos* have information about an oncoming health department crackdown, and without their alerts, everything else Daniel had built on that corner would not matter.

Street patrols and alerts were one important strategy that vendors employed on the street to evade crackdowns. The patrols and alerts provided real-time information about the location and route health inspectors and police officers were taking. These alerts were often carried out by *paisanos* looking out for each other or their own pushcart investments. Accurate information about ongoing crackdowns could maximize the amount of time a vendor stayed on the streets, which increased profitability. It was often not enough to know that crackdowns were occurring; this general information would frequently result in the hiding of pushcarts and produce for an extended period of time, which could lead to a loss of sales or even customer contempt. Vendors had to carefully balance how much they were willing to vend within the window of time they were given before inspectors arrived. When information was accurate, a vendor could finish ongoing transactions and still have enough time to hide the pushcart. In less ideal circumstances, a vendor would simply walk away from the pushcart to avoid a citation or arrest, though this typically meant sacrificing the pushcart and product altogether. When Daniel got the signal from the black pickup, he had no customers and was given enough time to pack up his things, tuck the pushcart into an alley, and walk away. It was an ideal use of his *paisano* ties, despite the fact that it was ultimately a false alarm.

Sometimes, the importance of these alerts was demonstrated more clearly in their absence. When Jesús was arrested the first time, it was because a fellow, non-*paisano* street vendor duped him. As Jesús explained:

> One day, the cops were following this man with a cart selling ice cream. I would see the man regularly. He would head up toward a school [to sell]. . . .

He'd always walk by. He'd greet me, and I'd greet him. [One day,] I saw him walking up. He would come back [down] around 5:00 in the afternoon, heading home. That day, I saw him—I saw that he was running, pushing his cart, running as fast as he could! So I ask him, "What happened? Why you running?" He said to me, "I just forgot something at home, so I'm headed home." But he'd already seen the police coming. He didn't warn me because he knew that if he warned me, I was going to hide. So then they'd catch him. And since they were close behind, what he did was just to run straight [past me], . . . so the police arrived and saw *me* there!

The man with the ice cream cart had no kinship or *paisano* link to Jesús and therefore, as Jesús saw it, no obligation to keep him safe. Jesús interpreted the man's actions as a deception that gave the man time to escape. As Jesús explained, had the ice cream vendor been kith or kin, this interaction would have been very different. These warning systems allow vendors, who typically work alone on street corners, to feel the safety and protection of a group. Information about ongoing crackdowns serves vendors in the short term by allowing them to finalize or maximize sales and serves them in the long term by helping them evade health department and police officials so they can go on to vend another day.

Given Jesús's interpretation of events, this case presented a test for the weak tie he had with the ice cream vendor. It failed the test disastrously for Jesús; he was jailed for vending, and his pushcart was confiscated. When he was arrested, his network of *paisanos* was undergoing financial hardship and could not afford to bail him out. He noted that this arrest brought about one of the most difficult periods of his life. He neither slept nor ate during the two nights he spent in jail. When he was released, he was unable to recover his belongings, including his wallet. He recalled with much chagrin the irony of coming to this country to work and make money only to end up in jail and later on the streets begging for change:

We [Jesús and other vendors that had been arrested during the crackdown] were released [from jail] at 6:30 in the evening. I wasn't able to collect my personal belongings because it was late. . . . I half remembered the telephone number for the house where I was staying. So I went out, and being new to LA, I didn't even know which bus I could take to bring me there. I didn't know what to do. I began asking for money on the street so that I could call the house. They [the other vendors] were embarrassed to ask girls [for money]. I would ask guys, and they'd be rude in responding: "How about you get a job? You lazy shit, asking for money on the street!" And I'd ask the women, but nothing. . . . I spent an hour trying to get fifty cents.

Jesús eventually managed to get back, and a few days later he borrowed another vendor's pushcart and was selling on the street again. He started working in a different neighborhood and never saw the ice cream vendor again. But the arrest and his time in jail took its toll. This episode occurred two months after his arrival in the country, and it gave shape to his disenchantment with the United States and his *paisanos*. Because he had only spent two months on his corner before the arrest, he had not developed networks of ties to distinct people on the street. He did not even know that he could be arrested for vending. The experience tainted his view of his ties, both within and outside of his *paisano* network. He readily admitted that this event and others like it made him bitter, setting the stage for his eventual return to Mexico.

The dependence on *paisanos* helps vendors counteract the negative effects of crackdowns and financial hardship. The risks tied to fruit vending are greatly diminished by kinship and *paisano* networks; in fact, some vendors argue that this occupation could not be performed successfully without heavily relying on social networks. Financial bailouts offered by social network peers allow vendors to get back to work, but the reappearance of vendors often prompts the health department and police department to renew their efforts and conduct crackdowns again.

However, the bounded nature of kinship and *paisano* networks means that if one vendor suffers financial hardship, it will weigh heavily on all the vendors in the network.[3] This is the trap of social networks.[4] While social networks may ease financial hardship by distributing it over many shoulders, the web of reciprocal obligations impedes individual and collective upward social mobility.

TURNING THREATS INTO RESOURCES

While LAPD officers frequently patrol the streets where vendors are located, policing street vendors generally is a low priority, and officers recognize that policing vendors can be controversial.[5] Officers are used in combined health department–LAPD sweeps during major crackdowns, but they rarely conduct sweeps of their own because they are unable to confiscate items without representatives from the health department being present.[6] Police officers will ask a fruit vendor to move and issue a citation only after several complaints have been made by private citizens or by business owners.[7] More often than not, police officers and fruit vendors see and interact with each other in civil and quotidian ways. Yet the experiences of fruit vendors do reflect racialized and gendered policing practices.[8] Civil interactions are often facilitated by a shared ethnic background and language. Thus, Spanish-speaking Latino cops are more likely to develop civil relationships with Latino fruit vendors. *Fruteros* embrace these types of interactions, using them to turn the threat that police officers present into a possible resource.

Interactions between fruit vendors and police officers are quite common. While one might expect these encounters to be more like confrontations than interactions, the vast majority of vendors develop positive or neutral relationships with cops through sustained civil interaction. The reasons for this vary. Vendors, as a steady presence on street corners, can take on the role of a "public character" (Jacobs 1961) and in this way assist police officers in monitoring the streets. They become police officers' "eyes on the street" and help make the street corners where they work "safer, stabler, and more predictable" (Duneier 2000, 8). As fixtures in the urban landscape, vendors can also provide a respite to cops from the doldrums of police work by offering casual conversation and a healthy snack. Fruit vendors sustain these interactions in an effort to gain useful information and to develop friendships that might help them down the road. In this way, fruit vendors curb—that is, bring to the street corner and bridle—the officers that might one day be charged with citing or arresting them. However, these vendor-officer relationships are tenuous.

It is important to acknowledge the very disparate power dynamic that exists between police officers and vendors. Police officers represent an imminent threat that can result in citations, arrest, and, in the era of Secure Communities, the possibility of deportation.[9] Police officers represent a population with rights and privileges that extend above those of an average citizen, while fruit vendors represent a population whose presence in the country and whose work on the street corner are both illegal. Thus, interactions between these two groups must be analyzed through the lens that this power differential affords. Regardless of the type of interaction, police officers always have the upper hand, and this can be leveraged in different ways. Police officers have complete discretion and can decide to cite or arrest a vendor at any point because vendors are always in violation of antivending ordinances in the county and city codes. However, officers are also charged with protecting these vendors, who are often ideal targets for criminals looking for vulnerable victims. Fruit vendors are always cognizant of this power differential. To vendors, police represent both the punitive and the protective arms of the state. And, like the other strategies presented here, befriending a police officer diminishes but does not entirely remove the threat that officers represent. While a vendor may have civil relations with a police officer one day, the police officer's official duties might bring her to the street corner in an oppositional role the next day.

On a slow Tuesday afternoon, I was working a corner in Echo Park with José. He did not have much fruit left, and so potential customers would look into his cart and walk away without purchasing anything. After close to an hour without any customers, José called the cart owner, one of the García brothers, and asked to be picked up. He was told he would have to wait another hour or two because of traffic. José leaned on his cart with his back to the street and chucked ice cubes into a box full of trash a couple of feet away. I was sitting on a milk crate nibbling on some leftover coconut pieces when I saw a police patrol car coming down the street. As the police approached us, they slowed down and came to a rolling stop in front of us. I sat up straight and averted my eyes, which caused José to glance over his left shoulder. He saw the cops but did not react, and his stance remained relaxed. The Latino cop on the passenger side, who was closest to us, leaned his head partially out and asked in Spanish, "*Todo calmado?* [Everything calm?]" José responded by apathetically nodding yes, and just as quickly as they showed up the cops were gone again.

José explained that those were neighborhood cops. He had been working at that gas station parking lot for a while, and about a year prior there had been an armed robbery at the gas station convenience store. When the police came to file a report, they asked José if he had seen anything; he had not. For several days after the incident, the cops maintained a stronger presence in the area and began to "drop in" on José to ask if he had seen the suspect or if he had noticed any unusual activity. Though José remained in the dark about the theft and whether the suspect had been captured—he never asked the police officers follow-up questions and did not maintain a relationship with the rotating crew of gas station attendants—he continued to interact with the police officers through brief encounters such as the one I witnessed. After a year, whether the convenience store robbery had been solved or not, the continued check-ins by police officers signaled to José that he had become a source of potentially valuable information. Though José did not care for the cops, he knew that these brief encounters served a purpose, and given the power differential, he never did anything to dissuade the cops from "dropping in." José did not care to establish a positive relationship with police officers; he preferred to be completely off their radar. However, since he was on their radar, he preferred to maintain a neutral relationship with them.

Among the male vendors I interviewed with similar relationships to police officers, none reported having extended conversations or interactions. This seemed to be the result of both parties' unwillingness to engage for long periods of time. When remembering conversations and in observed interactions with police officers, male vendors tended to give short, non–open ended responses to questions put forth by police officers. Police officers, on their part, did not leave their patrol cars during these interactions, and sometimes they only slowed their vehicles to a creeping roll to take part in them.

José's regular interactions with these neighborhood cops were benign, which means, in terms of relationships that can exist between civilians and cops, that they can be perceived as positive interactions.[10] For the police officers on the neighborhood beat, José functioned as an informal, if hesitant, lookout. The regular visits the police officers made to José allowed them to view him not as a threat but as a resource. In a similar way, José turned the threat of these police officers into a potential resource. The police officers' familiarity with José's routine and José's familiarity with theirs enabled them to better protect him if the need ever arose. This familiarity allowed José to approach the officers with any complaint or question that he might have. The police presence also helped to keep

José's business safe and prevented "rent-collecting" *cholos* (gang members) from visiting his street corner. In this way, José was able to use these mundane and routine interactions to advance his own interests.

The interactions that Carmen had with police officers on her street corner were markedly different. As a young woman selling on the street, Carmen had more playful and flirtatious interactions with officers. Carmen first met the two neighborhood police officers when they approached her to buy fruit one early afternoon. They parked their patrol car in the northernmost lane heading west on Wilshire Boulevard—a major boulevard that runs through most of the city—and purchased two bags of fruit salad. Carmen gave them much larger portions than her regular customers, and with time, their visits became routine. Only one cop could speak Spanish, but both would try to converse with Carmen while they waited for their fruit. Carmen's good-natured demeanor set the officers at ease, and the interactions went from perfunctory to playful after several encounters.

One day, in anticipation of another wave of customers, I busied myself peeling mangoes and cucumbers while Carmen sat down and rested. She was giving me the latest gossip while sitting in a fold-out chair facing me, her back to the busy boulevard. Suddenly, I looked up from the cutting board and saw, through the Plexiglas top of the pushcart, a police car parked in front of us. I gestured with my eyes to Carmen. She leaned back and turned her entire upper body to look at what I was gesturing toward. The cops said nothing, and then Carmen, while smiling, yelled, "Go away! I don't have time to shoot the shit right now, can't you see I'm working?!" The Latino cop chuckled and said, "Alright, we'll see you later!"

Carmen's relationship with the police officers drew on normative expectations of manhood and femininity. The two police officers, a Latino and an African American man, often visited Carmen to chat and kid around. They teased her and asked her if she had friends with whom they could go on dates. Often, the Latino police officer would converse with Carmen in Spanish while the African American cop, who did not speak Spanish, would stand by and listen, interjecting occasionally to ask, "What did you say?" or "What did she say?" Carmen never took them seriously but did string them along, telling them she had good-looking cousins who were young and single. Often, she would show the police officers pictures of her attractive twenty-something cousins dressed in tight and revealing dresses. The cops would sometimes roll through just to ask, "When are you setting me up with your cousin?"

The relationship Carmen established with the police officers was casual, and they often purchased fruit from her. Later, when Carmen got into trouble or heard of another vendor in some type of trouble, she would call these officers, whose phone numbers she had, and ask for assistance. When Manuel had a nasty interaction with a police officer at a new vending location, Carmen told these police officers. They told Carmen that Manuel should file a complaint with the police headquarters of the neighborhood where the incident took place. (Though Carmen passed on this information to Manuel, he never went to file a complaint.) Carmen benefited from her relationship in at least two ways: she improved her sales by selling fruit regularly to these visiting cops, and she diminished threat by using them as a resource for information and assistance. Not only would these cops come to chat with Carmen, but they would also look out for her safety. Unlike José's "eyes on the street" relationship with cops, Carmen's interactions with these officers helped them stave off boredom by giving them someone to "shoot the shit" with and offered them some flirtatious talk in the process.

Of course, routine interactions and positive social relationships with police officers have limits. Friendly relationships with cops can be trumped by pressing issues of public safety. For a time, Jesús was working in front of a bank near a Sears store east of downtown Los Angeles. The manager of the Sears store had an issue with Jesús after Jesús's interactions with a drunken group of men were misinterpreted. Although Jesús and the manager of the Sears store had the same goal—to create a safe and civil public space that would attract potential customers and increase sales—they each had opposing visions of how that space could be created. Although a vendor's street corner actions are always meant to reduce risk and remove threat, they are not always interpreted this way by different parties. Jesús explained what had happened:

[The second time I was confronted by a cop] was [due to] a group of drunken men from El Salvador and Guatemala. They drank a lot and would gather near my street corner. . . . [While drunk,] they would pick the mango pits from my trash box and eat them. I didn't like this, and I would give them fruit and tell them to go away. The manager of the Sears told me that he didn't want me having all those people there. He assumed they were gathering there because I was providing them with food. That is to say, the food I'd throw away.

The manager told me to get the drunk men away from there. But I couldn't make them go away, that's where they lived [in an apartment complex next to the Sears]. I *would* give them fruit sometimes, and then they would move a little further away. But since there was a [surveillance] camera there, at the entrance [of the Sears], it captured everything, and that's what the manager would see. The police would make me move over and over. They would chase those drunk guys away. The police officer, he was a nice guy. . . . There were actually two police officers [that would always show up], and both of them knew me. And they'd make me move. Sometimes he'd say to me, "You know the deal. Just take down your umbrella until we leave." I would take down my umbrella for a little bit, until they went away, then I'd put it back up again and continue selling. I wouldn't move my cart. . . . I worked like that for about four months. And one day the police officer showed up and told me that he'd received a report that two guys had come to blows there. Drunk, they'd come to blows. And since there's a lot of gang activity around there because of the Mara [Salvatrucha], a *cholo* had shown up and beat them both up. But I didn't work that day [that the incident happened]; I didn't go sell there. But the police officer said that he'd been reprimanded and that he had to come to make me move for real this time.

Even though the Sears manager called the police to enforce his own vision of safety and civility, Jesús's interactions and relationship with the neighborhood police officers staved off conflict for a few months. However, in the end, the violence of drunken men and the threat of *cholos* compelled the neighborhood police officers to banish Jesús and his street vendor peers from the corner. The Sears manager never understood that Jesús offered fruit to the drunken men not to befriend them but to get rid of them and to keep them from digging through his trash. The manager misinterpreted the fruit gifting because he viewed it out of context through the surveillance camera. He saw Jesús in the same light as the drunken men. To the manager, Jesús was part of the problem and not the solution. And though Jesús had a good relationship with the police officers, quelling the threat posed by fighting drunks and gang members was more important to them than allowing Jesús to keep vending in that location. For

Jesús, there was a social distance between him and the men on the corner. However, the surveillance of the manager and the enforcement of the police ultimately lumped them together in the same category. They were policed not as workers and loiterers on the street corner but as brown male bodies "inappropriately" occupying public space.[11] Despite this, Jesús was able to rely on his friendly relationship with the cops to hold on to the profitable vending location for longer than would have otherwise been possible.

Although some fruit vendors invest time and effort into nurturing their relationships with police officers, those relationships can quickly turn negative and/or end. Almost inevitably, police officers are ordered to enforce the law and act against vendors' interests, and when they do, by chasing vendors from their street corners for example, they also extinguish the opportunities to engage in regular social and civil interactions with them. Vendors acknowledge that maintaining police officers as resources is an ephemeral endeavor. Some assessed the mercurial quality of vendor-officer relationships in a resigned way, as Ricardo did when he said, "On a day-to-day basis, [street vending] is annoying and boring. There are problems. Sometimes the police will give you a hard time, some days they won't. One week they will harass you and not the next. Sometimes they'll throw away your cart, and sometimes they'll just give you a warning." Few *fruteros* held grudges against officers who had turned into threats after long-standing civil relationships; they recognized that police officers' occupational duties were often at odds with their interests as vendors. Vendors also knew that if and when the time came, they would employ evasive tactics to avoid police officers' attempts to issue citations, confiscate goods, or arrest them.

PERFORMING PERSONAL, PROFESSIONAL, AND SYMBOLIC HYGIENE

Though fruit vendors operate in violation of health code regulations, they still attempt to create a hygienic establishment for their customers. Fruit vendors cannot certify their carts and operations completely because of their positioning in public space and the lack of necessary infrastructure (e.g., running water and restroom facilities). However, the hygienic standards fruit vendors do maintain function as buffers to compensate for this lack of official certification. But as I will show, this can sometimes backfire. The performance of hygienic practices among vendors—who lack any other visible certification—allows customers to engage in acts of scrutiny before commissioning their services. Performing hygiene serves as a useful interaction strategy because it can attract and maintain regular customers. These customers keep fruit vendors open for business. However, some of the markers used in the performance of hygiene also identify vendors to passing health inspectors and LAPD officers.

Vendors have three types of hygienic practices: personal, professional, and symbolic. They are not mutually exclusive but rather capture different types of hygiene, some more viable than others. Personal hygiene entails those activities that vendors engage in to cleanse themselves or that prevent contamination, like hand washing and wearing gloves. Professional hygiene is meant to improve the presentation and appearance of fruit vendors; the use of aprons is one example. Symbolic hygiene includes all the markers and objects that vendors use when setting up on street corners. These objects may or may not be used, but their very presence serves an important purpose. The presence of brooms and hand sanitizing lotion or informative stickers applied to pushcarts are some examples of symbolic hygiene. All three types of hygienic practices lend some form of legitimacy to an otherwise illegitimate operation.

Vendors know that they must perform personal, professional, and symbolic hygiene if they hope to acquire and maintain customers. Personal inspection by discerning customers can lead to or destroy a regular customer base. Vendors often keep cleaning supplies in view to broadcast their hygiene; they also spend time between customers cleaning their carts. Carmen and Cristian each kept a large hand sanitation bottle on top of their carts and a Windex spray bottle on the ground next to their carts. On one occasion when Carmen and Cristian were working together, a little boy with filthy hands ordered a bag of fruit. Carmen took the hand sanitation bottle, leaned over to the boy, and asked him to stretch his hands out. In front of another waiting customer, Carmen made the boy scrub his hands three times, handing him napkins after each time. Cristian, who was preparing the fruit salad as this happened, asked the boy casually, "Were you working?" The boy shyly nodded. The middle-aged Latina customer waiting to be served stood back and nodded approvingly of the interaction between the vendors and the child.

On another occasion, as I helped Carmen vend, an Orthodox Jewish man approached and asked Carmen about her knives. Carmen, who does not speak English, asked me to translate. The man asked Carmen if she used the knives for cutting anything besides fruit. Carmen looked puzzled as she shook her head and said, in broken English, "Only fruit, only fruit, clean, I wash." The man nodded and ordered a $4 bag of fruit. Though the man asked about the knives for religious purposes, Carmen interpreted the man's questions through a health code lens. Because most customers who express hesitation must be "won over" by a vendor's hygienic practices, Carmen immediately made an appeal to the man by saying her utensils were sanitarily clean, even though his questions were about kosher cleanliness.

Attempts to broadcast hygienic practices can also have negative consequences when they help to identify vendors during crackdowns. The day Jesús was arrested, he had seen the police and health inspectors closing in and had begun to walk away from his pushcart, but he had forgotten to remove his apron. Police officers were able to easily identify and catch him before he traveled too far. Yet vendors continue to wear aprons because it visually communicates professional and symbolic hygiene. Because most vendors wear jeans and hooded sweatshirts to work, the apron becomes a type of uniform in the most minimalist sense. Aprons also allow vendors easy access to the large number of bills they handle throughout the day. In the end, the practical and symbolic purposes of the apron outweigh the risk associated with donning it.

Although vendors put a great deal of effort into the street corner presentation of their pushcarts and the performance of hygiene, they expend less effort in the "backstage" preparation of the cart. In the backstage preparation spaces, efficiency takes precedence over hygienic practices—both symbolic and actual. This contradiction is an intrinsic part of "backstage" space behavior, "where the impression fostered by the performance is knowingly contradicted as a matter of course" (Goffman 1959, 112). I helped vendors prepare pushcarts in the early morning hours on many occasions. The staging locations were often not commissaries (i.e., storage warehouses that offer preparation space, trash bins, and running water) but backyards, where dogs were running around and roosters could be heard crowing from adjacent yards. Gloves were rarely used while fruit was being handled, and day-old fruit was often washed and repeeled in an effort to make it appear fresh. The backyard space was an informal and unregulated substitute for the regulated space provided by commissaries. Despite the fact that both Manuel's and Carmen's carts had commissary information on them, there was an extended period during which they did not house their carts at the commissary. Instead, they kept the pushcarts in the backyard of the house that Manuel and Chava rented, under a large white tarp. Three pushcarts were stored there, and along the right side, on a makeshift shelf, they kept boxes of unpeeled produce. Prohibitively high rental rates prevented them from being regular and consistent users of commissary spaces. The lack of gloves in this backyard space augmented the symbolic nature of the use of gloves in the public setting of the street corner.

While hygienic practices, both in presentation and in preparation, serve a purpose on the street corner, the vendors' activity in the backyard space falls outside the purview of discerning customers. Early morning pushcart preparation work is characterized by quick, efficient actions. On a daily basis, vendors must purchase fruit and ice from the wholesale market, drive it to the preparation location, unload it, peel several pounds of fruit, prepare their carts, and load the heavy carts onto trucks so that they can be dropped off at the vendors' designated vending corners. And all this occurs in the morning hours before the street corner workday officially begins. Yet the backyard space was also used to craft professional and symbolic hygienic practices. Vendors themselves often regulated the presentation of the pushcarts and policed their own appearances.

In the mornings, as we prepared pushcarts in Manuel and Chava's backyard, the conversation was often light, and teasing was common. Chava often woke up early and prepared his cart before Manuel and I returned from the wholesale market, so we rarely saw him. When he did share the space with us to prepare his cart, we were often more reserved. One morning, Chava was particularly chatty with us. Carmen had spent the morning teasing Manuel about how dirty his water bucket was, and she asked me to take a look at it.

"Look at his bucket and tell me that's not dirty," Carmen said to me.

"The bucket is just for water so I can clean my hands. No one cares," Manuel protested.

Manuel's pushcart was packed with produce and covered with a black cloth, but it was not yet loaded onto the pickup truck. I walked over and opened the bottom compartment of the pushcart, crouched, and looked in. Inside was an orange bucket from Home Depot with a corresponding lid. It was filthy.

"It's dirty, right?" Carmen asked me.

"It's almost as if your day job is as a mechanic! [*Hasta parece que trabajas de mecánico!*]" I teased Manuel.

Carmen and Chava guffawed.

"For real, Chio? [*A poco, Chio?*]" Manuel said, smiling.[12] He walked over to the bucket and pulled it out. It was heavy because it was full of water. He dumped out some of the water and began wiping down the outside with a damp cloth.

"Don't get mad at me," I said, concerned that I had gone too far in teasing Manuel.

"I'm not mad, this is how we get along," he said.

"You have to keep your stuff clean, Manuel!" Carmen said over her shoulder as she got in the passenger seat of the truck.

When we finished loading the pushcarts, and as Chava pulled out in his pickup truck, he waved to us and yelled at Manuel, "See you later *me-cá-ni-coooo!*" The nickname stuck around for a while and functioned to ensure that Manuel kept his bucket and other street corner things clean to prevent more teasing.

Performing hygiene on the street corner serves the purpose of attracting customers and generating income, but LACDPH and LAPD officers know that this performance by vendors does not replace actual certification. This performance does not address health risks related to airborne contaminants or lack of refrigeration. Constant regulation and inspection by health department officials (of informal and formal businesses) is an indication that many vendors, if left to their own devices, would fall short of the established standards. Vendors are unable to seek normal routes to health certification and therefore engage in informal sanitation and hygienic practices, but these can have both positive and negative consequences.

If vendors do not perform hygiene adequately, they may lose customers and income, but when they perform hygiene too well, they become more conspicuous to passing LACDPH and LAPD officers. Still, like other inter-actions and strategies, the performance of hygiene is a short-term cure for a larger problem rooted in suspended informality.

CONCLUSION

LACDPH and LAPD enforcement continuously undermines fruit vendors' best efforts to operate and generate profit. In response, vendors implement interactional strategies to remedy problem situations arising from their precarious positioning. These strategies include claiming space and build-ing alliances; relying on *paisano* street patrols and alerts; building rela-tionships with police officers to turn them from threats into resources; and performing personal, professional, and symbolic hygiene. All of these strat-egies serve to decrease vendors' vulnerability on the street and/or to increase income generation. In the end, these strategies offer short-term remedies for a problem rooted in prohibitive vending regulations.

The main and most reliable survival strategy is depending on kinship and *paisano* networks for financial support. When other survival strate-gies fail—that is, when crackdowns occur and financial hardship arises—vendors lean on their social networks to survive. Unfortunately, one ven-dor's hardship adversely impacts all of the members of the network because it depletes the limited resources of the group. And because large-scale crackdowns typically target and apprehend many vendors at a time, it is likely that one social network will absorb the hardship of many fruit vendors at once. This collective hardship and web of obligations makes it difficult for individual members of the group to save enough economic capital to pull forward. Street vendors therefore deploy other street-level, risk-averse strategies meant to diminish everyday vulnerabilities in an effort to avoid leaning on social networks. In many instances, these strate-gies force vendors to make tradeoffs between income generation and risk.

These strategies allow vendors to operate in the gap between codified law and enforcement, but they do not dislodge vendors from their infor-mal liminality. For *fruteros,* the trap of informality, the limited benefits offered by these strategies, and the continuous enforcement of antivending regulations contribute to economic stagnation and poverty. Accounts provided by fruit vendors—about fear of arrest, begging on street corners, recurrent fines and confiscations, economic hardship, and increased vulnerability—continuously point to the ways in which economic and social precarity arises from their liminal positioning. This type of liminality and subsequent hardship might be expected from an immigrant group whose demographic characteristics include undocumented status, limited education and financial capital, and little to no English language proficiency. Fruit vendors are subjected to crackdowns that enforce what some scholars have called poverty-intolerant legislation (Light 2006). That is, local policy that disproportionately impacts poor, immigrant communities. Health department crackdowns have accentuated and even perpetuated poverty among immigrant fruit vendors. The regulatory backlash encumbers *fruteros*' potential to thrive. Without the vending prohibition, *fruteros* might be able to accumulate profit instead of merely saving for hardship.

4 Personal and Professional Entanglements

Strong *paisano* ties among *fruteros* mean that vendors' personal and professional lives often mix. Groups of men who work together often also live together, the few young women on the job often date the young men, and business deals can be facilitated because of the intimate details associates know about one another. Strong ties between *paisanos* based on connections of various kinds—as employers, as roommates, or as romantic partners—give the social network of *fruteros* vibrancy. These strong ties can reverberate with feelings of trust, support, and solidarity. In a business enterprise based largely on various types of informal agreements, trust is essential. Immigrants often rely on "interpersonal trust networks" (Tilly 2007) to carry out long-term, crucial enterprises.[1] Yet when these enmeshed relationships and trust networks are compromised, the consequences can be devastating. In this context, there is a fine line between harmony and discord, reciprocity and estrangement—all of which showcases the various vulnerabilities of those living and working inside the ethnic cage.

ROMANTIC ENTANGLEMENTS

In November 2007, Cristian left Los Angeles to visit his parents in Dos Mundos. Cristian was homesick, plain and simple. His mother had threatened to stop answering his phone calls if he did not return for at least a short visit—a fact I verified when I spoke to her years later in Dos Mundos. Cristian had saved enough money to live comfortably for a few months in Dos Mundos and wanted to leave Los Angeles before another health department crackdown hit or financial crisis befell the group, which might force him to tap into his savings. Cristian's plan was to drive to the border in his white pickup truck with Raúl. Although Cristian paid for his truck and owned it in practice, it was Raúl, a U.S. citizen, who was the owner of the truck on paper, as the title was in his name. The plan was for Raúl to drive the truck into Tijuana. Together, they would make their way to Puebla. Cristian's American-plated vehicle was allowed in Mexico for a maximum of six months, at which point the permit issued to the vehicle would expire. Therefore, Cristian planned to stay in Dos Mundos for no more than six months. Raúl would stay in Dos Mundos for a week before flying back to Los Angeles. As a U.S. citizen, Raúl had more freedom to travel in and out of Mexico.

In the weeks leading up to his departure, Cristian would often discuss the details of the trip with Carmen. For several days in a row, Carmen and I shopped around town, but especially in Chinatown, for items that Cristian would take to her family in Mexico City and to his in Dos Mundos. Carmen packed the items, mostly clothes and undergarments for her mom to sell at the *tianguis* market, in a large duffel bag. When word got around that Cristian was headed home, other *paisanos* dropped off items intended for their own families in Dos Mundos. Soon, one large duffel bag became two. In the conversations Carmen and Cristian had about the trip, the pickup truck came up often. One evening after work, as they reviewed the plans yet again while I sat in the backseat of the truck, Cristian and Carmen had a small argument about the vehicle.

"And do you *have* to take the truck?" Carmen asked, somewhat innocently. When Cristian did not reply, she added, "Doesn't your dad have a truck in Dos Mundos?"

Carmen had told me privately that she was concerned about what she would do when Cristian left. Although she was happy for Cristian to reunite with his family, his absence also presented a problem for her. She would be losing her romantic partner with whom she split the bedroom rent. And she would be losing her daily rides to her street corner in the pickup truck as well as Cristian's assistance loading and unloading the heavy pushcart.

"I'll get home faster and be able to come back faster. I won't have to waste my money on a crowded bus," Cristian responded.

"But what if Raúl drives you and you leave the truck with me?" Carmen asked.

"What are you going to use the truck for? You can't work on your own! Someone else is going to drive my truck to be your *raitero?* It's *my* truck."

"Fine then [*Está bien pues*]," Carmen responded as she turned her body toward the passenger window to signal the end of the conversation.

Cristian's truck was a great source of pride and status for him. He believed it would help herald his triumphant return to Dos Mundos, and he was eager to show it off to his father. The truck would also help ensure that Cristian would return to Los Angeles in about six months' time—the truck itself, by virtue of needing a vehicle import permit to enter and remain in Mexico that expired after six months, structured the length of time Cristian would spend with his family. It was agreed that, when Cristian was ready to return to the United States, Raúl would drive the truck across the international border and Cristian would use a *coyote.* Cristian was anxious and excited in the weeks leading up to his departure, and he called home often.

In the year before Cristian's trip home, Carmen had managed to purchase an older-model sedan by pooling her money with Cristian and by participating in the Dos Mundos community *tanda.*[2] One of the major benefits of dating a Dos Mundos *paisano* was access to this *tanda,* which was reliable because of the tightly knit members and their trust network.[3] Individuals in trust networks bind themselves to each other with these long-term rights and obligations. Thus, these trust networks operate simultaneously as sites of social insurance and social control (Tilly 2007).

Before the cycle of money collection and distribution began in the *tanda,* each participant drew a number that dictated their position in the distribution order. Often, this number was exchanged with others in the group as participants plotted out the major expenses they had coming up—such as warehouse commissary rent, pushcart purchases, car payments, or rent/mortgage payments. Each participant gave $100 on Monday, and funds were distributed on Tuesday. Sometimes, two participants shared a number, each contributing $50 a week and splitting the payout, or one participant paid for two numbers, giving $200 every week and getting a double payout. For each full cycle, the number of participants varied. In the span of four years, the *tanda* peaked at thirty-one participants and dwindled, in winter months when funds were low among all *fruteros,* to six participants.

Cristian and Carmen had relied on the *tanda* for several major expenses, including the purchase of Cristian's pickup truck and Carmen's sedan. While Carmen's sedan offered her freedom and allowed her to help fellow *fruteros* run errands, it was useless for the transportation of pushcarts. Besides, Carmen could not do the job on her own because she needed help loading and unloading the heavy pushcart. Before leaving, Cristian asked his cousins, Raúl and Andres Martínez, to look out for Carmen while he was away. A verbal arrangement was made. Carmen would continue working as a fruit vendor using Cristian's pushcart, but she would also work as a part-time employee for Raúl and Andres. She would get rides with them, pay them gas money, and alternate between working one week for them (as an employee) and one week for herself (as an independent vendor). Because Raúl was planning on staying in Dos Mundos with Cristian for a few days, Andres agreed to give Carmen rides to her street corner and help her load and unload the pushcart until Raúl returned. To facilitate the process, she would store her cart in the backyard of the house that Raúl and Andres shared.

During the six months that Cristian was in Dos Mundos, Carmen worked with Raúl and Andres without any significant issues. However, an ongoing conversation that Carmen had with Cristian was about the pickup truck's paperwork. Cristian had looked everywhere in the truck for the title but could not find it. Cristian surmised that Raúl had kept the paperwork but was not sure if he had done so intentionally or not. When Carmen offered to ask Raúl about it, Cristian told her not to do so and to keep the information between the two of them. Cristian did not think it would be a productive conversation, and he did not want to upset Raúl, especially in the weeks before he was preparing to return to Los Angeles.

Raúl was crucial to Cristian's plan of returning; without Raúl's help, Cristian would be unable to get his truck back into the United States. Not only did Raúl have U.S. citizenship, but he was also the owner of the truck on paper. Border patrol agents would not be suspicious of someone crossing the international border in his own vehicle. But, if Raúl and Cristian fought over the fact that Raúl took the paperwork with him, Raúl could rescind his offer to help drive the truck back into the country.

Mixed legal status among intimate partners, relatives, and friends can do much to structure those relationships. The power dynamic between individuals is impacted by governmental policies that benefit some while exposing the vulnerabilities of others. In effect, these policies can sanction legal violence when legal rights, protections, and benefits are unevenly distributed in a process that creates "toxic ties" between documented and undocumented individuals in the same network (Del Real 2019). Thus, even though Cristian would characterize his relationship with Raúl as a strong friendship—in addition to being a kinship tie—he was aware of the power differentials between them rooted in their different legal statuses.

In May 2008, Raúl flew to Puebla to help Cristian make the journey back. Cristian, Raúl, and Alejandro—a neighbor and first-time migrant to the United States—left Dos Mundos for the Mexico-U.S. border on a Friday. A few days later, in the early morning hours, as they neared a border town in the Mexican state of Sonora, a truck attempted to pass them without leaving enough time to avoid oncoming traffic from the opposite lane.[4] When the passing truck attempted to reenter Cristian's lane, Raúl, who was sitting in the passenger seat, panicked and pulled the steering wheel, causing the pickup truck to roll over several times before coming to a rest, upside down, in a ditch. When I visited Dos Mundos in 2011, Cristian recounted the tragic story:

> We rolled over two or three times. And when the truck stopped rolling, I don't know, I was out of it. I tried to get out through the front, because the windshield had been shattered, but I couldn't. Something was holding me back. I didn't remember that my seatbelt was buckled. When I finally crawled out, I felt my face, and it was wet. I had blood all over my head, all over my body. My chest hurt, I couldn't breathe. A driver that had seen the accident came over and then left to get help. I lost all sense of time. I didn't know what was happening. I tried to remember, and I sensed that someone

had been with me, and then I remembered Raúl. I went back to the truck and got him out. . . . I also took out the other guy [Alejandro]. He was dead. I pulled them out of the truck and then [dragged them] some ten meters away because I was afraid. I don't know, I was afraid the truck might blow up or something.

Alejandro, who had been sitting in the back seat, had not been wearing a seatbelt and had died instantly. Cristian and Raúl were badly injured. After being transferred to a nearby hospital, Raúl, as a U.S. citizen, was airlifted to a hospital in Arizona. Cristian remained behind in a Mexican town near the border. The truck was wrecked, and they abandoned it.

News of the accident reached the *frutero* community in Los Angeles quickly. Carmen was constantly on the phone with Cristian's parents in Dos Mundos. Andres traveled to Arizona to see his brother and help bring him back to California. The Dos Mundos community in Los Angeles collected money to help the Martínez family while Raúl recovered. Similar collections took place in Dos Mundos for Cristian. Carmen was devastated. She continued working with Andres and sent money to Cristian's family in Dos Mundos. After a few months, it became clear that Cristian would not be returning to Los Angeles. He was bedridden; his parents cared for him in Dos Mundos while he recovered. Raúl spent eight months unable to move and then had to learn how to walk again.

In Los Angeles, life continued for the *frutero* community. About a year after the accident, and likely because Andres filled the void that Cristian had left, Carmen and Andres became romantically involved. However, Carmen continued to maintain a long-distance relationship with Cristian. Carmen did not confide in me initially, but on several occasions she asked me to drive her to random locations, and because I did not have a car, she would lend me hers so that I could run errands. I did this several times before realizing the role I was playing in her trysts with Andres.

One afternoon at the end of the workday, after Carmen and I had finished putting everything away, Andres arrived at her corner to pick up her pushcart. They exchanged glances and giggles but did not talk much. She had driven her car to her corner, and when Andres picked up the pushcart to take back to his home, she and I headed to her apartment to eat and hang out. The long workday had made me drowsy. After dinner, I napped on her bed while she showered and got ready. She had asked me to drop her off somewhere, and told me to keep her car until the next workday. When we finally left her apartment, I could feel her excitement as I drove. It had started to lightly rain, so Carmen told me to pull off into an empty street in an industrial neighborhood and wait with her until it let up. She had asked me to drive her to a bus stop, where she was going to be picked up.

"Are you doing anything fun tonight?" I asked.

"You could say that," she responded coyly and laughed.

It had been a long day, and I was too tired to play along with whatever game she had going, so I simply nodded and said, "*Qué bien* [That's nice]." We listened to music and sat quietly. The rain fell gently, obscuring our line of vision. Then, a black pickup truck appeared at the bus stop and turned on its emergency lights. Carmen's phone rang.

"He's here!" she announced as she picked up the phone. She exchanged some flirtatious talk with the person on the other end and then hung up. Carmen looked at herself in the visor's mirror, flashed her sexy eyes, and gave her breasts an upward pump. I turned on the car's wipers to get a better look at the truck.

"That looks just like Andres's truck," I said, and Carmen flashed me a look that conveyed pity.

"It *is* his truck," she replied, laughing, and then stepped out of the car. She covered her head with her arms and ran to the bus stop. I waited until they pulled away and then drove home, contemplating what I had just observed.

Andres's house was the staging ground where Carmen would prepare her pushcart in the mornings and store it in the evenings. Andres would drop her off and pick her up on her street corner five days a week. She had been spending much more time with Andres than ever before, so the development of a romantic relationship would not have been unusual. But Carmen had never broken up with Cristian. It was Cristian who had asked Raúl and Andres to watch out for Carmen while he was gone. Cristian and Raúl were incredibly close and talked often. Raúl and Andres shared a house where they lived with their respective wives and also stored the pushcarts.

As I drove home in the rain that night I thought, "This could get ugly." And it did.

Raúl found out about the affair between Carmen and Andres. Cristian and Carmen talked on the phone and fought; Cristian admitted to having slept with someone else while in Los Angeles, and Carmen told him she had too. Cristian told Raúl that he did not want Carmen working his pushcart any longer. He asked Raúl to take away the pushcart as punishment, but both the Martínez brothers thought that was unwise and refused to do it. The Martínez brothers knew Cristian would not return to Los Angeles, and he had lost any claim he had on the pushcart when he left. In talks with Carmen, they told her what Cristian had asked and said they were not going to enforce his cross-border punishment. They did not want to take away Carmen's livelihood, and they believed the pushcart rightfully belonged to her now.

The Martínez brothers' actions after the fallout could be categorized as "benevolent sexism"—that is, "a subjectively favorable, chivalrous ideology that offers protection and affection to women who embrace conventional roles" (Glick and Fiske 2001, 109). They presented themselves as Carmen's protectors, unwilling to punish her in the way Cristian requested and viewing her as a victim in need of help, all the while benefiting financially from her continued use of the pushcart.

Still, mornings preparing the pushcart in the Martínezes' backyard were strained. Raúl and Andres fought often. The brothers' wives eventually figured out what the fighting was about and abruptly pulled the welcome mat out from under Carmen's feet.

In one fell swoop, Carmen lost access to the backyard storage space and the daily transportation. She became a persona non grata in the Martínez household and with the other *fruteros* who worked for Raúl and Andres. She officially broke up with Cristian, who remained in Dos Mundos. Though Carmen was not a Dos Mundos transplant, she was deeply invested in their *paisano* community and did not want to lose the benefits that came with her connection to it. For years, Carmen had prepared for this type of precarity by performing highly gendered scripts of deference, flirtatiousness, and friendliness with other *fruteros*.[5]

Carmen's interactions with male *fruteros* were structured in part by the precarious nature of the informal work and by her token status as a young woman in an occupation dominated by men. The risk associated with the job and the looming threat of health department crackdowns meant that a request for help was always around the corner. Carmen knew she needed to stay in the good graces of multiple *fruteros* in order to more readily request and receive help, and she used her femininity to do so.[6] As a young woman, she was often viewed as a potential romantic partner. In an effort to receive assistance, she leveraged her token status and performed a highly gendered script of "job flirt." She was always friendly and flirtatious, often stringing along men who promised to take her out on a date. When she was kicked out of the Martínez working group, she began dating a series of *fruteros*, trying to use romantic relationships to regain access to the Dos Mundos community and to get assistance with storing and transporting her pushcart.

In addition to working with Dos Mundos fruit vendors, Carmen participated in weekly *tandas* with other Dos Mundos community members. This system of forced saving had been instrumental in helping her save money to buy her used sedan. As Carmen explained, "If you have it [money], you get it from your *cajoncito* [little drawer] and spend it. This way, [by taking part in a *tanda*,] you get some responsibility instead." The goodwill and trust she had generated while participating in the *tandas* and in the community *colectas*—the pooling of monetary donations to help community members in crisis—also helped her maintain access to the community.

After a series of failed romantic pairings with fellow vendors, Carmen asked her uncle for help finding a *raitero*, and he suggested his friend Alberto. Alberto was a middle-aged man from the Mexican state of Guerrero who owned a pickup truck. He began giving Carmen rides to her corner. However, Carmen did not like Alberto's reckless driving and how much he charged her for the service ($85 a day). She was not making a profit from her work under this arrangement. She would frequently tell me she was unhappy with Alberto, often immediately after he dropped us off. Carmen could not renegotiate the *raitero* arrangement because she did not have leverage. She felt powerless in this arrangement because Alberto was an older man and her uncle's friend. Alberto's interactions with Carmen were often paternalistic. Carmen had similar experiences with her uncle, whom she had lived with when she first moved to Los Angeles, and this is why she had moved out of his house as soon as she could. Carmen knew she needed to find a new *raitero* before she could drop Alberto.

After some time, Alberto learned enough about the fruit vending business to want to become a vendor too. He bought a pushcart, but he had difficulty finding a street corner. He was not a *paisano* in the Dos Mundos network, which could have offered him some help getting his business going. Alberto was chased away by police officers from every location he selected. Established vendors had their own corners. It was summer at the time, and decent street locations were getting difficult to find because there was an increase in the number of *fruteros* working. Competition was fierce in the summertime. Carmen and the other Dos Mundos vendors complained continuously about the increased number of "fair-weather" *fruteros* who worked only in the summer months and made things difficult for year-round *fruteros*.

Alberto took his frustrations out on Carmen, and she eventually left that work arrangement and returned to the Dos Mundos fold. She began working with Manuel, a Dos Mundos *paisano*, and started storing her pushcart in his South Central home's backyard and getting rides from him. Initially, they might have had a romantic relationship, but it ended, and they continued to share the backyard space and transportation as friends.[7] Carmen had a knack for finding ambitious and upwardly mobile *fruteros* to date, and Manuel did not fit the bill. A few months later, she began dating Gonzalo—who was also from Dos Mundos and had come to Los Angeles the same year that Cristian had left. When Carmen talked to me about Manuel and his economic insecurity, she wondered whether he just had bad luck or whether he made poor business decisions; as a result, her treatment of him often ranged from pity to contempt. Manuel's trajectory proved to be complicated not by bad luck but by constant run-ins with the health department during work hours and the police during non–work hours, which perpetuated his economic and personal insecurity; by his involvement with the Dos Mundos hometown association, which extracted much of his disposable income; and by the resulting crippling debt he got into with the wholesale merchant.

FINANCIAL ENTANGLEMENTS

Carmen's judgment of Manuel did not only occur in private conversations between us. She often gently ribbed him and offered advice that might help him make more money on his street corner. One hot October day in 2009, Carmen sold out of fruit in the early afternoon and called Manuel to ask if he could bring more. Manuel had not had a good day vending at his corner, and he agreed to come over. When he arrived, he unloaded his pushcart from his truck and wheeled it over to us. It was full of produce.

"You need to move to a different corner. That one isn't worth shit," Carmen said, looking over his product. We began moving the produce from his pushcart into hers, and within minutes, customers began arriving. Manuel pulled up a milk crate and sat down to watch us work.

"I like my corner. It's calm," he said. Manuel had a distinctive shy demeanor. Because he was missing a front tooth, he often muffled his laugh with his right hand, which he would then use to rub the top of his bowed head.

"Too calm!" Carmen said, teasing him.

Carmen would often give Manuel advice about how to vend and pointed out corners that might be more profitable. Manuel always listened quietly and nodded his head but rarely acted on anything she suggested.

Establishing a new corner to vend at always required a bit of effort and risk-taking. The corner needed to be unoccupied by other vendors who might object. The location also needed to be tested for hostility from nearby business owners and for profitability and accessibility. Certain neighborhoods around the city were "hot zones" for the health department, and while vendors still operated in those areas, they knew they had to be extra vigilant and ready to move at a moment's notice. Manuel had been cited multiple times and had been sent to jail on two occasions for vending while working under the García brothers. Manuel also knew he was at a higher risk if he got caught vending because he used an unlicensed pushcart without a proper drainage system—the type the health department was particularly keen on getting off the street. The cart had cost him $800, and the only reason he was able to buy it was because the wholesale merchant who sold it to him allowed him to pay for it in installments. As a result, he was very risk averse. Now that he worked on his own, he stayed away from Hollywood, where he had previously been cited and arrested, and operated in the shadow of what he described as an "Asian clinic." He was not very visible to passing cars at this location, but he had some regular customers among the clinic's staff. Manuel opted for safety instead of profit.

That October day, Carmen suggested to Manuel that he take me to the wholesale market, and he agreed. This arrangement, where I would meet Manuel in the predawn hours to go shopping together, continued for several months. During this one-on-one access, Manuel began to tell me about his financial entanglements and his complicated trajectory. While Carmen thought profitability was Manuel's major problem, he had other issues with which to contend. His financial problems extended well beyond the street corner. Layered on top of Manuel's financial problems related to vending arrests and citations was a significant financial obligation to his *paisano* community.

In 2008, Manuel was elected to serve on the board of ministers for the Dos Mundos hometown association. Every year, Dos Mundos nominated individuals to serve on one of two town ministries. Each ministry consisted of seventy members and included people who lived in the United States as well as Dos Mundos residents. The priest from the town parish and the Dos Mundos mayor headed up the ministry in Dos Mundos. The ministry in Los Angeles elected a group leader, known as the mayor. In Dos Mundos, these ministries raised money for town festivities and their accompanying costs. These two groups would spend the year competing to see which group could raise the most money. These ministries, a variant of hometown associations (HTAs), were responsible for raising funds for the benefit of the hometown.

In other towns, HTAs are responsible for infrastructure projects, such as paving roads, constructing drainage systems, or building town plazas (Moya 2005; Smith 2006). Scholars have written extensively about migrants who are able to translate their economic success in the United States into improved circumstances back in their sending community via HTAs (Orozco 2002, 2003).[8] HTAs are composed almost entirely of first-generation immigrants; their purpose is to bring people from the same town or state in the sending country together in the receiving state. In doing so, these groups of people are able to create social and economic links to their hometown, promote social exchange, exercise structured political influence, pursue low-scale development goals, and retain a sense of community as they adjust to life in the United States (Orozco and

Lapointe 2004). Academics focusing on HTAs are overwhelmingly positive in their assessments of these types of organizations and their influence; some have even noted that HTAs might promote political participation and empowerment not only within Mexico but also in the United States (Duquette-Rury and Bada 2013; Zabin and Escala 2002). Scholars consider the relationship between HTAs and sending communities to largely be mutually beneficial.[9] However, most studies on HTAs focus on the size and impact of the contributions to the sending community; they rarely focus on individual HTA members and how their involvement in such an organization can impact their personal livelihood.

Manuel considered his election to the board of ministers an honor. But membership and involvement with the ministry ran for six years, and all members were expected to make contributions of between US$200 and US$600 four times a year. After the six-year term ended, Dos Mundos migrants were expected to make only one contribution a year, of an average amount of US$500, in May, for the festival of the town's patron saint, which was held the following month. Despite the financial problems Manuel faced in Los Angeles, he never faltered in making his ministry contributions. However, the required financial contributions were a strain on Manuel, who often put these expenses ahead of others.

Manuel never missed a payment to the hometown ministry because he wanted to save face among his *paisanos* in Los Angeles and back in Dos Mundos. Even within an occupation riddled with unexpected financial calamity, vendors in Los Angeles had very low regard for migrants who failed to meet the financial obligations of these ministries. Members of the committee were expected to be responsible providers for the town of Dos Mundos, and election to the committee was recognition of their time (and thus success) abroad. If a member failed to meet his committee's obligations, the group ridiculed him. Manuel avoided this ridicule by forsaking remittances to his grandmother in Dos Mundos. So while his family's household was one of the poorest in Dos Mundos among those that had a son working in the United States, his reputation as a contributing member of the hometown association remained untarnished. In Los Angeles, Manuel also carried a sizable debt with the wholesale merchant.

When I began visiting the wholesale market with Manuel, I saw a more extensive community of *fruteros* and of *paisanos*. Manuel and I typically arrived at the wholesale produce market before sunrise, and it was always a frenzied scene. The market was busiest between four and seven in the morning. Customers in pickup trucks were constantly driving in and out of the parking lot, young teenage boys pushed steel hand trucks laden with boxes of produce between stalls and waiting vehicles, and food trucks and sidewalk merchants selling quesadillas and *champurrado* (a thick hot drink made of chocolate and maize) lined the outer perimeter and sold to market customers, stall owners, and their many employees. The wholesale produce market was a large warehouse consisting of stalls catering to different clientele, though several of them catered to various kinds of street vendors.[10]

From my first visit to the wholesale market with Manuel, it was clear there were issues. When we finished walking through the small stall that catered to *fruteros,* Manuel asked me to supervise the young teenagers as they loaded the produce into the back of his truck. It was a request I immediately understood to be more about getting me to leave his side than about me ensuring everything was loaded properly. From a distance, I saw Manuel interact with Gloria, the owner of the wholesale market stall. He talked to her while covering his mouth with one hand and motioning with his other hand. Gloria shook her head and eventually pulled out a notebook and wrote some things down. Manuel never exchanged money with Gloria.

"Is everything OK?" I asked Manuel when he got back to the truck.

"Yeah," Manuel offered.

"How much did it come out to?" I asked once we were on the road.

"Less than $100," he said.

"How much exactly?" I insisted.

"Like $80," he responded.

"Do you pay the woman at the end of the day?" I asked, letting him know that I did not see him pay. It was my first time at the market, and I knew nothing about how things worked there. I was prying because I wanted to understand the transaction interaction.

Manuel smiled and sighed. "The thing is, Chio, I owe Gloria money, and she has a running tab for me."

"Do you owe her a lot?" I asked, embarrassed about forcing the information out of him.

"A bit," he said.

Manuel would later tell me that he owed her nearly $5,000. Several *fruteros* would periodically make financial arrangements with the wholesale market owner, and he was not the only one in debt. A couple of years later, in 2011, I sat down with Gloria to get a sense of her personal trajectory and how she operated her business.

The Wholesale Market Owner

The majority of *fruteros* bought produce from Gloria's market stall. Like the vendors, Gloria was from the Mexican state of Puebla; her hometown was a twenty-minute drive from Dos Mundos. And like the majority of *fruteros*, Gloria was undocumented. When she first arrived in the United States, she worked at a garment factory, making jackets. Later, she married, had two children, and became a homemaker. A friend of Gloria's, Tatiana (Tati), owned a small stall in the produce market. Tatiana bought pallets of mangoes and sold them to large companies. Tatiana explained to Gloria how the business worked, and Gloria began working with her.

"Tati taught me everything I know. She taught me how to go through the pallets and take out rotten fruit so that the whole pallet would not spoil. We made about $240 profit per pallet," Gloria explained as we sat on crates in the back of her market stall.

Tatiana, also an immigrant, eventually returned to Mexico and sold the business to someone else, who went bankrupt. Gloria bought the business from that second owner. Like Tatiana, Gloria sold wholesale produce to large companies that bought pallets of product.

"Those companies would often buy on credit and tell me that because they were large companies, they would 'naturally repay what was owed.' But they didn't."

Many of those large companies would file for bankruptcy before repaying Gloria. After a few of these cases, Gloria's own business was on its way to bankruptcy as well.

"One day, I met Benjamín García, who convinced me to cater exclusively to fruit vendors by selling the produce they stocked in their pushcarts and not just the watermelon and mango pallets I had been selling." Benjamín García told her that fruit vendors needed a one-stop shop.

Starting around 2007, Gloria began stocking cucumbers, pineapples, limes, melons, jicamas, and coconuts. Then she began selling bags of ice, plastic forks, and the clear plastic bags used to serve the fruit salads.

"Benjamín said, 'Buy those supplies in Chinatown like we do, sell them for a dollar more, and we save on gas.' . . . Some days, I make more selling plastics because they don't go bad and I can store them forever."

Later, when trash disposal became an issue for vendors, they came to her. Some fruit vendors used to sneak into the parking lots of large grocery stores to throw away their trash, but after several of them got caught on camera, they had to stop. Other vendors would make arrangements around the city to get access to large trash containers. For example, Manuel used to pay off a security guard at a parking structure to allow him to dispose of day-old trash before he headed to the wholesale market. Gloria made a deal with the trash collectors in front of her shop to pick up more often and took on that cost herself. When vendors asked to deposit trash into that large container, she charged them a bit more for the produce they bought.

"I don't charge a fee for trash, but I'll sell them fruit for a few cents more," Gloria explained. "To vendors who do not use me for trash disposal, I offer them a better deal on fruit. But trash collection is another reason vendors buy from me, it's an extra that I offer."

This arrangement was ideal for some vendors, like Manuel, who would dispose of the previous day's trash immediately before buying that day's produce. After he arranged this with Gloria, he stopped going to the parking structure in the mornings. But Gloria was also central for fruit vendors' livelihoods because she sold produce on credit. When I asked Gloria who her biggest borrowers were, she said she had small-scale and large-scale borrowers. Small-scale borrowers were those vendors who worked only their own pushcarts—independent vendors. To them, Gloria extended a $5,000 line of credit. Among the large-scale borrowers were the García brothers, who owned eight to ten pushcarts and had several workers. To them, Gloria would extend a credit line of up to $10,000.

"The Garcías usually carry an $800 debt, but they make large repayments and catch up quickly," she explained.

Another large-scale borrower was Nancy, a middle-aged woman from the Mexican state of Michoacán who owned multiple carts and employed many vendors. Nancy was the only female large-scale employer I ever met in the vending world. She was universally disliked by all the Dos Mundos workers I met—both the ones who had worked with her and the ones who had not. I often wondered if that had anything to do with the fact that she was a woman. She was strict in her operation and was often seen in the commissary warehouse chastising vendors whom she suspected of stealing from her during the end-of-day cash counts.

"Nancy owed me a lot at one point," Gloria told me. "Because she owns so many carts, her daily expenses were between $1,000 to $1,500, so it was easy for her to rack up the debt. But I did have to stop the credit line when she hit $25,000." When Gloria stopped extending credit, Nancy stopped buying from her and started repaying her debt. "Nancy is good at paying, and she got back on track," Gloria confirmed.

Gloria accepted payments only in cash. She was intimately aware of the risk vendors operated under on account of the crackdowns by the health department. She knew the health department confiscated carts, and she also knew that sales were low during the winter months due to decreased foot traffic. Gloria often extended lines of credit and accepted smaller repayments after crackdowns hit and during the winter months. "It's a cycle," she explained. "Vendors usually catch up on payments only to ask for credit again."

Gloria extended credit to vendors only after knowing them for some time, and usually she began with a small limit of $1,000 to $2,000. This extension of credit allowed vendors to save up a little. *Paisanaje* mattered a great deal to Gloria, and she was often willing to extend credit to a vendor from Dos Mundos after a shorter period of time based largely on that connection. When I asked Gloria about delinquent vendors and how she collected overdue payments, she said she had intimate knowledge of vendors' lives that helped her make decisions about lines of credit and collect overdue payments. She could easily find the vendors who owed her money because they often continued to live in the same household even if they started shopping at another market. She also could find their families back in Dos Mundos because of her own connections in Puebla. Gloria had this kind of information about *fruteros* in part because of her *paisano* connection to them. The way she used this information was central to how vendors experienced the ethnic cage as both protection, when credit was extended, and an enclosure, when payment was due. Gloria also knew that *fruteros* were trapped in the network and, thus, in the job—she understood the ethnic cage and profited from her knowledge of it.

"Sometimes vendors will disappear, but they stay in the fruit vending business because that's all they know," Gloria explained. "The vendors will stop coming here and will go to another wholesale market and buy there. But I maintain contact with other market owners. Sometimes, we will call each other up and say that so-and-so has started shopping here. If there's a person that happens to owe me money, I will call the wholesale market person and tell them to call me if they show up there, and when they do, I head over there to see if I can get my money back. All the wholesale market owners help each other out with favors; we call each other about the debt owed by different customers. But I eventually get them back because they all hit a point where they have to start buying on credit from the new market owner, and those people might not know them as well as I do. So they come back to me."

"What do you mean this is all they [vendors] know?" I asked.

"Even if they go into another job, they come back to vending because it's a fairly easy job. They aren't killing themselves in this line of work. It's not like other jobs they could and sometimes do have. They make good money in the summers. They have connections in this job. This is all they know [*Es todo lo que saben*]. So they return."

Gloria explained that *fruteros* had many connections on the job to fellow *paisanos*. These connections were a great resource that they stood to lose if they left the business of vending. Gloria clearly stood out as a major resource in the community, and she routinely encouraged former vendors to come back into the fold.

Ultimately, Gloria did not want to lose *fruteros* as clients. As she explained, "There's profit there with them [*Hay tengo ganancias*]. Even if they owe me money, I let them pay me in installments. If I lose vendors as clients, it's worse down the line. If I ask for all the money back at once, I might lose them as clients. And I know the details of their lives that cause them to get behind on payments."

She knew, for example, when Manuel was struggling to find a group of vendors to work with and was jumping from household to household. When Manuel moved in with Chava, Gloria knew he needed to make a large rent deposit, so she extended credit to him for a time. Gloria was also aware of the ongoing *tandas* and knew which vendors participated and what week they expected to get an influx of cash: "Sometimes, when a vendor owes me money, they will tell me their *tanda* date [the date they will receive the group payout], so I know they will be able to make a large payment to me then. But I prefer small, consistent payments instead of a large promised sum."

Over the years, Gloria became more selective about extending credit and learned who was good and who was bad at repaying. "For example," she explained, "if someone promises to pay something back the next day, then I won't make a note for it. If they pay late, even if it's a week late, they are already making false promises. If they screw me with small payments, they will screw me with large payments."

Gloria had a group of twenty regular customers. These customers would buy produce from her daily, and she considered herself to have a good relationship with each of them. Of those twenty, she extended credit to ten. The García and the Martínez brothers and Manuel were among the ten.

In 2009, when Manuel owed Gloria $5,000, she cut off his line of credit. He scraped by for a year making small payments but could not get out of debt. Carmen helped him strategize. In the fall of 2010, Manuel decided he had to make a drastic change. He decided to return to Fresno, where he knew the pay was good and cost of living low, to earn enough to repay Gloria. Manuel had no intention of staying in Fresno. He went during the grape season because the work during that period paid well and was not as physically taxing as harvesting other crops. He left in the fall of 2010 and returned to Los Angeles just in time for the New Year celebrations.

"When Manuel left for Fresno, I was definitely scared he would not come back," Gloria admitted. "I just took a deep breath and waited. I knew he left Los Angeles to be able to repay me, that's what he had told me. When he came back, he told me I was his first stop. He paid back most of his debt in one go. It was a relief for me."

What Gloria understood, and what allowed her to run a successful business, was that in the world of *fruteros* and among *paisanos*, respectability was a currency. She would openly shame vendors who owed her money and disappeared before paying. She could tarnish reputations, and while vendors might be able to evade her warehouse stall, they would never be far from the judgment imposed by other fellow *paisanos*. Gloria's reach extended all the way to Mexico, where the shame of a vendor's failure to pay in Los Angeles would fall on family members in Dos Mundos. Yet respectability was not a currency unique to Gloria's business; it permeated the entire *paisano* community. Maintaining respectability was the reason why Manuel never missed a payment to the Dos Mundos ministry.

When Manuel returned to Los Angeles from Fresno, he made a big show of repaying Gloria, according to her. He also made a big show of the money he had earned while away. After he got back, he texted me to invite me to dinner, stating that he would pay for whatever I wanted, wherever I wanted. He invited me to the Dos Mundos New Year celebration, but I was in Texas for the holidays. According to the vendors who did attend the celebration, Manuel arrived with several boxes of beer to imbibe and to share. In addition to the New Year, he was celebrating being back in Los Angeles after a dreary few months in Fresno. That night, he drank a lot. In the early hours of the morning, Manuel drove home while intoxicated and was arrested on the highway headed to Pasadena—the opposite direction of his home. His truck was impounded. When I returned to Los Angeles a few days later and talked to Manuel, I learned that he had spent the night in jail. He had paid a sizable sum to recover his impounded truck. He was given a hefty citation. In the weeks that followed, he was given a community service assignment cleaning MacArthur Park and had to attend mandatory DUI classes three times a week in the evenings—missing a single class would result in a heavy fine. Just as soon as Manuel had managed to get out of one hole, he had dug himself into an even bigger one. Such was Manuel's luck, Carmen surmised when she tried to make sense of his trajectory.

CONCLUSION

The strong ties between *fruteros* are apparent in the various ways in which *fruteros* relate to each other. They can be coworkers, business associates, roommates, and even romantic partners. While these connections add depth and meaning to their relationships, they also create more vulnerability. The different types of connections they have to each other can both provide cover from harm and expose them to harm, thus the dual nature of the ethnic cage. Being romantically involved with a coworker might make the job easier by reducing living expenses, but a fallout means much more than losing a partner—it can also lead to the loss of a livelihood. In extreme cases, fallouts can also mean losing connections to other *paisanos*. Strong ties between *fruteros* can also signal devastating consequences when trust breaks down and things fall apart.

Carmen's fallout with Cristian and the Martínez brothers upended her work situation. The fallout led to trust being compromised between various individuals: between Carmen and Cristian, between Carmen and the Martínez brothers, between Cristian and the Martínez brothers, and even between brothers Andres and Raúl. When personal romantic relationships mixed with professional work arrangements, things fell apart in multiple spheres. After a series of unstable and uneasy work arrangements, Carmen connected with Manuel. Carmen could more easily influence and maneuver Manuel than she could Alberto, her previous *raitero*. Carmen's ability to exercise some control over Manuel and Manuel's willingness to take criticism and advice from her led to a successful work arrangement between the two.

By 2009, when Carmen and Manuel began working together, Manuel was experiencing his own fallout with other *paisanos*. Manuel had been fired by the García brothers for getting cited and arrested too often as their employee and becoming a liability in the process. While Manuel retained a good standing within the Dos Mundos ministry, to which he had been elected, he was compromised financially by his commitment to it. In the fruit vending community, Manuel was getting a reputation for being a bad luck charm. Employees of the García brothers routinely ridiculed him for his poor business decisions, and this filtered down to Carmen, who also treated Manuel with pity or contempt. It was widely known that Manuel was in debt to Gloria, the wholesale merchant. In a way, Carmen and Manuel found each other when their reputations were both tarnished in the *paisano* community.

However, Carmen was actively repairing her reputation in the community, but Manuel was struggling to do the same. By laughing along with other vendors who made fun of Manuel, Carmen was creating distance from the stigma attached to him. Eventually, even Manuel wanted some distance from his bad luck in Los Angeles. In an effort to repay his debt to the wholesale merchant and start with a clean slate, Manuel returned to work in the fields of Fresno. His decision to leave allowed him to earn enough money to pay back Gloria. However, the shadow of misfortune returned just as soon as Manuel got back to Los Angeles. As I show in the next chapter, his troubles extended further than the DUI he received shortly after his return.

Carmen and Manuel were enmeshed in *paisano* trust networks that bound them to each other and to others in the community. Their long-term rights and obligations meant that they did not leave the ethnic community or the vending job even when relationships soured due to romantic trysts or accumulated debt. As sociologist Charles Tilly (2007) warned, though, trust networks often narrow the range of opportunities for work, housing, socializing, and welfare. When things fell apart for Carmen and Manuel, they had to weather the storm and maneuver their limited options inside the ethnic cage.

5 Ethnic Ties in Crisis

Manuel's problems did not end when he returned from Fresno and paid off part of his debt with the wholesale merchant, nor did they end after he began to recover financially from the DUI he received at the beginning of 2011. In fact, the biggest crisis he would ever experience was on the horizon, and all of his *paisano* ties would be tested as a result. This crisis—a traffic violation arrest that led to a deportation scare—would create a ripple effect in his network that would ultimately showcase the precariousness of *paisanaje*. But in the days leading up to the crisis, things were relatively stable at work and at home for Manuel. By late 2011, with the help of Carmen, whose advice he had begun to take more seriously, Manuel had seemingly bounced back from the financially taxing DUI that he had gotten at the beginning of the year. The DUI arrest literally sobered him up; he gave up drinking, he limited his attendance at late-night social functions with his *paisanos*, and he started working seven days a week as opposed to six.

Gloria, the wholesale produce merchant, acquired a *carro pirata* (unlicensed pushcart) and sold it to Manuel at a great price. After some vetting by Carmen, Manuel hired Doña Alicia, a woman in her fifties who had frequented Carmen's corner asking for a job. Doña Alicia was Central

American, had lived in the United States for just over a year, and rented a small bedroom in an apartment near MacArthur Park. She was a reliable worker who sent most of her money home to her children in El Salvador. Doña Alicia seemed content with her arrangement working with Manuel and Carmen. For the three of them, the days were mundane and routine. Manuel gave rides to Carmen and Doña Alicia. He dropped them off with their pushcarts in the mornings and then went to work on a slightly more profitable corner than the one he had worked on previously. Carmen continued working her corner in the Mid-City area. Carmen had asked the Martínez brothers for permission to use one of their unused corners near MacArthur Park so that Doña Alicia could set up her pushcart. The Martínez brothers owed her that much, she told me. Manuel was easing into this financial stability, and he started sending his grandmother in Dos Mundos money to build a house for his return, someday in the distant future.

Life was stable for Manuel in his living arrangement as well. While his early years in Los Angeles had been characterized by constant moves, at this point he had managed to keep his room in South Central for over a year.[1] He rented a small bedroom in a three-bedroom home. The room was wide enough to hold his twin-sized bed and a small desk with a chair in the corner. Chava, another *frutero* from Dos Mundos, rented a larger bedroom in the house. A middle-aged Mexican woman owned the house and lived in the largest bedroom, facing the street. She was widowed and had refinanced the house in order to renovate the kitchen and add two restrooms so that she could rent the vacant rooms. A third man, Don Martel, lived in the basement storage room, which could only be accessed through a door in the backyard. Don Martel was in his late sixties and did not work. He served as the home's caretaker; he would keep an eye on everything when everyone was at work. Before living in the storage room, Don Martel had been homeless. He would wake early and sweep the front porch or backyard while Manuel, Chava, Carmen, Doña Alicia, and I would get the pushcarts ready. Don Martel entered the house only to use the restroom near the back kitchen. He spent most of the day outside in the backyard or on the front porch sitting or napping on an old couch.

The woman who owned the house gave the men limited access to the public spaces of the home, like the living room and kitchen. In fact, when

Manuel and Chava moved in, she told them that she preferred that they eat out instead of using her clean, recently renovated kitchen. For the most part, Manuel and Chava obliged, though they did keep some food in the pantry. Manuel would occasionally use the kitchen to prepare a bowl of food, but he would always eat it in his bedroom. Manuel and Chava both had locks on their bedroom doors that could be accessed only with the keys they each carried. Although they lived together, Manuel and Chava had a strained relationship. They never socialized, even in or around the house. They each stayed in their rooms when they were home. Chava would often drop off his pushcart in the evening and then leave again, only to return late in the night.

The South Central Los Angeles neighborhood where the house was located was not exactly walkable, especially for a young Latino man like Manuel. It was bounded on one side by a heavily transited avenue that did not have a crosswalk or intersection with streetlights, which forced residents to run across between speeding cars. It was also unclear how many residential blocks Manuel could walk away from the avenue without being on someone's turf, he explained to me. When Manuel moved in, Chava had warned him that people might not appreciate his presence if he walked around the neighborhood. For this reason, Manuel never walked around in his neighborhood, day or night. His interaction with the neighbors never lasted longer than the time it took him to get out of his truck to open and close the driveway gate. However, he saw his neighbors often. They were a multigenerational black family, and a group of young men, family and friends of the family, would often be sitting on the couch on their front porch listening to music when Manuel arrived from work. They would greet him warmly, and he would respond in Spanish with a generic nicety and move on. I likely had longer interactions with the neighbors than Carmen or Manuel because I spoke to them in English.

THE CRISIS AND THE ENSUING SCRAMBLE

In early September 2011, the Dos Mundos community in Los Angeles was planning a celebration. Carmen urged Manuel to go, and Manuel urged me to go. I could not attend. As Manuel explained to me later, he had planned to attend the party that evening. That afternoon, he had come home from work with Doña Alicia. Carmen had driven herself home from her corner that afternoon so that she could get ready for the party. Just like every other evening, Manuel unloaded the three pushcarts from the bed of the truck. Unpeeled fruit was stored on the shelves; ice and buckets of water were dumped. When everything was done, Doña Alicia walked to the corner bus stop and headed home. She would return early the next morning to work. Unlike other days, Manuel did not drive Doña Alicia home because he needed to get ready for the evening celebration. He wanted to get a fresh haircut for the party with his *paisanos*.

Because Manuel did not walk in his neighborhood, even a trip of a couple of residential blocks to the next boulevard over meant jumping into a vehicle. So, that Friday in September, he got into his truck to drive to the local barbershop. He drove down two long blocks and spotted a parking space directly in front of the barbershop. To get to it, he made an illegal U-turn. He didn't realize that he had done it directly in front of a passing police car. As he explained later, the police car pulled up behind him with its lights turned on. He did not notice it immediately but looked up after the officers blared a warning *woop* from their siren. Manuel did not have a license, and he was arrested. He remembered the hefty fee he had paid previously when he was arrested for the DUI and his truck had been impounded. He asked the police officers not to have his truck towed. One of the officers parked the truck in front of the barbershop. Then Manuel was taken to the South Central Los Angeles precinct jail and booked. The citation he received, which he showed me later, was time stamped 6:45 p.m.

No one at the party that night noticed when Manuel failed to show up. Carmen had attended the party but had left early in the evening with Gonzalo, her boyfriend from Dos Mundos. As Carmen explained in a phone conversation on Saturday afternoon, it was Doña Alicia, when she showed up to work on Saturday morning, who noticed that Manuel's truck was not in the driveway. She called Manuel, and when he did not pick up, she assumed he was driving back from the wholesale market. Time passed, and because Manuel had not yet returned, she took some unpeeled fruit belonging to Chava. She was expecting to replace it as soon as Manuel arrived. When Chava emerged from the house and realized what she had done, he grew furious. He yelled at her and told her that he did not want her poking around without Manuel around. Doña Alicia yelled at Chava, saying that Manuel owed her back pay and that she needed to work with or without Manuel. Doña Alicia stormed off in anger, pushing a half-full pushcart in front of her. She said she would use her own yard to prepare and store it.[2]

When I spoke to Carmen on Saturday afternoon, she relayed the conversations she had had with both Doña Alicia and Chava. Carmen had not worked that Saturday and, like me, was catching up on everything that had happened during the morning blowout. Carmen called other *fruteros* and found out that none of them had seen Manuel at the party.

"Do you want me to file a missing person's report?" I asked Carmen as we strategized on the phone.

"Let me talk to Chava and call you back." She hung up, and a few minutes later she called me again. "Chava wants you to check the inmate website and the coroner's office," she said plainly.

"Coroner's office?" I asked, growing a bit concerned.

"Well . . . yeah," she said slowly, and then added, "Check the jail first."

I had previously had to check the Los Angeles County Sheriff's Department inmate information center website for other vendors, so I did that quickly. I found Manuel in custody at the precinct jail and gave Carmen the information. Carmen went directly to the precinct jail and was told that Manuel had a $2,500 bail. She mobilized and called her uncle and other vendors to start collecting money over the weekend. On Monday morning, Carmen and I went to the precinct jail. Carmen was afraid of putting her name down on any document in a jail setting, so she told me to visit Manuel.

That Monday, before going to the jail, we stepped inside a bail bond office directly across the street. The receptionist working at the office quickly did an online search and informed us that an ICE hold had been placed on Manuel and that there was no longer any bail amount to post. Carmen gasped. As we walked to the precinct jail, Carmen kept repeating, "*Híjole! Híjole! Híjole!* [Gosh! Jeez!]" She began to cry. She called her uncle and asked for advice, which she then gave to me to pass on to Manuel. She called Chava and told him about the ICE hold. Chava told her he knew of an immigration lawyer but said that he charged at least $4,000. After a few minutes, she walked to her car, and I walked into the precinct jail.

I signed up for the visitation and waited for an hour before I was called. I was told I would have fifteen minutes. Inside the visitation area, I waited another forty-five minutes before Manuel was brought out. When he saw me sitting in the booth, he looked a bit surprised and embarrassed. He smiled nervously, revealing his missing front tooth, and sat down. We talked on a phone with a glass wall dividing us, and he told me he had not slept in days. He looked very tired.

We spoke quickly. I updated him on everything, including the ICE hold and our inability to post bail because of it. I told him we had seen the $2,500 bail posted over the weekend and that Carmen had collected money. He asked why no one had posted the bail when the amount was listed. I told him no one had known he was arrested until Saturday afternoon and that it had taken Carmen time to collect the money. He nodded and took everything in silently. I told him that Carmen had instructed me to tell him not to sign anything related to his immigration case. I asked Manuel if he had signed any papers or anything indicating a "voluntary departure." He shook his head no. This bit of information seemed to concern him, and I reassured him that we would be at court the following day to see what could be done. I told him that Carmen had asked Chava about an immigration lawyer and that it might cost $4,000 to secure one. Manuel shook his head and said that the amount was too much and that he would rather be deported.

Manuel's chief concern was his truck. The police officers had parked it for him instead of towing it. He wanted to release his keys to me. He asked if I could take his wallet and cell phone also, but I told him he might need them if and when he was released. Later, Chava would tell me that he knew some people who never received their property when they were deported. I asked an officer about the property transfer and was given a form to fill out for the exchange. Under "family relation," I wrote "cousin," which was the perfunctory designation I got in most circumstances when the vendors introduced me to strangers. Manuel was given the form to sign as well. He told me to keep his truck safe. Shortly after, the police officer standing nearby informed us our time was up.

When I walked out to the waiting area with Manuel's keys and instructions, I did not see Carmen. On the phone, she said she had driven to Manuel's home and was on her way back. When she arrived to pick me up, she was crying. She told me that she had had a confrontation with Chava. "Without Manuel there, he doesn't want me or Doña Alicia using his backyard to prepare our pushcarts!" she exclaimed. She began fretting about where to store her pushcart, which was still in the backyard.

I asked her what had happened. Carmen told me that when she had discussed the immigration custody issue and Manuel's possible deportation with Chava, he told her it was fitting since Manuel had not managed to do anything with himself while he was free. Chava also told her that if Manuel was going to be deported, he wanted the keys to his pickup truck. Manuel owed rent, and the truck would be used to pay off what he owed. According to Carmen, who had recently bought a used sedan, it had upset Chava to see her "parading" the new car around. Chava knew that Manuel drove Carmen and her pushcart to her corner. As he asked for the truck keys, he told her, "Let's see how you pay off your new car now that you won't be able to get to work." It was that comment that had made Carmen despondent.

Chava never interacted extensively with me. He was hardly ever in the house after workdays when I helped Manuel and Carmen unload the carts, and when I did see him, he was always churlish toward Manuel. Chava ignored me for the most part. Carmen and Manuel always brushed him aside and told me, "Just ignore him, he's like that." On one occasion, I overheard Chava berating Manuel, and when I walked into the room, Chava stopped abruptly and stepped out. I knew that Chava acted differently around me, perhaps because he did not understand my presence. Still, I was not sure if Carmen's interaction with Chava that morning was sparked by some preexisting grievance or was an extension of the argument Chava had had with Doña Alicia.

In the end, Carmen decided to keep the truck herself so she could continue working. "Manuel would want it that way," she explained to me. Together, we picked up the truck and then went to Manuel's house. Don Martel greeted us from the porch. He told us Chava would not want us there, and Carmen explained that I had just met with Manuel at the precinct jail. "Manuel gave Rocío the keys to his room so that she could get some paperwork for him. She's trying to *help him*," Carmen said abrasively, though Manuel had never mentioned anything about paperwork. Don Martel stepped aside, and we opened Manuel's bedroom door with his keys.

Once inside, Carmen began looking through Manuel's desk. "Help me find any important papers so that I can take them with me, anything he might need if he gets deported," she said as she opened and closed drawers. In one drawer, she found a wad of cash. We both saw it at the same time. She picked it up and slipped it in her bra. "I'm only taking this in case he needs it later. He might need it later," she repeated. I said nothing and watched her go through the rest of the drawers.

Before we left, Carmen locked the bedroom door. As we walked away from the house, Carmen began fuming. "Chava turned Don Martel against us," she said angrily. "Chava is glad Manuel got arrested and might be deported! He said Manuel deserved it because he had done nothing with himself while he was here. Even after he knew Manuel was in jail, he didn't tell anyone who might have helped with the bail. Did you see I was the only one doing anything about it?"

I was not sure if what Chava told Carmen was true. The argument had happened while I was visiting Manuel, and I never became close enough to Chava to verify it. Chava would not have been likely to tell me anything since he always appeared to watch his language and attitude around me. But Carmen used that argument to justify why she decided to take Manuel's truck, and it was the story she repeated to other vendors who later saw her with his truck.

Carmen called Chava while we drove. She asked if she could keep the pushcarts in his backyard until the following day, when she would pick them up. She needed to secure a space at the commissary storage warehouse. He agreed. We drove to the commissary, and Carmen filled out the necessary paperwork and paid the monthly fee for a space. It was early afternoon, and some *fruteros* were returning from their corners. In conversations with them, Carmen would lead with the line, "They're going to deport Manuel!" At that point, we were not certain that deportation was imminent, but it was the narrative circulating among the *fruteros*, aided in part by Carmen's retelling.

By evening, when news had hit the community more widely, we realized that Manuel had been struggling financially. Gloria began telling people that Manuel still owed her money for the pushcart that Doña Alicia used and that he had an outstanding bill for produce. Doña Alicia told us that she had been working without pay because Manuel said he was paying off the pushcart. Doña Alicia told Carmen that she planned on keeping the push-cart regardless of what Carmen told her. Carmen could not argue with her; she figured Chava would not let Doña Alicia work out of his backyard any-way, and neither Carmen nor Doña Alicia could afford to pay the commis-sary to store the cart. Meanwhile, Chava complained to Carmen that Manuel owed money for rent. He said that he would have to pay double rent if Manuel were deported until he found someone to take the room. The land-lord of the home they rented did not seem to care that Manuel was in the middle of a crisis. And although Carmen had secured Manuel's pickup truck, she still needed help loading and unloading the pushcart. Everyone that Manuel was connected to began worrying about how to survive in his absence. This invariably meant that all of Manuel's possessions began to be divided up among his small network of home and work relations.

Carmen continued to justify keeping the truck by saying that she needed to keep working to be able to continue paying off Manuel's *tanda* contribution. Both Manuel and Carmen participated in the Dos Mundos *tanda*. Carmen had two tickets, so she contributed $200 per week, and Manuel had one ticket, so he contributed $100 per week. With Manuel in jail, Carmen would be making his contribution as well as her own, paying a total of $300 per week. Manuel had signed up to be one of the first to receive the money in a group of thirty-one tickets, and so it was especially bad if he did not continue making payments during the full group rota-tion. Rotating credit associations, or *tandas*, can turn into liabilities when there are too many numbers taken by the group. When a person has a payout at the beginning of a large rotation, the weeks that follow—in which they are continuously making payments but no longer expecting any return—can feel endless.[3] When Carmen started paying Manuel's weekly contribution, it felt particularly difficult, because she would not benefit from his payout at all.

On Monday night, at Carmen's urging, I called Mexico and talked to Manuel's aunt Rosaura in Dos Mundos. I explained what had happened to Manuel. Rosaura asked if it would be possible to have his truck taken across the border to Mexico so that he could bring it back to Puebla if he got deported. I told her I would do whatever Manuel wanted but explained that Carmen was using the truck to work. Later, Carmen told me that she had spoken to Rosaura and that the aunt had allowed her to keep all of

Manuel's belongings and told her not to let Chava have them. Again, I did not witness this conversation, so I do not know what Carmen said to convince Rosaura or even if the conversation had actually happened.

Carmen put me in charge of dealing with Manuel and his court case. On the Tuesday after he was arrested, she went to Chava's house to pick up the pushcarts. She enlisted the help of another male vendor. I went to traffic court to see Manuel. Carmen asked me to talk to the bail bonds people to see if he could be released and to keep her updated. She loaned me her sedan so that I could go to and from the court and jail quickly instead of waiting for the bus. In our subsequent interactions, as I updated her on issues, Carmen seemed distant, and I felt like she had charged me with doing the emotional labor of caring. When I tried returning her car at the end of the day, she told me to keep it for a while longer. "You can keep visiting him if you have the car," she said.

At traffic court on Tuesday, I sat in an empty courtroom for a while before a bailiff told me to wait outside. The bailiff said he would call me when the cases began, but he never did. When I entered the courtroom again, Manuel's case had already been discussed. Manuel was sitting in a special area next to the judge, along with several other men. The view was obstructed so that he could not see me and I could barely see him. After the men's cases were discussed, they were escorted out through a side door. I approached the bailiff who had asked me to step out, and he gave me Manuel's booking number so that I could keep track of him.

Later, when I spoke to Manuel, he told me he was allowed to make phone calls only to landlines. Everyone in his circle, including me, had only cell phones. He also did not have any important numbers memorized and could not access his cell phone to look them up. I relayed all this information to Carmen, and she gave me the number of a friend who had a landline. Meanwhile, I asked people in my own social network who worked on immigration issues for more information. I was told Manuel had a difficult case. His DUI record would not help. He did not have U.S.-born children or a wife with citizenship, and he had spent a limited amount of time in the country. All these factors, I was told, meant he did not have a very good chance for leniency from the immigration courts. Yet his case was only heard before traffic court and was not transferred to the immigration courts.

By Wednesday, Manuel was transferred to the men's central jail in downtown Los Angeles. I deposited $70 into his commissary account but had no way of letting him know that I had done so. A week and a half later, Manuel was released with a monitor attached to his ankle. As a condition of his release, he had to do a weekly check-in on Fridays at the downtown immigration courts. Manuel emerged from his incarceration completely defeated. Although the teller at the central jail told me that Manuel would receive the money that I deposited if he were released, he never did. But Manuel had no interest in reclaiming the commissary money owed to him. "Let them keep it, I don't care," he said. He had no interest in recovering the pushcart Doña Alicia had taken. He had to pick up the pieces of his life and find a new place to live because Chava did not want him living in the house any longer.

PICKING UP THE PIECES

In the weeks that followed, talk about Manuel's money management was circulating in the *paisano* rumor mill. Chava was telling people that Manuel was a bad employer and a bad business owner; several *fruteros* verified that Chava was spreading this story. Before he was arrested, knowledge of Manuel's financial troubles had been confined to a small circle consisting of Carmen and Doña Alicia, whom he worked with, and Gloria, the wholesale produce owner, but now the larger community was aware of the financial problems that had driven him to work in the fields of Fresno the year prior. For some in the *frutero* community, the fact that Manuel had not been paying his worker elicited bad memories. In conversations among vendors, a negative narrative began forming around Manuel's unfortunate circumstances. While he had sat in jail, his *paisanos* had been justifying his arrest and imminent deportation. When he was released, many of his *paisanos* moved away from him in an attempt to create real and symbolic distance from his misfortune.

Manuel's arrest and the threat of his potential deportation created a ripple effect of economic and personal crises in other people's lives. This, in turn, showcased how the misfortune of one individual weighs heavily on others in the tightly networked community of *paisanos*. Everyone in

Manuel's immediate circle took or attempted to take his few assets. Possession of his pickup truck was a contested battle between Carmen and Chava; even Manuel's aunt Rosaura, in Dos Mundos, inquired about the truck immediately after learning about Manuel's arrest and possible deportation. His extra pushcart was ceded to Doña Alicia—first by Carmen, who did nothing to prevent Alicia from taking it, and later by Manuel, who did nothing to reclaim it. Chava fought with Manuel over everything that had happened, and Manuel was kicked out of the house. Chava had the support of the home's owner, who also wanted a more stable tenant. The immigration court–ordered monitor around Manuel's ankle did not inspire confidence that his presence in the country would last.

Manuel reclaimed his truck from Carmen. He spent several weeks trying to find a new place to live. He eventually landed in the home of some fruit vendors who were more marginalized members of the *paisano* community. One of these *paisanos*, Lucío, offered him a room in the Compton home they shared. Manuel joined their small vending working group. In Compton, Manuel was farther away from members of the larger *paisano* community, who worked and lived in central and northeast Los Angeles. Because his home was located so far from Carmen's work corner and the commissary warehouse where Carmen was now storing her cart for a monthly fee, Carmen and Manuel's work partnership ended. Manuel had been useful to Carmen not only as a *raitero* but also because he provided a free place for her to store her pushcart. Now that she was paying for that service at the commissary warehouse, the usefulness of Manuel was greatly diminished. They spoke less and less and would ultimately go several months without seeing or speaking to each other. Manuel stopped attending the regular social gatherings, and we heard very little from him.

No one in the *paisano* community seemed particularly concerned with Manuel's disappearance. Initially, I struggled to understand the animosity directed at Manuel. He had been arrested for an issue that any other *frutero* could have been arrested for; the large majority of people in the *paisano* community lacked a driver's license, and plenty of them owned and operated vehicles, which meant they could be arrested for a similar issue. A few of them had DUI arrests on their records. After many conversations with multiple *fruteros*, I came to understand their behavior toward Manuel as rhetorical self-preservation. They opted to find fault with

Manuel's individual characteristics so that the crisis that he endured was specific to *him* and would not befall *them*. To hear them say it, Manuel had been arrested for being foolish; he had lost his pushcart and his housing because he was a poor businessman; he had almost been deported because he did not deserve to be in the country; and he had squandered his chances and was now paying for it. Yet everyone else in the community was struggling in almost exactly the same way; almost all of them were vulnerable to economic and immigration issues as well. Street vending was riddled with risk. Even the most profitable *fruteros* had outstanding debts with the wholesale merchant, and anyone could lose their pushcarts at any time because of a health department crackdown. Living in the country without authorization was also an everyday risk, but *paisanos* were loath to be reminded of it. Manuel's presence, and his ankle monitor, were a reminder they did not need or want. By making Manuel's crisis unique to him, they could deny the precarity of their own social and economic positioning. In the end, instead of helping Manuel during his crisis, his fruit vending *paisano* network opted to banish him. Coethnic ties may grant entry into the community, but they do not guarantee benevolence—that is the nature of the ethnic cage.

6 Dos Mundos Transformed

I visited Dos Mundos for the first time after I had spent five years interviewing and working with *fruteros* in Los Angeles. The small town of Dos Mundos loomed large among fruit vendors in Los Angeles; the hometown structured the community's social ties and social calendars. Every seven days, a group of Dos Mundos emigrants met in Los Angeles to pray a rosary for the hometown's patron saint. Every summer, there was a large patron saint celebration in central Los Angeles that mirrored the one taking place in Mexico. I arrived in Dos Mundos wanting to know what these *fruteros* left behind and why. Through the narratives of departure provided by family members in Dos Mundos and by *fruteros* in Los Angeles, I began to piece together the impact of migration on social relations. In Dos Mundos, I began to see the cascading issues, emotions, and social fractures associated with international migration. While *fruteros* in Los Angeles were trapped in an ethnic cage of restructured *paisanaje*, their family and friends in Mexico were living in a community transformed by departures and the migration industry that enabled them.[1]

THE SENDING COMMUNITY

Most of the streets in Dos Mundos are unpaved, rutted dirt roads. The town has many undeveloped plots of land between homes where weeds grow wild. A few of these plots are planted with *milpa* (maize fields). There is one central paved road that runs through town; it has two lanes, and along its sides are sidewalks paved with large red bricks. On this paved road, near the entrance of town, there is a small structure that houses an altar with the town's patron saint. Dos Mundos residents will sometimes drop in and pray there on their way out of town. The small ornate door is kept locked except for a few hours every weekday. Inside, the white walls and marble floors are kept immaculately clean. This structure was one of the first things built with remittances from migrants abroad.

Older homes in Dos Mundos are concrete, flat-roofed dwellings. Yet dotted throughout the rural landscape, two-story homes with American architectural features—such as gable roofs, porticos, and large modern windows—are springing up. These homes are the physical manifestation of the financial and cultural remittances of Dos Mundos emigrants. These homes also function as markers of success that motivate other would-be migrants in town to leave. However, their impressive presence obscures the hardship that many Dos Mundos emigrants face abroad.

In 2010, the inhabitants of Dos Mundos numbered just under 1,400. The town's principal economic activity is agriculture (INEGI 2010). There is an increasing belief in Dos Mundos that a life working the *milpa* fields and herding animals is not sustainable. The wages from this type of work are low, and residents who rely only on agricultural work are generally the poorest in town. It is increasingly common for residents to work outside of Dos Mundos in other industries. Town residents who do not work in agriculture often commute to adjacent cities for work. The type of work sought and the distance traveled is partly determined by an individual's gender. Men typically take weeklong or month-long construction jobs in urban centers like Mexico City and Monterrey. Women take jobs closer to home in Puebla City as maids, nannies, or laundresses; they commute daily. A relatively new and young generation of Dos Mundos residents migrates north to the United States in search of work.

Unlike other towns and cities in Mexico, Dos Mundos does not have a well-established "culture of migration" characterized by high rates of out-migration, where international migration and the aspiration to migrate is "transmitted across generations and between people through social networks" (Kandel and Massey 2002, 981). Historically, communities in western Mexico—in the states of Jalisco, Michoacán, Guanajuato, Nayarit, and Zacatecas—have sent the majority of migrants to the United States (Jones 1988; Massey and Espinosa 1997). The sons—they are typically male—that Dos Mundos sends often do not have older relatives who have traveled north as migrants themselves. In fact, fathers sometimes discourage sons who want to migrate north into the United States. The social networks that connect migrants in Dos Mundos to communities in the United States are, accordingly, nascent ones. Yet they are quickly becoming strong forces pulling young men across borders.

But these young migrants are also responding to a paradox rooted in international migration. Gonzalo explained this paradox one night after having dinner in my apartment. That night, I sat on my living room floor holding Carmen and Gonzalo's newborn baby. Carmen looked over my shoulder at her son in my arms, and Gonzalo sat at the other end of the room musing out loud while a digital recorder captured the conversation. Of life in the United States, he said simply, "Here, without papers you are no one [*Aquí sin papeles no eres nadie*]."

Yet he believed that he and others like him had been able to lift their hometown up because they had left Dos Mundos. According to Gonzalo, Dos Mundos began to matter to local politicians only after the town began to boast more migrants. These migrants sent back remittances and built up the town's infrastructure. This provoked more attention from state politicians, who contributed more resources to the town—resources that they had needed far more when there were fewer migrants.

"Why am I worth more here, suffering, than I am when I'm in my own country?" Gonzalo asked, letting the question hang in the space between us. Understanding this paradox, of having a greater worth in absentia, likely also drove migrants out of Dos Mundos and into the United States.

LEAVING DOS MUNDOS

A journey out of Dos Mundos begins with a mile-long walk along the main road to the outskirts of town. Once the last home is passed, *milpa* fields spread out on either side of the road, and the occasional goat or sheep can be seen grazing.[2] At the edge of town, there is a large metal arch that is decorated with brightly colored *papel picado* during the summer's patron saint celebration (see figures 4 and 5). Just past this arch, local residents stand on the dusty highway shoulder to wait for the bus that will take them to the state capital, Puebla City, which is about seven miles away. Both coming and going, the bus fills with people quickly. The bus services multiple towns along the way, and it is always packed shoulder to shoulder, front to back with a pressing mass of bodies. With multiple stops, a half-hour drive turns into a two-hour public transportation commute. Once in Puebla City, migrants must make a transfer to a city bus, which arrives at the main bus terminal in the city. It is from this bus terminal that Dos Mundos residents make the long journey to a border town.

Dos Mundos migrants leave home and travel thousands of miles to the United States for many reasons. Some are complex, and others less so. An underexplored reason is the desire of young people for adventure and change. Yet even an individual desire for change is deeply rooted in globalization processes that have made subsistence farming, which past generations of Dos Mundos residents depended on, unsustainable. Some migrants leave Dos Mundos because they have more pressing needs, such as needing to make money to alleviate extreme financial hardship due to unforeseen expenses. The decision to migrate to the United States, instead of to another urban center in Mexico, is driven by issues like collapses in construction industries, where would-be migrants might otherwise find jobs, and the devaluation of the Mexican peso, which makes a job earning American dollars much more profitable.

Often, departures are hurried decisions made on receiving knowledge that a neighbor or friend is going to cross the border. In these cases, young men from Dos Mundos accompany their neighbors out of convenience and leave parents behind wondering how it all happened so quickly. But

Figure 4 (top). The entrance to Dos Mundos in 2011.

Figure 5 (bottom). The entrance to Dos Mundos in 2017, after the highway was constructed.

even these hurried decisions are a result of the cultural and economic remittances that abound throughout the small rural town and that young people observe and absorb.

THE MIGRATION INDUSTRY IN DOS MUNDOS

Manuel's grandmother, Doña Julieta (see figure 6), is giving me a tour of Dos Mundos. We walk along dirt roads, and every time we pass a house under construction, she points and says, "They [the owners of the houses] are on the other side [in the United States] too." At this time, Doña Julieta's grandson has been in the United States for six years.[3]

Manuel calls Doña Julieta his *mamá* (mother) because she raised him after his biological mother, Doña Julieta's daughter, abandoned him as a baby. Doña Julieta is the archetypical Mexican grandmother, the kind depicted in the Disney movie *Coco*. During my visits, she wears shin-length skirts or dresses—never pants. Over her simple and clean outfits, she wears a *delantar* (apron). On her feet are well-worn black shoes, the kind worn by nurses of an older generation, dusty from the unpaved roads in town. Doña Julieta wears her gray hair in two simple braids. She is in her seventies, and her sun-kissed skin is lined with wrinkles. Doña Julieta smiles with her eyes, which seem to be filled with an intangible innocence. Manuel arranged for me to stay with his grandmother while I visited Dos Mundos—his hometown and that of most of the other fruit vendors I interacted with in Los Angeles.

Doña Julieta and I pass a well-kept two-story home with a black iron gate and flower garden, and she whispers, "The money lady lives there." She is referring to the moneylender who financed Manuel's trip to the United States by giving him a loan with a 15 percent interest rate. I look back in the direction of the home and point to it.

"There?" I ask in my regular speaking voice.

She pulls my hand down and shushes me.

"Can she hear us?" I whisper, looking around at the empty street.

"Let's not risk it," she whispers back, and we continue walking. Manuel's family in Dos Mundos is poor, which is why the family went to the local moneylender when Manuel decided to cross the border. Many others

Figure 6. Doña Julieta outside a home in Dos Mundos.

before and after Manuel also used the local moneylender to finance their journeys north.

For international migration, the phrase "it takes a village" is apt. Migrants who have traveled to the United States often send for or come back to guide other aspiring migrants. The local moneylender in Dos Mundos is available to provide loans to pay for these journeys. Yet international migration involves many actors beyond the individual migrants traveling. Throughout the process, a "migration industry" develops that profits from, facilitates, and sustains that movement (Hernández-León 2005). The entrepreneurs, businesses, and service providers that make up the migration industry are often not far removed from migrants themselves. International migration, and the migration industry that emerges as a consequence, transform the social relations between all of the actors involved.

Layered on top of the webs of information sharing and money lending are complex emotions tied to the uncertain and clandestine passage north. Different needs and desires set international migration in motion. And because unauthorized entry into the United States tends to carry an air of finality, these departures are often emotionally taxing. It is in this space of emotional tumult that migrants must rely on others for assistance, and when social ties are tested and fail, they create conditions where individuals feel abandoned, cheated, or used. As she explained on our walk, Doña Julieta was intimidated and angered by the moneylender. She was intimidated by the money and power this woman had in her small community. She was angered by the interest rate that this woman had given Manuel, which she felt was unnecessarily high. Doña Julieta was also upset by the fact that Manuel spent so much of his time in the United States working just to be able to pay off the debt he owed the lender.

Migration scholars often focus on large-scale transformations created by the movement of people across international borders. They seek to understand how immigrants fare once they arrive in the destination country or how a sending community is transformed by the social, cultural, and economic remittances that emigrants provide. However, it is also important to understand how international migration changes the nature of relationships between people in sending communities. Ultimately, in the wake of these departures, social relations in town and between *paisanos* are inevitably altered by the monetization of the migration industry.

BORROWED DREAMS

"I was the one who was supposed to go," Manuel's aunt Rosaura interjects in a belligerent tone when I ask Doña Julieta how Manuel decided to migrate to the United States.[4] In her arms, she cradles her sleeping baby, her second child, while sitting on a bed where her older toddler is also taking a nap.

I am interviewing Doña Julieta, Manuel's seventy-one-year-old grandmother, but Rosaura sits to the side, watching and interjecting when Doña Julieta's memory fails her. Rosaura is a major part of the story, and her presence functions to set the record straight.

Manuel's family in Dos Mundos is among the poorest I encounter during my visit. Doña Julieta's house is a two-room cinder block structure with a flat roof. The room is dimly lit by a bare light bulb hanging two steps from the front door; the farthest corners of the long rectangular room are cast in shadows. During the day, the large metal front door is kept open, and a twin-sized bed sheet serves as an improvised curtain to keep flies out of the living quarters. At night, when the door is closed, a large machete is visible, tucked into the nooks of the metal door's frame. There is no running water, so the cinder block outhouse doubles as a place to take bucket showers. There is no kitchen. Instead, Doña Julieta cooks on a low wood-burning stove in an adjacent room with a thatched roof.

Doña Julieta had nine children, four of whom died in their infancy. She had no formal schooling. Her whole life, she has worked in the fields and cleaning houses in Puebla City. In Dos Mundos, she lives in a two-room house with her daughter Rosaura and her two grandchildren. She also takes care of her son's three children while he works on construction jobs throughout the country and his wife works as a maid in Puebla City. Despite her age, she still cleans houses in Puebla City two to three days a week, a fact she tells me to keep from Manuel because he would not want her working at her age.

Doña Julieta explains that Rosaura was the one who had the dream of migrating to the United States. Rosaura had not only talked about making the trip but had also begun planning it. It was her talk of leaving that made Manuel decide to leave, which meant Rosaura would have to stay behind. The cost for both of them to migrate was too great, and they knew they would be a burden upon arrival to the neighbor who was planning on helping them make the journey. Manuel's logic was also motivated by gendered expectations: he believed that Rosaura would be a better caretaker for Doña Julieta in her old age, that the journey north would be too dangerous for a woman, and that he would be able to work harder and earn more money in the United States than Rosaura could.[5] In the end, Doña

Julieta gave her blessing to Manuel. He left, and Rosaura remained unhappily behind.

Although Rosaura is thirty-nine years old, she has the tired and lined countenance of someone much older. She is short and wide. Her straight black hair is pulled back in a low ponytail, and her bangs hit just above her eyebrows. Her skin is dark from the miles she walks to and from work. Her hands are tough from the years she has spent working in the fields herding animals and as a laundress in Puebla City. Rosaura's resentment about the turn of events is palpable. She had dreams of going to the United States. She had told neighbors and friends she was leaving.

Doña Julieta explained the ongoing issues: "He [Manuel] didn't want to take Rosaura. Later, she would tell him, 'Hey, send me money, and I'll go,' and he would respond, 'And what are you going to come for? You think it's so easy that with a broom you'll sweep up all the money here? Here, you suffer.'"[6]

"This is what he would say to her when he first left?" I ask.

"After a year of being there. She still wanted to go. She would tell him that," Doña Julieta explained.

Turning to Rosaura, I ask, "Do you still want to go?"

"Yes," she replies without hesitation.

Because it was a borrowed dream, Manuel knew who would take him and where he would go. Twenty days before leaving, Manuel bought Doña Julieta a cellular phone so they could stay in touch. The amount of planning that Manuel did and the departure date he set in the somewhat distant future contrasts sharply with the hurried departure narratives of other young men in town who left when they were roughly the same age. Manuel also had a job waiting for him in Fresno once he arrived, which was given to him by Margarita, a reliable long-time family friend. Margarita was Doña Julieta's *comadre* (a fictive kin relationship based on a godparent role), and she had initially offered the job to Rosaura. When Manuel left, he told Doña Julieta he would return in two years.[7]

In Dos Mundos, Manuel had worked in the fields earning Mex$50 a day (roughly US$4.46).[8] The family had to borrow Mex$9,000 (roughly US$800) from the local moneylender for the trip, which had a 15 percent monthly interest rate and was to be paid back in six months' time. Manuel's first paychecks in Fresno went straight to the moneylender in Dos Mundos and to the *coyote* who crossed him over the border. The money borrowed from the Dos Mundos moneylender was not sufficient to pay the *coyote*, so when Manuel arrived in the United States, he was indebted to two different people, one in the sending country and one in the receiving country. The *coyote* was known to Margarita and therefore was willing to take payments in installments from Manuel.

The debt Manuel had incurred by the time he arrived and the ease with which he could make installment payments showcases the elaborate migration industry that continuously profits off of migrants. The commercialization of international migration is not a new phenomenon—though the strengthening of border controls can contribute to the migration industry's expansion as more actors step in to profit off of helping migrants navigate tighter restrictions and border controls.[9] In Dos Mundos, a community in which previous generations did not migrate, the act of profiting off of people's departures was new and felt unsavory to many, as Doña Julieta's attitude toward the moneylender demonstrates. After Manuel left, Doña Julieta would walk to the moneylender's home once a month and make an installment payment. She recalled to me that each time she visited, she noticed all the nice things this moneylender had in her house. It was frustrating for Doña Julieta to make those payments when she wanted instead to be helping her grandson build his house.

Many migration scholars have extolled the social networks and social capital that migrants rely on to cross borders and build lives in strange new lands (Massey et al. 1987). The migration industry literature that has emerged more recently has begun to question the motivations behind those social networks by focusing more concretely on the ways in which different actors profit from the movement of people across borders. The migration industry, as conceptualized by sociologist Rubén Hernández-León (2008), is less concerned with the altruism behind the actions than with the profits those actions bring about.[10] Doña Julieta could have felt grateful to have a moneylender in her social network who would give her grandson a loan with no collateral, but instead she was consumed by contempt for the "greedy" profit-making venture of her neighbor. Still, unlike his peers, Manuel left Dos Mundos with no pressing urgency and with a solid contact that provided him with a relatively well-paying job in the

United States, which softened the blow that *paisanos* working within the migration industry can deal to migrants.

Manuel worked steadily in Fresno and later in Los Angeles to repay the moneylender in Dos Mundos. After a little over six months, Doña Julieta had enough left over from the remittances to begin buying building materials. Manuel wanted to have a home in Dos Mundos waiting for him when he returned. Meanwhile, buying the materials filled Doña Julieta with hope that her boy would return soon. However, the money that Manuel sent to his grandmother soon slowed as he experienced the economic hardship associated with street vending in Los Angeles.

In Dos Mundos, when I asked Doña Julieta how often Manuel sent money, she said it was about every two months, though Rosaura retorted, "[He goes without sending for] more [months] than that! He doesn't even send anything [as of late] [*Pues ni manda ya*]." In an apologetic tone, Doña Julieta explained,

> But it's because he says he doesn't have enough for his expenses. He tells me, "I pay electricity, water, rent," and I tell him, "Work to sustain yourself, and so you can eat." He does send [money] for—well, because he's an elected town minister on the church committee—he does send [money] for the day of the festival. That he does. Since he's part of the group of elected ministers, he's committed to sending money for the weeklong patron saint festival, or for the New Year [festivities], or for the Holy Week [festivals]. . . . They [migrants abroad] send money for food, to feed the musicians, to pay the muscians. The New Year contribution is bigger, because for New Year they get food and hire different bands to play. That's the time when they send more money.

Manuel understood his family in Dos Mundos could benefit from his remittances and knew they were among the poorest in town. In the first few years I knew him, Manuel did not talk much about life in his hometown. However, when I began to talk about visiting Mexico and interviewing vendors' family members there, Manuel began opening up about the circumstances of his family back home. Manuel arranged for me to stay with his grandmother, and as my departure date approached, he began revealing more details in an effort to, as he put it, "prepare me" for the poverty I was to encounter.

One evening, as Carmen, Manuel, and I sat in the small bedroom he rented in South Central Los Angeles, he said, "We're very poor people there [in Dos Mundos], not poor like what you see here." He pointed to the restroom just beyond his bedroom door and explained, "There is no running water [at the house where you will stay]. You will have to shower with buckets of water."

Manuel had left Dos Mundos to improve life for his grandmother in Mexico, but he had been unable to do so in the years he had been in the United States. Manuel had promised to build his grandmother a suitable kitchen to replace the thatched roof room that she used to prepare food. He had also promised his grandmother that he would build a bigger house on the plot of land the family owned.

One evening in Dos Mundos, as Doña Julieta and I were walking through the back part of the family lot trailed by her nine grandchildren, she pointed to a small pile of bricks lined up against a neighbor's wall and told me she had bought them with the money Manuel had sent her. She told me the bricks were for the house Manuel was going to build. Those bricks represented the six years Manuel had spent working abroad. At that time, they were little more than props in the children's game of long jump. Only later, when I returned in 2017, had Manuel managed to send enough money to build the house. The three-bedroom house remained unfinished and unoccupied, but it represented the burden that had been lifted once his ministry tenure ended.

LIKE FATHER, LIKE SON

Jesús's father, Don Camilo, was one of the few from his generation to have migrated to the United States. He had gone to Los Angeles to get the family out of debt and to make enough money to build a house. When he arrived in Los Angeles in the early 1980s, he worked as a carpenter, but he only remained in the country for seven months before returning to Dos Mundos. In that time, he made enough money to build a small house for his growing family, and he and his wife were able to move out of his in-laws' crowded home. He had never intended to stay in the United States. He had journeyed north as a "target earner," hoping to make enough money to complete certain projects before returning to Mexico.[11] When Don Camilo returned to Dos Mundos, he continued doing work in construction, when it was available, and in the *milpa*. Jesús's mother, Doña Fátima, had always been a homemaker.

When I spoke to Doña Fátima in Dos Mundos, Don Camilo had recently died. She recalled her husband's sacrifice fondly. "Thanks to those days of adventure, he left me with a home to live in." With her hand, she motioned to the space around us.[12] Her home was long and narrow, like a shotgun house. It did not have many windows to let in sunlight, and the concrete floor and cinderblock walls kept the house a few degrees colder than the outside temperature. The furniture was sparse. In the front living area, there was only a formal wooden dining table with chairs. When I arrived, Doña Fátima pulled the dining chairs to the middle of the room so that we sat a couple of feet apart facing each other. During the interview, her soft voice echoed throughout the largely empty space.

Doña Fátima knew that her husband's time abroad had been difficult. Even the most basic things had been challenging, she explained:

> I think it's hard [to live in the United States]. Because, like I said, my husband would ask for food, right? As he would tell me, he would enter restaurants, and he would ask for food, but they wouldn't understand. He would tell me, "I would just enter, and they would just pick something for me. They would give me what they picked. But I didn't want that." So of course it's hard. You don't know anything there. You can't read any English, nothing. It's very . . . very sad for me [to think about].[13]

Don Camilo told these stories of hardship to Doña Fátima, and they both later passed them on to their three sons. When Don Camilo returned, he did not want any of his three sons to go to the United States, and they never had aspirations of going. But hardship that would necessitate a venture north landed on Jesús's doorstep nonetheless. When Jesús's wife needed medical treatment, the family found themselves in serious debt due to the expensive medical procedures. Jesús decided to go to the United States to make money quickly. Just like his father decades before, Jesús left to pull his family out of debt. And like his father, Jesús maintained a sojourner mentality, endured difficult times working in Los Angeles, and eventually returned to his family in Dos Mundos. In the end, Jesús stayed in Los Angeles for three years and five months before returning to Dos Mundos. By 2011, when I visited Dos Mundos, Jesús had returned.

"I knew he was going to return. He would tell me often that he was getting ready to come back," Doña Fátima explained. She was aware of some of her son's tribulations: "[He would tell me that] it was difficult. He couldn't get his bearings. He'd cut his fingers [while working as a fruit vendor] because he didn't know how to do it [prepare fruit]. And he'd tell me he wanted to return, but necessity would make him stay there. He always, always told me he wanted to return."

Interestingly, Doña Fátima did not know much about the ways in which Jesús's employers, the García brothers, withheld pay and verbally abused him. He later explained that he did not want his mother making a scene in Dos Mundos about the issues he was confronting in Los Angeles with the brothers, especially when it was Gerardo García who had "done him the favor" of getting him across the border in the first place.

When I asked Jesús's mother if he had made enough money to get out of debt before returning to Dos Mundos, she replied, "I think he just wanted to return more than anything, to see his kids and us too. His daughter was a baby when he left, and his wife was three or four months pregnant. We would also tell him to come and see his children. He would talk to me about his wife and kids and how he missed them."

Unlike Manuel's grandmother, Doña Fátima had no ill will toward the local moneylender. Instead of anger, she felt sadness about the circumstances that had led to Jesús needing to leave his family. Doña Fátima's concern for her son was due to his homesickness and to what she perceived as a dangerous job. While she was aware of the difficulty of the job, she did not know the role that the García brothers played or how Jesús jumped from one set of employers to another. Similarly, Jesús felt betrayed not by the moneylender, who did not figure prominently in his migration narrative at all, but by his *paisano* employers. The lack of communication to his mother and others about the specific circumstances surrounding his employment would play a role in the continued migration of others in town.

IMPROMPTU OPPORTUNITIES

A fundamental reason for international migration is a desire to seek a better life, not only for oneself but also for family left behind. Every fruit vendor working on the streets of Los Angeles leaves home for precisely that reason. However, the relative need of each vendor and of his family in Dos Mundos varies. The distinction between families that are more in need and those that are less in need differentiates migratory experiences. Among those who believed they were not in desperate financial need prior to migration, justification for leaving was rooted in the idea of seeking adventure. Beyond the reasons why young men in Dos Mundos migrate, the type and strength of their social networks matter a great deal in the passage, settlement patterns, and outcomes. Here again, the distinction between those who have strong networks and are able to use them effectively and those with weak networks further divides migratory experiences. The stories of Cristian and Gonzalo represent two different migratory experiences that hinge largely on the strength of *paisano* networks.

There are many young Dos Mundos migrants in the United States, and the call to migrate north continuously beckons residents in Dos Mundos. They are further encouraged to head north because someone in Dos Mundos is always talking about leaving or making plans to leave. When Cristian and Gonzalo came of age, they heeded this call and made their own journeys north. Both left Dos Mundos—Cristian in 2004, and Gonzalo in 2007—spurred on by peers who were also making the passage north.

According to Doña Agustina, Cristian's mother, he made the decision to go to the United States very quickly. As she recounted,

> He said, "Mom, I'm going to work so we can have a better life [*Voy a trabajar para tenerla major*]." I told him, "No, that's not true. Your father never had to leave, and thanks to God, we've done something here." But he said he wanted to know the world out there and that he would leave for only a year. He said, "I want to go see how things are. I don't want people to fool me [about life out there]." And finally I said, "Okay, son." . . . He had that enthusiasm. He wanted to know Los Angeles because they would tell him that over there you could earn a lot of money, and I don't know what else. And I would tell him, "Don't go, son. I'm going to miss you. Over there you don't just sweep up the money; it's the same as here, you have to work like you do here." I would tell him, but he had that dream [*andaba con esa ilusión*].

Cristian's father was also saddened by his son's sudden departure and saw no need for him to leave. As he explained, "One gets sad when they leave. You know they're going to suffer, but one doesn't even know how [*Pues más que nada pues van a sufrir, no sabe uno ni cómo*]."

Because his decision was sudden, Cristian sought out the local money-lender for a loan to make the trip. Four days after telling his mother he wanted to leave Dos Mundos, Cristian set out on his adventure with neighbors and cousins, and as his father had feared, his journey was riddled with difficulties. After a difficult passage across the border, Cristian went to Utah to work in construction and later to Los Angeles to work as a street vendor. In both jobs, his employers refused to pay him for the work he had completed.

Cristian's parents had tempered their expectations regarding any remittances he might send. And given the misfortune Cristian encountered, they were correct to expect little. Cristian did not have steady income for several months when he first arrived in Salt Lake City. Understandably, during this period he did not remit. In fact, for the first year and a half that he was in the United States, Cristian did not send home any money at all. The remittances he eventually sent his parents were always small in quantity and infrequent.

As Cristian explained, "I didn't send anything for over a year. I was paying off the *coyote*, and then when I did work they wouldn't pay me. I couldn't save any money. Sometimes I would buy a phone card [with the money I did have], and even then I would call only every two or three months."

In Dos Mundos, Doña Agustina verified this: "For a year and a half he just couldn't [send any money]. Then, [after Utah,] he began working in the fruit business, and he couldn't make ends meet. They [the health department] would toss his fruit. He would have to go to court to pay tickets. He would tell me, 'Mom, I have to pay off citations. They take my fruit away. The situation here is ugly.'"

During this time, Cristian's family gave up on any expectations they might have had regarding financial contributions from their son and instead began worrying about his personal livelihood. When asked how much he would send when he did remit, Doña Agustina simply stated that it was not much and then added, "I'm going to be sincere. There were times when he'd send 600 pesos [US$57], or 800 pesos [US$76], or 1,500 pesos [US$143], even as high as 2,000 pesos [US$190]. I'm not going to say he sent me some big fortunes."[14]

In fact, these remittances were augmented at times by contributions from Carmen—who dated Cristian and lived with him in Los Angeles. While running errands with the couple in Los Angeles, I had witnessed Carmen adding money to envelopes meant for his family Mexico. Although Cristian had promised his mother he would stay only a year, financial troubles and bad luck with employment and employers kept him in the United States longer so that he could save more money. Cristian did return to Dos Mundos in 2007 after spending nearly four years away, and though he meant for that visit to be a quick one, he had an accident on his way back to Los Angeles that left him immobile and convalescing for months, and he ended up staying in Dos Mundos.

Gonzalo, like Cristian, left Dos Mundos in a hurry after being invited to go to the United States by a friend. His parents, Doña Magdalena and Don Pablo, just like Cristian's parents, were shocked by how quickly things moved. In 2007, just as Cristian was returning, Gonzalo was leaving Dos Mundos. He was seventeen years old when he left. Unlike Cristian, Gonzalo went directly to Los Angeles, where he had lined up work as a fruit vendor. He went to work for the García brothers, and when he arrived, they had a pushcart ready for him to work. Less than a month after arriving, Gonzalo sent his family in Dos Mundos his first remittance. A couple of years later, in 2009, Gonzalo began dating Carmen (who had broken up with Cristian by that point). While several parts of Cristian's and Gonzalo's narratives overlap—such as their decisions to leave on a whim, their desire to seek adventure, and their families' discouragement and relative lack of need—their outcomes are distinct, with Gonzalo staying in Los Angeles and faring well, and Cristian returning after carrying debt and not getting paid for his work. In 2017, when I visited Dos Mundos for the second time, Gonzalo and Carmen were living in Los Angeles with a newborn baby, and Cristian was living in Dos Mundos with a wife and a toddler.

During my 2017 visit to Dos Mundos, I spent an entire day with Gonzalo's parents. They shopped in a neighboring town for items for me to take to Gonzalo and Carmen. When we returned to their home, they began packing the items. Doña Magdalena had purchased a blue toddler-sized T-shirt printed with an image of the patron saint of the neighboring town for Carmen and Gonzalo's baby boy. She also purchased roasted pumpkin seeds, *dulce de camote poblano* (sweet potato candy), and assorted candies for Carmen, and a religious amulet. While Doña Magdalena scavenged around the house for a shoebox, Don Pablo and I sat at the dinner table rolling glass bottles of perfumed scents in newspaper. Each of the five bottles was a different color, and the labels said things like "protection" and "fortune." Don Pablo gently placed them in the shoebox his wife handed him and then taped up the box with clear tape. Later, when I delivered the box to Gonzalo in Los Angeles, he exclaimed, "I've never been able to find these in Los Angeles!" He explained that these perfumes are meant to bless and protect the pushcarts.

I arrived in Dos Mundos with a backpack full of items from vendors in Los Angeles. Carmen and Gonzalo sent eight-by-ten-inch photographs of their baby and newborn clothes for Gonzalo's sister, who was pregnant. Other vendors in Los Angeles sent their family members new jeans and athletic shoes, straight-brimmed baseball caps with Los Angeles team logos, and envelopes with unused Mexican pesos and American dollars. I returned to Los Angeles with a backpack full of items for vendors from their families, mostly small food items. Gonzalo's parents packed the most items; they had more disposable income for the purchases. By comparison, Manuel's grandmother, Doña Julieta, gave me only a package of roasted pumpkin seeds and a few plastic containers of leftover *mole* sauce from the recent patron saint celebration feast. When Doña Julieta handed these items to me, she apologized for not having more to send.

After Gonzalo's parents finished packing everything, I sat with Doña Magdalena to talk more formally. Don Pablo stepped out into the yard while we talked. I asked how Gonzalo came to leave Dos Mundos.

"He left from one day to the next," she told me.

"How did he tell you he was leaving?"

"Well, it was very sudden. He said he was going to leave. We didn't have any money on hand. But, from one day to the next really. The next day, he left early. It was around 10:00 a.m., right? When your brother left?" Doña Magdalena turned to her left to the small loveseat where her very pregnant daughter, Alicia, was pleating her little daughter's hair. Alicia did not look up from her work, but she nodded.

"Did he ever mention that he wanted to leave?" I asked.

"No. Did he talk to you, *hija?*" Again, Doña Magdalena looked to Alicia.

"No," Alicia responded.

"He left suddenly, from one night to the next," she repeated.

"What reason did he give you?" I asked.

"He said he was leaving so we could live better, so that we could have better things. And well, yes, from that day to now, we've been better off."

Gonzalo left with a cousin who was two years older. Neither of them had migrated before. A neighbor, who was in his forties and had migrated north several times before, took them. When Gonzalo explained to me why he left, he said that he was struck with courage when he heard of his cousin and neighbor's plans. He knew he had to act quickly. Gonzalo wanted to experience something different. He wanted adventure, and he knew that his small town could not offer any of that. He was very close to his family, and he believed that if he thought about the decision too long, he would lose his courage to leave and the opportunity.

Gonzalo left in the middle of the week. He had told his mother he was leaving as soon as he had made his decision, but he did not tell his father until a few hours before he left. He walked to the school to say goodbye to his little siblings and then to the patron saint chapel to pray for a safe journey. Outside the chapel, he saw his parents for the last time. They said a prayer for him, and he walked down the road to begin the first leg of the journey.

Gonzalo is the oldest of four children. Prior to his departure, he had never talked to any of his family members about leaving. Like his parents, his two younger sisters and younger brother were also in shock when they heard of his plans to leave. His younger brother, who was in grade school, took it particularly hard and was depressed for several years after Gonzalo's departure. He did not tell his father he was leaving because he was afraid of not getting his blessing, but his father said he would never have denied his son the opportunity to leave, even if he did not understand why it was necessary.

According to Doña Magdalena, Gonzalo's father never had the urge to migrate north and found that urge strange in his son. As she explained, "[My husband] never wanted to [go to the United States]. He said, 'Not even if I was crazy would I go.' He worked as far north as Tijuana, but he returned from there. He told me a man there wanted to cross him and some friends over, but he said no. He never wanted to go."

When he left, Gonzalo told his parents he would return in three years. Over the years, different events led Doña Magdalena to believe he had no plans of returning. "I cried when they [Gonzalo and Carmen] got together," she told me. "Instead of being happy for them, I was sad. I got ill. My husband had to take care of me. . . . I thought, 'When am I going to see him again?' I would cry, and my husband would say, 'Why are you crying? He's happy. He's better over there.' But I don't really know the girl. I don't know what she's like. He says she's good to him and treats him well. She's not from Dos Mundos. But she calls us almost daily, and she tells him, 'Send your mother money.' He's never stopped sending us money."

The remittances from Gonzalo came early and often. She explained, "He's always sent money. Maybe twenty days after being in Los Angeles he sent the first bit of money. Even after he got with this girl, he's sent money. He would call and say, 'I've sent money. Go pick it up, go out and enjoy.'"

Gonzalo sends money to his family twice a month in varying amounts averaging about Mex\$1,000 (US\$56).[15] With that money, the family built the three-bedroom house they live in. When Gonzalo left, the family lived in another part of town in a smaller, rented home. They already owned a plot of land, and with Gonzalo's help they built the house on it over the years. The latest purchase for the house was a giant water heater that they had placed on the roof above the restroom, which Doña Magdalena pointed out to me as I left. Gonzalo also sent money for his sister to attend cosmetology school and to discourage his little brother from dropping out of middle school. When his little brother started skipping school, Gonzalo promised him new clothes and shoes if he kept attending.

Gonzalo had a relatively stable life in Los Angeles, but his journey across the border had been perilous. He did not often talk to me about it. He also did not tell his parents how difficult it had been because he did not want them to worry. It was only years later that he began opening up to them about what had happened.

"At first he didn't tell me about how it was to cross over," Doña Magdalena told me. "He just said that it was very sad. He said he arrived like a poor man, his shoes and pants were all torn up. He said one of the García brothers, Omar or Benjamín, gave him money so he could buy himself shoes and clothes. And Gonzalo remembers this. Now, everyone who has just arrived, he'll take them clothes and give them a hand. He'll show them around town. Because he remembers how he suffered."

Despite his rushed departure, Gonzalo lined up a job in Los Angeles before leaving Dos Mundos.

"Did he know he was going to work selling fruit?" I asked Doña Magdalena.

"Yes, he went with his job secured," she replied.

"Who gave him the job?"

"The García brothers. Benjamín and Gabriel and the other one, Omar."

I spent my last day in Dos Mundos with Gonzalo's parents. Before leaving, I had to return to Doña Julieta's house to pick up my things and say good-bye. Although her house was only a fifteen-minute walk from Don Pablo and Doña Magdalena's house, they offered to drive me because it was starting to rain. Doña Magdalena hopped in the covered truck bed and left the passenger seat for me. Throughout the day, while we were shopping, Don Pablo had remained quiet in my presence. Now he sat next to me in the truck.

"Even if no one told me you were Gonzalo's father, I would have known the second I saw you. You have the same facial expressions," I offered.

"Really?" he replied, smiling softly.

"He's going to look just like you when he's your age," I added.

Don Pablo backed the truck out of the yard in silence. Once on the road, he said, "Gonzalo left home when he was only seventeen. He was a child with a child's face."

I remained silent, not knowing what to say. Don Pablo kept his gaze on the road and added, "He's become a man over there."

7 Conclusion

By taking a fine-grained and long-term look at the lives of immigrant *fruteros* in Los Angeles, we see the dynamic nature of a *paisano* network. When this *paisano* network operates in a hostile context of reception—as street vendors do when working in the local prohibitive and punitive informal economy—we see the contours of network relations and how unevenly resources can be distributed. Importantly, we see how a *paisano* network both offers help and justifies exploitation. Research on immigrant social networks has often flattened complex narratives in order to make sense of their outcomes. This book is an attempt to add depth to the depiction of immigrants by focusing on their everyday work and social lives. In telling the story of these *fruteros*, I expand the analytical frame we use to understand immigrant networks and the purpose they serve. The ethnic cage concept is meant to capture the complexity of what a *paisano* network provides for new immigrant arrivals. This concept can also help us better understand the role that hometown connections have in immigrant adaptation.

To be clear, other scholars have examined the "underside" and dynamic nature of coethnic networks (Cranford 2005; Hagan 1994; Mahler 1995; Menjívar 2000; Portes and Sensenbrenner 1993). Jacqueline Maria

Hagan's (1994) study of undocumented Maya immigrants in Houston examines how networks weaken for some while expanding for others. In that study, we see how networks among Maya immigrants are deeply impacted by gender and the workplace.[1] Cecilia Menjívar (2000), focusing on Salvadorans in San Francisco, examined the transformation, reconstitution, and dissolution of social networks.[2] In her work, she found that giving and receiving help is conditioned by the structure of opportunities in the receiving context; state policies affecting citizenship status; and the local economy, all of which influence the amount and type of material resources a network carries and thus also its viability. Meanwhile, Cynthia J. Cranford (2005) addresses the power differentials and exploitation that occur between Latino immigrant workers and their employers within the Los Angeles janitorial industry. Cranford also places great importance on context. In the decentralized, deunionized industrial context of her study, undocumented immigrant workers are recruited because they are more easily exploited.

Context and structure matter for *fruteros* as well. Local laws that police both immigrants and poverty represent the threats from which the ethnic cage provides protection. Even when local contexts become more immigrant friendly—by becoming sanctuary cities, for example—federal laws remain adversarial to the presence of undocumented immigrant populations. In the current political climate, and under the Trump administration, we see California becoming less punitive toward immigrants while the nation becomes more hostile toward immigrants in both policy and rhetoric. Although Los Angeles is a sanctuary city, antipoverty and quality-of-life local ordinances often target poor, undocumented immigrants and indirectly serve the same function as hostile federal immigration laws (Light 2006). Indeed, the hostile context of reception and the protective nature of ethnic communities are major reasons why the ethnic cage— much like the ethnic enclave—is formed in the first place. But in this book, I also show the hostility that exists in the sending community, where relationships are structured along class and status lines. These relationships, at times problematic and exploitative, in the hometown of Dos Mundos are often reproduced in the new context of Los Angeles and are amplified in the face of multiple forms of vulnerability and marginality. The ethnic cage is a phenomenon that reveals itself in the receiving country, amid the hostility of the local context and the restructuring of hometown relations.

While structure and context matter, the ethnic cage is impacted by human agency as well. In this book, we continuously see the messy ways in which work, social, and romantic entanglements manifest themselves. Individual emotions and motivations play a role in the ethnic cage as well. *Fruteros'* actions are not determined solely by the hostile macro-level structures in which they operate; they are also propelled by individual feelings of love and anger, trust and mistrust, goodwill and resentment. This is why it is important to observe immigrant networks through an ethnographic lens so that we see how *paisanos* become coworkers, roommates, and lovers. With time, we also see how they move and fall away from one another while remaining inside the ethnic cage. This method allows us to see how these relationships form, what they provide, how they become undone, and what they withhold. Structural constraints may give form to the ethnic cage, but human agency gives it its function.

As several scholars have warned, it is also important to exercise caution when the concept of immigrant social networks is used in relation to "social capital" (Cranford 2005; Menjívar 2000). The assumption has long been that social networks automatically result in social capital, but this logic is problematic. As I show in this book, *paisano* networks provide different members different and disparate resources. The allocation of these disparate resources is conditioned by both the structural context and human agency. Sometimes help cannot be given, and sometimes network members do not want to offer help. Ability and willingness play important roles in the process. Furthermore, the assumption that social networks beget social capital is too abstract a conceptualization. Cranford critiques the conceptualization of social networks as a form of social capital because this distinction makes it difficult to explain "who benefits from social networks, to what degree, and in which context" (2005, 379).

Again, my aim is not to refute the benefits of immigrant social networks—they are crucial to the integration of newcomers and help to create and sustain community. They have also been shown to reduce the financial and psychological costs of migration (Bailey and Waldinger 1991; Browning and Rodriguez 1985; Massey et al. 1987). The purpose of the ethnic cage concept is to make room for the fact that webs of social relations are messy and complex and have the capacity to both assist, by offering resources, and exploit, by withholding resources. *Paisanos* can help and harm each other. A cage can protect and enclose.

Fruit vendors in Los Angeles serve as an important case study to assess the ethnic cage. As I detail in chapter 2, the business emerged and was structured by Mexican immigrants who helped funnel other *paisanos* into the job. The *paisano* network provided migrants passage across the U.S.-Mexico border as well as work and housing on arrival. Vendor bosses often had resources, in the form of financial capital and legal documentation, that allowed them to land on top of the occupational hierarchy. The street vending job was not without its risks. In chapter 3, I explore these risks from the street level and show the survival strategies that fruit vendors employed to withstand local government assaults on their livelihoods. Chapter 4 moves beyond the street and into the social lives of vendors. Here, we see how personal and professional entanglements, rooted in trust, form and dissolve. In chapter 5, an extreme case of hardship, created after Manuel's encounter with the police, shows us the fragility of *paisanaje* when confronted with the power of the state. Still, while some network members distanced themselves from Manuel and his misfortune, other marginalized members took him in, allowing him to remain living and working with his *paisanos*. Finally, in chapter 6, we return to Dos Mundos to understand what *fruteros* left behind and what they hoped to build by leaving. In the town of Dos Mundos, we see how social relationships are transformed by the emergence of a migration industry that profits from migrant departures.

HOW LONG DOES THE ETHNIC CAGE ENDURE?

In the receiving context, *paisanos* do not live in isolation. Immigrant life is social and full of interactions with people and communities outside of one's own *paisano* group. Los Angeles is home to a sizable population of immigrants from across Latin America (and various parts of the world). Increasingly, *fruteros* are incorporating recent arrivals from Guatemala and El Salvador into their work and social networks. Years from now, ethnic succession might lead these new migrants from Central America to dominate the fruit vending business. International migration, on its own, invariably alters *paisanaje*. Settlement and work patterns also change across time and across generations. Even within the first immigrant generation, *paisanaje* changes, and this, in turn, alters the size and strength of the ethnic cage. Within the Dos Mundos community in Los Angeles, changes did manifest themselves, specifically after an election that led to the fracturing of the hometown association. This event might demonstrate one of the ways in which *paisanos* fall apart from each other over time in a new country.

A Hometown Association Divided

Toward the end of my time in Los Angeles, I heard of a major dispute in the Dos Mundos hometown association. It took place in the summer of 2012, on the night of the Dos Mundos patron saint celebration. According to several *fruteros* who were present, the event had been well attended. After attendees had prayed the rosary while kneeling before the nearly life-sized statue of the patron saint of Dos Mundos and eaten dinner, they prepared to vote for the association's next ministry mayor. This person would lead the group's fundraising efforts for the following year. Elections were simple and did not require ballots or booths. Instead, nominated individuals stood up, and attendees stood behind the person they supported.

That night, three men stood up as the nominees: Gabriel García, Alberto, and Lucío. Gabriel was the leading contender going into the vote, and many *paisanos* believed that he should be next in line for the post. Slowly, the people in attendance began to form lines behind each of the three men. Defying expectations, Lucío, the host of the evening's event, won by a landslide. His election was controversial, however, because many of the people standing behind him were not fellow *paisanos*. For example, many of Lucío's votes came from his wife, her extended family, and family friends, who were from a different town in the Mexican state of Puebla. Meanwhile, most of the Dos Mundos *paisanos* stood behind Gabriel.

A protest began with a question asked by someone in the crowd: Should people not from Dos Mundos get to vote? This evolved to speculation that Lucío had rigged the process because he was hosting the event, which suspicious guests thought might have guaranteed him a majority of supporters in attendance. Lucío and his family responded that although Lucío's supporters were not from Dos Mundos, they still contributed hundreds of dollars to the town every year and should have a right to vote. Sides were taken and lines were drawn. Manuel voted for Lucío. Since getting kicked out of his South Central Los Angeles home, Manuel had moved to Compton, where he rented a room in Lucío's house, and formed a work association with a smaller contingent of Dos Mundos *paisanos* living and working there. The Martínez brothers also sided with Lucío. Alberto, the third nominee and the one with the fewest votes, withdrew his nomination and threw his support behind Gabriel. Gabriel also had the support of his brothers, Benjamín and Omar.

The discord grew into a larger argument that culminated in Lucio kicking the opposing group out of his home. This was frowned on by many present (including Manuel, who had not been kicked out). That night, the Dos Mundos hometown association split into two. This was no minor altercation. A few days later, Lucío's smaller faction sent word to Dos Mundos and the local Catholic diocese there. A new patron saint statue—similar to the one at the celebration, encased in cherry wood and adorned with intricate robes—would have to be commissioned, blessed, and shipped to Los Angeles as soon as possible. Gabriel's group had taken ownership of the original saint statue after the fallout. When the newly commissioned saint arrived, months later, the new group was official. Los Angeles had two Dos Mundos hometown associations, each with the ability to host patron saint celebrations in the presence of the saint's statue.

The larger and, arguably, more powerful group was Gabriel's. Although Gonzalo and Carmen were not at the patron saint celebration when the split occurred, they were affiliated with Gabriel's group by virtue of geography (they lived and worked in central and northeast Los Angeles) and friendship (Gonzalo and the Garcías were close friends). Manuel remained affiliated with Lucío's smaller group.

I spoke to Gonzalo in June 2017, and he explained that the two groups had remained split since the 2012 argument. For five years they had hosted separate patron saint celebrations.

"I think they haven't come to an agreement. But perhaps it's because they are resentful," he explained after I asked him for an update on the situation.

"*They* are?" I asked, referring to Lucío's group.

"Well, both sides, I think. I mean, I can't tell you what other people think . . ." He trailed off.

"But you said both groups sometimes get together for the rosaries?" I asked.

"There are times when they do get together, both groups. But just the same, people get together with their own group. They do comingle but . . ." Again he trailed off.[3]

Gonzalo went on to estimate that Gabriel's group consisted of forty members while Lucío's group had only eight or so Dos Mundos *paisanos,* plus other members from other towns. Lucío's group would organize patron saint celebrations by incorporating other Poblanos who came from small towns adjacent to Dos Mundos or incorporating migrants who liked the atmosphere of the celebrations. In this way, their celebrations were more "diluted," according to Gonzalo.

"Do you think relations will ever be fixed?" I asked.

"No, I don't think so," he responded. "It's difficult. For my part, I have no problem [mending the relationship], but there are many others who don't think like I do. It's a story with no end [*Es el cuento de nunca acabar*]. Think about it, there are maybe six or seven people in our group who don't want to fix things. In their group, let's say there are eight members, and four of them don't want to fix things. So instead of [the two groups] becoming united again, they lose members, and then we lose members. Even if the groups get back together, we're still divided. The day it happened, I wasn't there. But many took it very personally. Various things were said. They fought among each other. Verbally, not physically, fought. Many are still bitter."[4]

"Dos Mundos is a small town. Do you think breaking up the *paisanos* into two [groups] has affected the community?"

"No, I don't think so. In Mexico, they don't take it into account. They don't live it like we do here. It doesn't affect them. And truthfully, we are of the belief that it doesn't matter where you celebrate the patron saint and your hometown. You are celebrating it, that's all that matters. There are times when I don't have money to give for the celebration, and so I celebrate in my own home, on my own. I can celebrate the community even there, on my own."

Despite the fracture in the Los Angeles ministry, each group retained powerful connections to the hometown. That was something Gonzalo admitted could not be denied. International migration may have changed relationships between *paisanos* in Los Angeles, but it did not shatter their *paisanaje*. Not, at least, in this first immigrant generation.

However, we know that *paisanaje* endures in the receiving country. Throughout the United States, we see the endurance of ethnic communities across several generations. We see the permanence of *paisanaje* in the Ticuani community of New York City (Smith 2006), among Basque Americans in Bakersfield (Petrissans 2018), and among Baghdadi Chaldeans in El Cajon, California (Mohajer 2018). It is important to note that I eschew the notion that the way forward is for *paisanaje* to disappear. Assimilation is not necessary for upward mobility or for integration in the United States. It is possible to be upwardly mobile and have a sense of belonging in this country while being a member of an ethnic community. The way forward is to ensure that the ethnic cage does more good than harm, that it functions to corral community and uplift its members. It is also vital that the context of reception remains welcoming and open to newcomers.

The Ethnic Cage Years Later

In 2018, twelve years after I met the young *fruteros* in this study, I found myself in a large banquet hall in East Los Angeles celebrating the baptism of Carmen and Gonzalo's two children. The venue was located in an industrial block of the neighborhood, bookended by two busy gas stations. Inside, the ornate decorations were reminiscent of an upscale *quinceañera* or wedding reception. Large glass flute centerpieces held bouquets of fresh white flowers at every table. The celebration—complete with waiter service, dinner, and an open bar—cost nearly $9,000. There was seating for just over two hundred people, and by the end of the night the venue would be full to capacity, primarily with *paisanos* from Dos Mundos, Gonzalo's hometown. The majority of those in attendance worked as *fruteros*. They sat at tables that mirrored their smaller working groups. Bosses, when not sitting next to their wives and children, sat surrounded by their employees. That evening, however, they sat together as *paisanos*.

Throughout the night, I danced with many of the men I had met while doing fieldwork. They greeted me warmly and treated me like an old friend. In the hall, these men represented the old heads of the *frutero* world now. Interspersed among the guests were the faces of recent arrivals, a new generation of young men from Dos Mundos.

Late into the party, a pregnant and tired Carmen asked me to keep her company at the main table while Gonzalo made the rounds. I sat next to her, holding her infant son on my lap. Late arrivals made their way to the main table to greet her and to give her gift cards or presents for the kids. Among the late arrivals was Chava, the *paisano* who had lived with Manuel in South Central Los Angeles. The last time I had spoken with Chava was in the midst of the fallout following Manuel's arrest and deportation scare. He and Carmen had fought about Manuel's possessions, and I had struggled to remain neutral given my association and friendship with Manuel. When Chava walked by, Carmen exclaimed, "Rocío is here!" He turned to me, focused on my face, and I saw the flicker of recognition in his eyes. He smiled, seemingly happy to see me, and instantly pulled me out from behind the table to dance with him. I returned baby Ethan to Carmen and obliged.

"Are you still selling fruit?" I asked, as we danced to the live *banda* music.

"Still [*Todavía*]," he replied.

I asked him what street corner he was vending on now so that I could drop by sometime and visit. Chava stopped dancing for a second, inched closer to me, and said, "But don't tell anybody [*Pero no le vayas a decir a nadie*]."

I chuckled and said, "Of course."

He gave me the street names of his vending corner. I thought of the neighborhood where it was; it was a very exclusive beach enclave.

After dancing a bit longer, I asked, "Why don't you want me to tell anyone?"

He looked over his shoulder at a table full of *fruteros* and said, "It's a new spot, and I don't want anyone to find out about it."

There was complexity in his disclosure. Chava enjoyed the company of his *paisanos* and celebrated happily with them that night, but he was still suspicious enough about them that he kept them at arm's length when it came to his scouting, strategizing, and plans to get ahead as a *frutero*. Our brief conversation while dancing revealed how the ethnic cage could simultaneously corral community and confine individuals within it.

The celebration that night represented many things: the enduring importance of community among transplanted *paisanos,* the economic stability of a group of entrepreneurial workers who confronted many obstacles in their informal occupation, and the perseverance of immigrants who arrived without legal authorization. Yet as an observer of this community over time, I also knew that many faces were missing from the celebration. Some had returned to Dos Mundos after several years in Los Angeles because they felt like failures, because they had accomplished what they had set out to do as international migrants, or because they had gotten stuck while visiting Mexico and had not been able to return. Others who were missing that evening, like Manuel and the Martínez brothers, still lived in Los Angeles but had become estranged from this group of *paisanos* following personal or romantic fallouts. This book is about both the *fruteros* in attendance that night and those absent from the celebration. It is a story of economic stability and insecurity, of settlement and return migration, of ethnic solidarity and exploitation. Among these *fruteros,* we see the promise and pain of community. Importantly and ultimately, it is my hope that this community of *paisanos* and the concept of the ethnic cage help us better understand immigrant adaptation in all of its complexity.

Afterword

In November 2016, a *Los Angeles Times* headline proclaimed, "Citing President-Elect Trump, L.A. City Council Members Announce Policy to Protect Immigrant Street Vendors." Obscured in that headline and behind the city council decision was a massive push by a street vendor–led mobilization campaign that began years earlier. According to Mike Dennis, an organizer at the East Los Angeles Community Corporation (ELACC), a group of Latino immigrant street vendors convened at the ELACC offices in 2008. This group of vendors was being harassed and displaced by police and inspectors during the construction of the Metro Gold Line (Dennis 2014). As a result of the meetings at ELACC offices, ELACC organizers and street vendors formed a coalition with the Los Angeles Food Policy Council and forty-two other organizations to form the Los Angeles Street Vendor Campaign (LASVC).[1]

This was not the first street vendor organization in Los Angeles that had attempted to address the city's street vending ban and lack of a legal permit system for street vendors. In the late 1980s, following several highly visible and financially devastating crackdowns in central Los Angeles, a group of street vendors came together and began organizing out of the offices of the Central American Resource Center with staff help from the Coalition for

Humane Immigrant Rights of Los Angeles. This group of vendors formed the Association of Ambulatory Vendors (Asociación de Vendedores Ambulantes, or AVA). At its peak, the AVA boasted close to five hundred street vendor members.[2]

The AVA's primary goal was to create sanctioned vending zones in various areas around Los Angeles (Southern California Library Archives 2001). After an extended bureaucratic process that took several years, one vending zone around MacArthur Park was created, with oversight outsourced to local business owners, community leaders, and organizers. Street vendors were largely left out of the regulation and decision-making process (Hernandez 2008). The vending zone had strict regulations as to who could sell (permitted vendors only), how products could be sold (out of specially made, decorative pushcarts only), when vending could occur (business hours only), and which foods could be sold (only tamales were allowed) (Kettles 2006; Romero 2006). Very few vendors participated due to limits placed on permits and pushcarts and to the inability or unwillingness to sell tamales in a crowded field of competition. Perhaps unsurprisingly, given the constraints placed on vendors, the vending zone was ultimately deemed a failure and criticized by many (J. Rodriguez 1995). The overregulation of vendors, partly due to the outsourcing of the decision-making process, contributed to the failure (Kettles 2004, 2007). The AVA eventually succumbed as well, splintering into two groups along ethnic and geographic lines. Central Americans working in the MacArthur Park area, just west of downtown Los Angeles, formed one group, and Mexicans and Mexican Americans from the Boyle Heights neighborhood, just east of downtown, created another (Southern California Library Archives).

Unlike its predecessor, the LASVC, which emerged in the late 2000s, was incredibly successful. The LASVC established a significant social media presence and set out to create a community of stakeholders that included customers and small business owners.[3] They held protests, rallies, and town halls in neighborhoods throughout the city. They also had an organized presence at all relevant city hall meetings and the support of two councilmembers, Curren D. Price Jr. and Jose Huizar, who represented two central Los Angeles districts with a high concentration of street vendors.[4] The primary goal of LASVC was to rid the city of its ban on street vending; it was a campaign that would stand to benefit thousands of street vendors across the city (Dennis 2014).

But the fruit vendors whose stories I tell in this book never joined the campaign. *Fruteros* would have been a key demographic for the mobilization campaign because they were often well received by the public and widely patronized by a range of customers of various ethnic and socioeconomic backgrounds. Their product, a mix of freshly peeled and chopped fruit and vegetables, is often sold in areas devoid of healthy, affordable, and readily available food options. On corners throughout the city, blue-collar and white-collar workers frequent *fruteros* for a healthy snack, dessert, or alternative to a fast food lunch. Why were *fruteros*—who had so much support from customers and the community generally and much to gain from this campaign's success—notably absent from the mobilization effort?

To a certain degree, the initial mobilization effort that turned into the LASVC belonged to the East Los Angeles street vendors who mobilized for it. Efforts to expand an advocacy campaign of this nature, which sought to encompass street vendors across a sprawling metropolis, would necessarily take time. Several *fruteros* in this book, including Manuel, did attend one informational meeting at the ELACC headquarters in 2014. They went seeking legal assistance with their citation problems. They wanted the help of a law firm and some type of legal representation in order to fight back when citations were issued, arrests were made, or confiscations were carried out. This type of help was not being offered by the organization at the time. Afterward, the general sense among the *fruteros* that attended was that the meeting had not been useful. To my knowledge, they did not return to attend any other event put together by the mobilization campaign. The sustained lack of engagement on the part of *fruteros* was due to many reasons, including not having time and energy to attend events, not believing the campaign could be successful, and thinking that street vendor mobilization members just wanted legitimization "handed to them."

The belief that street vendors in the mobilization campaign wanted legitimization handed to them underscored the sustained effort *fruteros* had put into building a network of *paisanos* to make vending viable. *Fruteros* had struggled, they had built up competencies and used their ingenuity, and they had developed a community of *paisanos* to respond to each threat. *Fruteros* were constantly finding ways to legitimize their work so that they could operate in a "semi-formal" sector. They purchased certifiable pushcarts with drainage systems that cost thousands of dollars to avoid some health department crackdowns that targeted only *carros pirata* (unlicensed pushcarts) with no drainage systems. These more expensive pushcarts could be taken to the health department to be inspected and receive a health department certification sticker. Although informal vending could still get *fruteros* cited and their wares confiscated, having a certified pushcart meant that the pushcart itself would not be impounded or destroyed. The fruit vendors' *paisano* network was big enough to facilitate the lending of money for expensive pushcarts and help vendors recover after financially devastating crackdowns. It was the *paisano* network and web of reciprocal obligations that gave *fruteros* their edge on the streets. It is not by chance that Poblanos are overrepresented among the city's *frutero* population. Fruit vendors criticized the street vendors in the mobilization campaign in part because they feared losing their dominance if legalization occurred.

That legalization did come. Local and state laws have undergone various changes in recent years. In January 2017, the Los Angeles City Council voted to draft a law that would decriminalize vending. A few months later, in April 2017, street vending was decriminalized, which meant that vendors were protected from dire penalties such as deportation but not from fines. In September 2018, Governor Jerry Brown signed into law the Safe Sidewalk Vending Act (SB946), a statewide act that limited the violations and fines imposed on vendors. This state law forced the hand of local city officials, and in November 2018, the Los Angeles City Council passed an ordinance legalizing and regulating vending on city sidewalks. On January 1, 2019, the law took effect, with certain restrictions in place: vendors had to pick up trash generated; ensure sidewalks remained accessible; stay clear of fire hydrants, driveways, curbs, and building entrances; and have all business and health permits required by city, county, and state agencies. In an effort to keep street vendors informed about all the new regulations, the LASVC has started hosting informational summits. Unfortunately, fruit vendors' lack of engagement might mean they miss out on this vital new information.

In the end, just as the *Los Angeles Times* headline that opened this chapter proclaimed, it was the racist, inflammatory, and anti-immigrant rhetoric of Donald Trump that played a major role in the creation of the new state and local laws. To be sure, punitive antivending measures had created economic precarity among street vendors previously. But while that precarity had been tolerated and even sanctioned, the existential threat that the new administration posed caused officials to react. It is worth asking why local officials, especially those charged with serving immigrant communities, failed to act until this threat emerged. So while the legalizing of street vending in Los Angeles is a silver lining, it came on a very dark cloud.

It remains to be seen how the changing and seemingly more progressive laws will affect the *fruteros* in this book. The city is still deciding how a permit program would work. Meanwhile, the Bureau of Street Services (known as *salubridad* among vendors) has suggested that fines be increased for breaking the rules going forward, and the city has proposed hiring more inspectors and administrative staffers at the bureau (Reyes 2018). Legalizing street vendors while increasing surveillance and punitive measures seems like a two steps forward, one step back approach. Meanwhile, various actors and institutions, including business improvement districts (BIDs) and neighborhood associations, have opposed and continue to oppose the legalization of street vending. These institutions, specifically BIDs, often have enough political and economic capital to hire their own private security to patrol and police neighborhoods. An unintended consequence of the local law might be that the policing of street vendors is outsourced to private contractors. All of which is to say that there is no easy road ahead for the *fruteros* in this book or for the thousands of street vendors who work in Los Angeles. In words that continuously ring true for Latino communities across the United States, *La lucha sigue.*

Acknowledgments

I owe a great debt of gratitude to the *fruteros* and their families who allowed me into their community. They welcomed me into their homes, broke bread with me, and gave me the gift of their friendship. I hope I captured their lives in a way that honors the trust we shared.

Fieldwork for this book began when I was a graduate student at the University of California, Los Angeles. In that space, I met some of the most wonderful people, who, throughout the years, provided friendship, laughs, comfort, ideas, and critiques. They helped me grow as a person and a scholar.

I am thankful for the friendship of Amada Armenta, Nazgol Ghandnoosh, Juan Carlos Aguirre, Anthony S. Alvarez, Wes Hiers, Barbara Soliz, Sylvia Zamora, Laura Bekes, Anthony Ocampo, Marisa Gerstein Pineau, Iddo Tavory, Brooke Minor, and Jed Ela. At UCLA, I benefited tremendously from the various members of the Ethnography Working Group. I am thankful that space was created to share our work and ideas. I am also glad a few of us revived it years later— thank you to my fellow EWG writing group members Laura Orrico, Mike DeLand, and David Trouille.

My chair and (forever) mentor Stefan Timmermans provided much-needed encouragement and intellectual support throughout the years. My committee members Rubén Hernández-León, Abel Valenzuela, and Roger Waldinger were unwavering in their support of this project.

Many other people have been generous with their time and feedback through-out the years. I am particularly thankful to Leisy Abrego, Vanesa Ribas, Glenda

Flores, Patty Fox, Jacob Avery, Tanya Golash-Boza, Zulema Valdez, and my UC Chancellor's postdoc mentor at UCSD, David FitzGerald. I am also thankful for the invitations to present this work. Colloquiums at Cornell University's School of Industrial and Labor Relations and UC Berkeley's Sociology Department provided insightful critiques and feedback.

I received generous financial and fellowship support for this project from the Mellon Mays Foundation, the Ford Foundation, the John Randolph and Dora Haynes Foundation, the American Philosophical Society, the UCLA Center for the Study of Poverty, the UCLA Chicano Studies Center, the UC Chancellor's Postdoctoral Fellowship Program, and the Woodrow Wilson Early Career Enhancement Fellowship.

In addition to UCLA, the UC San Diego Center for Comparative Immigration Studies served as an intellectual home for me. At UC Irvine, my colleagues have provided a welcoming and supportive environment in which to complete this manuscript.

I am grateful to UC Press for providing this book with a home. I'd like to acknowledge the anonymous reviewers for their helpful and insightful comments, and editor Naomi Schneider and editorial assistant Benjy Mailings for their attentiveness and support.

I would be remiss if I did not acknowledge the support of my family in El Paso. They have always come through for me. My father offered real world advice and kept me on my toes. My mother built me up emotionally and created a special fieldwork apron with a chest-level pocket for my digital recorder. My sister Veronica financed part of my graduate career; she also put her life on hold to help me move between institutions. My other siblings and nieces tolerated my endless academic talk throughout the years—sorry about that. I'm also thankful to Jovan Williams for his companionship and support.

I apologize to anyone I may have forgotten; it has been a long journey (and I forgot to keep field notes). I truly am lucky to have met so many wonderful people at every stage of my life. This book would not have been possible without them.

APPENDIX   A Personal Note on Research

How does research begin? When writing retrospectively, researchers often plot out the ideas, communities, and phenomena they wanted to study and how they set down a path to do it.

Yet we know that is not how research works (Becker 2009; Galison 1987; Latour and Woolgar 1986). As researchers, we err, we backtrack, we reposition, and if everything goes well, we create a grand narrative about intentionality. Successful qualitative research is an iterative process. As Howard S. Becker writes, "Successful researchers recognize that they begin their work knowing very little about their object of study, they use what they learn from day to day to guide their subsequent decisions about what to observe, who to interview, what to look for, and what to ask about," and they interpret data as they get it over time (2009, 547). Ethnographers have confessed to not knowing where their research was taking them and not feeling confident about completed work even after it was accepted for publication (Duneier 2000; Liebow 2003; Whyte 1993). The research on which this book is based is no different. It took several years before I recognized what the focus of the study was going to be, and even then, the data I collected took me in several different directions.[1] In this appendix, I reflect on a few dilemmas I confronted in the field and offer some guidance for how other researchers might respond to similar issues. The dilemmas encompass various parts of the field research experience, from how to collect data when data collection spans entire workdays to making sense of getting shut out and shut down by prospective respondents.

COLLECTING DATA ACROSS LONG WORKDAYS

On entering the field, the biggest obstacle I confronted was how to study *fruteros* as a community when they spent most of their time working alone on street corners.[2] Because Los Angeles is a sprawling metropolis and traffic congestion is a daily obstacle, "hanging out" entailed spending time with one person on one corner at a time. As a result, entire days and weeks were devoted to fostering relationships with individual vendors without knowing how the vendors I approached were connected to each other. While I knew *fruteros* likely existed as a community, I entered the field wanting to learn about their street-based work life. I could study street-based interactions with individual vendors. There was variation between vendors and neighborhoods, and much of what I saw was interesting. With time, however, I became interested in how vendors survived the various threats they encountered. Survival, in this informal operation, required community. So I began asking vendors for access to other spaces where I might see them interacting with more vendors.

To access these spaces, I had to become useful as a worker. I asked if I could help shop for produce at the wholesale market, unload it, and prepare pushcarts in the mornings. Only then did research move from the street to the backyards and warehouses where vendors prepared carts. Later, I followed vendors to their homes at the end of the workday for dinner and celebrations. Days spent with vendors stretched from early mornings to late evenings. These extended periods of time necessitated different ways of keeping track of information. I always carried small notebooks and jotted down notes continuously throughout the day. Later, I carried a digital recorder and kept it on as long as I could. My role as researcher was continuously apparent because I often had to take breaks to write down important conversation points. I also began dictating and recording field notes while still in the field. Despite my best efforts, many interesting interactions and events went unrecorded because it was also important for me to stay in the moment—laughing, complaining, and lamenting with vendors. While these moments may have been "lost" in the data collection effort, I did strengthen my connection to this community of *fruteros*. Ethnographers do not often talk about the moments that are forgotten or left unrecorded, of which there are many. Yet those moments still serve a researcher's purpose because they allow us to *convivir* (live together/coexist) with our interlocutors.

DIFFERENT WAYS OF BEING

Gaining vendors' trust and developing competencies as a worker allowed me to move into spaces beyond the street corner where I could observe more interactions between *fruteros*. Yet throughout my fieldwork, I continued to spend much of my time alone with individuals. With each vendor, I practiced different ways of being and different ways of observing. They, in turn, reacted in different ways to my presence in their lives. It bears repeating that our interlocutors are not passive agents; they have agency, and they exercise it in how they relate to us as researchers. They decide whether and how to accept, confront, entertain, or banish our presence. Every relationship I established with vendors yielded different types of information but also presented distinct obstacles. Below, I outline three strategies—opting out, opening up, and falling in—that developed as a result of my one-on-one time with *fruteros*. I then present an instance in which I was shut out—literally and figuratively—by one family of vendors and explain their justification for it.

Opting Out

Throughout my research, I was continuously surprised by the speed with which *fruteros* granted me access. As mentioned in the introduction, being a recent arrival to the city of Los Angeles facilitated this entrée. Vendors readily provided advice and guidance regarding how to navigate the city. Daniel, one of my earliest respondents, was instrumental in helping me understand the world of *fruteros*. Within weeks, he introduced me to his small *frutero* working group. However, as time progressed, it became necessary for me to opt out of that relationship. Opting out entails leaving a space, relationship, or interaction that can be problematic for respondents, the researcher, or both. In my conceptualization, opting out entails leaving a specific situation or person so that the larger research can continue and returning at a later time to renegotiate interactional boundaries. Opting out might be particularly important for women who enter male-dominated spaces and who must continuously negotiate how respondents perceive and engage with them. Ethnographers must enter the field with curiosity and interest—these characteristics are required to be a good social observer. Unfortunately, curiosity and interest can sometimes be mistaken for romantic interest. When interactional mistakes occur, opting out is one viable solution.

I met Daniel, a stocky and talkative vendor from a small town adjacent to Dos Mundos, early on during my fieldwork. Daniel was a vendor in West Los Angeles, and I initially approached him in the same way that I approached all vendors—as a customer. His concern for me, rooted in the dangers that might lurk in a city for a young woman, epitomized the way in which vendors conceptualized the city and being a newcomer within it.

After purchasing my fruit, I asked Daniel what direction Fairfax Boulevard was in. He pointed to his right and said I could walk or take the bus. I explained that I did not know the area well and was new to the city. Instead of walking away, I leaned on a nearby post and started eating my fruit.

"I just want to eat my fruit before starting my walk," I said.

"You're not from here?" he asked, looking at me sideways while he prepared fruit salads for a handful of customers.

I explained that I was from a smaller city in Texas, had been in Los Angeles only a few months, and was still learning how to navigate the public transportation system.

"Don't you worry about getting lost?" he asked.

"Not really. I can always ask someone," I replied.

"Do you speak English?"

"Yes," I responded.

"What if it gets dark?" he continued.

"Well, it gets dark."

Daniel laughed. "True. But I guess you can't really get lost here. All the major roads lead in one general direction. Like this one. You can take Venice [Boulevard] all the way to Los Angeles or in the other direction to Santa Monica. Easy."

After finishing up with his customers, he moved to my side of the cart and continued our conversation. "Have you ever been to Mexico City?"

"No. Are you from Mexico City?" I asked, stepping closer to indicate my interest in hearing the response.

"I'm from Puebla, but I went to work in Mexico City before coming here. That city will swallow you whole if you get careless [*Esa ciudad te traga si te apendejas*]."

I was initially puzzled by Daniel's expressed concern about the possibility of me getting lost. Several visits later, I learned that while he knew plenty of young women who braved far more dangerous landscapes than that of West Los Angeles, he thought there was some naiveté and lack of street smarts in my own person that would make me a prime target for victimization. This perceived naiveté was rooted in the openness with which I approached and talked to him and others on the street. In a sense, he believed "street smart" people kept to themselves and did not talk much. His logic fit with his expressed concern to not get careless, or *apendejarse*, which, in addition to meaning "careless," can be translated as acting stupid in a situation in which you might get taken advantage of. Not getting taken advantage of was very important for Daniel.

Gaining access and building rapport with Daniel and the small group of men that he worked with went fairly swiftly. I initially visited Daniel every other day and disclosed early on that I was a student wanting to do research on vendors. After each visit, he would see me walk off toward a bus stop. About two weeks after I started visiting him, he asked if I wanted a ride closer to my final destination. I could join him and the other workers at the end of the day, and they could drop me off. I accepted the offer. This is how I met Francisco and Juan.

Francisco was the group's *raitero* (ride giver). He owned a pickup truck and gave Daniel and Juan rides to and from their street corners at the beginning and end of the workday. Every afternoon, Francisco would arrive with Juan, who was picked up from a few blocks west of Interstate 405. Francisco would pull up into a nearby commercial driveway, and Juan would hop out and help Daniel load his pushcart onto the bed of the pickup truck. Because I would arrive late in the afternoon and spend time talking to Daniel, I would occasionally see Francisco and Juan, but I often took their arrival as my cue to leave. The day I was offered a ride, I lingered and helped Daniel pack up his pushcart.

Francisco's old truck, I soon learned, was always acting up, and on the first day I accepted the ride, the truck was overheating. Daniel worked across from a building that had a street-facing water spigot, and the three vendors often relied on that water when the truck overheated.

Francisco, Daniel, and I sat patiently in the pickup truck eating from a small cardboard box full of strawberries that we passed back and forth between us. Though the hood of the truck was open, blocking our street view, the crescent of space between it and the dashboard offered a sliver of visibility. It was through this opening that the three of us sat watching Juan pour water into the truck's radiator using a tattered plastic bag. Daniel, Francisco, and I were amused by Juan's perseverance as he ran back and forth between the truck and the adjacent building's water spigot, water leaking through the bag's various holes as he did so. It was a long wait, as more than half of the bag's contents would be gone before Juan reached the open hood. On one of Juan's multiple trips, Daniel stuck his head out the passenger window and yelled teasingly, *"Córrele, córrele, córrele* [Run, run, run]!"* laughing heartily with Francisco as Juan tripped and spilled the bag's water onto the street. When Juan finally finished filling up the radiator, he squeezed himself into the truck's front seat, and Daniel handed him the box of strawberries. Francisco pulled out a long screwdriver and inserted it into the truck's ignition—this was how he turned on the truck (which didn't surprise me because I had a car in high school that turned on the same way). Francisco looked over at me, pressed tight between him and Daniel, and asked if I knew how to drive in case he got pushed out the door by all of us jammed in there. I nodded confidently, and after a few faulty starts, we were off.

We drove out into the traffic-jammed boulevard and idled. After a few blocks, we pulled alongside a red convertible driven by a young, bleach-blond woman. Francisco said, "What do you think, guys?" motioning with his chin to the woman as he inched closer to the convertible. Daniel, Juan, and I turned to have a look. Daniel and Juan nodded approvingly. Juan, the youngest in the group and the one sitting in the window seat, giggled and covered his face when the woman turned—likely after feeling the eyes of all of us staring at her. In that moment, I thought how strange and wonderful it was to be in a truck with men I had met only a few days before getting this type of access to their own brand of the male gaze.

My visits to Daniel's corner continued for about eight months, but because I usually arrived early in the day, I rarely saw Francisco and Juan. After I met other vendors in different parts of the city, I visited Daniel less and less often. After a prolonged absence prompted in part by my inability to find Daniel at his usual corner and my growing connection to Carmen, Cristian, and Jesús, I returned to Daniel's corner and found him working. However, his demeanor with me felt immediately different.

I arrived at Daniel's corner late in the afternoon and helped him pack up. Francisco and Juan arrived shortly thereafter, and while they packed up the pushcart, Daniel asked me to go for a walk with him. This was different from our established routine, but I agreed. We walked away from the two men and around the corner toward the downtown area of Culver City. When I looked over my shoulder toward Francisco and Juan, I noticed they were grinning and felt that it might be because Daniel was taking me for a walk, which had an air of intimacy to it. Daniel and I chatted about random things, and then he said he needed to use a restroom. We passed a local coffee shop that was full of mostly white young hipsters, and I told Daniel that he could probably use the restroom in there. I walked toward the door, but Daniel remained behind, unmoving. When I noticed his absence at my side, I turned back. He looked apprehensively at the customers and the upscale-looking coffee shop and said, "I can't go in there." I immediately recalled the street vendors in Mitchell Duneier's *Sidewalk* and the many ways in which public urination became a feature of their lives due to inaccessible public or customer-only restrooms. In an effort to assuage his concerns, I told Daniel that I would buy a drink so that he did not feel the guilt of using a restroom without being a paying customer. I walked in and purchased tea while he used the facilities. When he emerged, he offered to pay me for the tea. I declined. We continued our walk, and he pointed out some idiosyncratic architectural features in the buildings we passed. I pointed out a house with a lush, picturesque garden that seemed at odds with the concrete business towers next to it. When we returned to Daniel's corner, Francisco and Juan were gone. I asked where they were, and he said they had gone to run an errand.

Across the boulevard was a parked food truck setting up for the early evening customers. Daniel offered to buy me a *torta*, and we crossed the street. The order was put in, but money was not exchanged. Daniel drifted to the far side of the truck to look at something. The order was called out, and at that point I was charged for the food. Because Daniel was on the other side and looking away, I pulled out my wallet and paid for the food. In that moment, Daniel turned around and saw me putting away my wallet and walking toward him with the food. "No, no, no! Why did you pay for the food?!" he asked me. I told him it was fine, that it had seemed easier to just pay myself. "No Rocío, that's not how it goes!" Daniel continued, visibly upset. He half-heartedly grabbed his *torta*. "I've lost my appetite," he said, and after a few beats he threw the sandwich in the trashcan. I could not make sense of his distress. Even though he had offered to buy the food, the price was inconsequential to me. I attempted to make sense of his discomfort through the lens of male chivalry but did not understand why he had thrown away the food. I kept repeating that it was no big deal and that he could get the bill next time, but to no avail. Feeling awkward, I told him we should probably walk back to his corner, which we did. I said goodbye shortly afterward.

It was this incident and Daniel's strange interaction with me that afternoon that made me decide to stop visiting his corner and opt out of that interaction. Though Daniel had been a great source of information, I thought that perhaps he had viewed me as a potential romantic partner or that he expected me to follow some gendered scripts with which I was not familiar, and which I would likely not be willing to follow given the platonic researcher-participant dynamic I wanted and needed to establish. I also felt that I had caused him much distress and was not sure how to recover from that. In the end, the conversations that I had with Daniel about *apendejarse* fluttered to the surface and prompted me to opt out before I did something that could be offensive to him.

Several years later, I did return to Daniel's corner. It was before I visited Dos Mundos. I was visiting all the vendors who I knew were from Puebla to ask if there was anything that they might want me to bring to their families and to inquire if I might be able to interview their family members when I was in Mexico. Daniel was happy to see me, and I was able to excuse my absence by saying that things had gotten busy with school and travel to Texas; people routinely fall in and out of vendors' lives, and in this way I was no different. Daniel was excited that I was visiting Puebla and told me that he wanted me to deliver something to his *mujer* (his woman), who lived in a town just fifteen minutes away from Dos Mundos. When I visited her to deliver the item, which Daniel had purchased at an electronic store, we spoke briefly while she gave me a tour of the town square. I asked her how long she had been romantically involved with Daniel, and in relating the story of their relationship, she disclosed that they had had several issues—due to distance—throughout their courtship and marriage. I privately wondered if Daniel's interactions with me had been influenced at all by the difficulties he was having with his *mujer* in Mexico.

Opting out of my interactions with Daniel meant that I avoided having a difficult conversation with him about what I perceived to be inappropriate behavior. On the one hand, a conversation like this might have led him to push me out of his life entirely and might have impacted my reputation within the larger *frutero* community. On the other hand, having this type of conversation might have helped me reaffirm my role as a researcher and establish healthy boundaries. I weighed the multiple options and possible outcomes and made the best decision I could at the time.

In the end, I opted out of my relationship with Daniel so that I could continue doing research among his *paisanos*. When I eventually returned to his corner, I updated him on the status of my research and explained that it was extending into Dos Mundos, where I would be conducting interviews. This information allowed me to renegotiate our interactional boundaries.

Opening Up

Embracing my mishaps and awkward interactions was something that suited me well in the field. My comic demeanor allowed me to break down Manuel's shy and quiet tendencies. His acceptance of my presence eventually gave me regular access to another space where *fruteros* spent time—the wholesale produce warehouse. I first met Manuel one afternoon in the fall of 2009 while I was working with Carmen. By this time, Carmen would routinely leave me working the pushcart alone while she went to the restroom at an adjacent business or went inside the bank to get smaller bills and catch up with her bank employee friends. Carmen and Manuel had spent some time working together, but I had been in Texas for an extended period in the summer of 2009 and therefore had not seen that work relationship develop.[3] That afternoon, Manuel walked up to the pushcart to help Carmen pack and load the pushcart, and we were introduced.

"This is my friend Rocío. She does research on *fruteros*. You should let her interview you," Carmen said, immediately getting to the point.

"Oh yeah?" Manuel replied as he moved closer.

Manuel looked very young. When he was not paying attention, I asked Carmen his age. She said he was twenty-one years old, but he looked like a teenager to me. Carmen explained that Manuel was her *raitero*, giving her rides at the end of the workday and making some extra cash in the process. Later, I would learn that both of them were storing their pushcarts in Manuel's backyard and that they also used that space to prepare their carts in the morning. In this way, Manuel was more than a *raitero*.

After a few minutes, Carmen told me to watch the cart while she went to the restroom. Within a minute of her leaving, there was a customer. The customer asked how the process of ordering worked. In front of Manuel, I explained that fruit came in three sizes that cost $3, $4, or $5. Manuel laughed, likely at my overly serious and formal presentation of the prices. The customer asked for a $3 fruit salad and picked out the produce. I cut up what Carmen had told me was $3 worth of fruit, and then the customer asked to add additional pieces of different fruit, which made the serving size larger. Each time I cut up the fruit, the customer asked for another item. As I prepared the fruit, I turned to Manuel and gave him a comical side-eye look that said, *Look at this guy trying to play me.*

Manuel chuckled and immediately covered his mouth with his hand, but not before I saw that he was missing a front tooth. Carmen returned while I was still chopping fruit and stood over me telling me how to slice different pieces.

"She new. I teach her," she explained in broken English to the customer, who nodded in approval. Softly, in Spanish, she asked me how much the fruit was for, and I whispered, "It's supposed to be a $3 bag, but I'll pay you the extra dollars since it's gotten so big."

When the customer left, Carmen told me not to worry about paying her and that I had to be careful about customers that would try to advantage of me.

"You'll learn," Manuel added, laughing at my review of events, in which I playfully said, "*Es que me ven la cara de pendeja, o que* [Is it because they see the face of a fool on me, or what]?"

Shortly after, I helped Carmen pack up, and we parted ways. She and Manuel headed toward South Los Angeles in the truck, and I jumped on a bus headed west. Because I was often dividing my time between different locations, I didn't see Manuel for some time after that. However, by October, I had heard quite a bit about Manuel from Carmen. Carmen told me I should visit the wholesale produce market with Manuel some morning. I asked if she could set it up, and she did. My first trip with Manuel to the wholesale market was on a Tuesday in October 2009.

Manuel and I agreed to meet in downtown Los Angeles at around 6:30 a.m. He would be driving north from South Los Angeles, and I would be coming east from West Los Angeles. The wholesale produce market was just east of downtown Los Angeles, and I wanted to make my incorporation into his morning routine as easy as possible. I got on a nearly empty Metro Rapid bus headed east. Shortly after I hopped on, the bus driver, who had been trying to balance a 7-11 Big Gulp drink while driving, squeezed the plastic container too hard and spilled it all over part of her lap and onto the floor near the front door. She cursed and was visibly annoyed. She treated all subsequent bus riders, who hopped on and complained about the sticky, wet floor, with contempt. This effectively meant that the mood on the bus was grim for everyone, but only a few of us knew the root of the problem. I thought this might be a good story to tell Manuel as an icebreaker when I arrived. I got off in the middle of downtown. The sky was still dark, and the air was damp. I walked to the corner of Broadway and Sixth Street, where Manuel and I had agreed to meet, and waited for Manuel's white pickup truck to pull up. In the predawn hours, downtown Los Angeles was only beginning to stir. The streets were largely empty except for a few city workers in city vehicles and shopkeepers hosing down their sidewalks. Several service sector workers in uniforms came and went from the bus stops, but the streets were nearly empty— an unusual sight in this very commercial corridor. I stood looking a bit forlorn on a street corner in front of a pawnshop. I had picked a corner with no public transportation stop nearby so as to not confuse bus drivers. After ten minutes, I saw a white pickup truck driving toward me. I perked up and smiled at the Latino driver as he pulled up in front of me. As I walked over, I noticed a strange decal on the truck and stacks of newspapers in the cargo bed. I had not paid much attention to Manuel's truck before this and wondered why he would have newspapers in the cargo bed. But since I was expecting Manuel, I felt my hand going for the door handle before my thoughts caught up with me. I opened the door and bowed down to say hello before hopping in. The man inside smiled wide, and all I saw and took note of was his full set of teeth. Manuel's defining characteristic was a missing front upper incisor. I quickly slammed the door and stepped back. The man grimaced, flipped me off, and drove away. A few minutes later, Manuel arrived, and I jumped into his truck. My Big Gulp story was replaced by my I-think-I-was-just-mistaken-for-a-prostitute story. Manuel laughed. This was the second time I had shown my naiveté to Manuel in just as many times meeting him, and he seemed at ease in my presence.

I continued to join Manuel on his market trips. These mornings at the market gave me access to the informal ways in which debt and credit were managed, and I saw firsthand how these too were structured within *paisano* networks. Manuel proved to be an invaluable source of information. Our one-on-one time at the wholesale market created a space where he could tell me about various issues he was having, such as his debt to the wholesale merchant, problems with his *paisanos,* and his feelings of estrangement in the United States. I often felt he disclosed more to me in this time than he did when Carmen was around.

Manuel sometimes talked about the hostility he felt in this country. Crackdowns were particularly unpleasant, and he often interpreted them as a form of anti-immigrant policing. One morning, as he recounted the specifics of a health department crackdown and an expensive DUI charge, he explained that he sometimes wanted to leave it all behind. Manuel often threatened to return to Dos Mundos, and while I initially took him on his word, I soon learned that this threat was part of his repertoire when he felt down. One morning, on our ride from the wholesale market to his home in South Los Angeles, we were listening to a Spanish language morning radio show.

"I'm going to return to Dos Mundos [*Ya me voy a regresar*]," he said solemnly, interrupting the silence between us.

"When?" I asked.

"Maybe next month. My [grandmother] is telling me to return already."

"But do you have a date in mind?" I asked again.

"Soon," he said.

"What are you going to do with your truck? And your pushcart?" I asked. He didn't reply. We drove in silence for a while longer.

"I mean, why *be* here if they don't *want* me here?" he finally said.

The "they" Manuel alluded to, as he explained in our conversation, included all of the actors and agencies—local and federal—that continuously undermined him, policed him, and threatened his continued existence in Los Angeles and the United States. The feeling of being unwanted was one that he expressed as a worker and as an immigrant. The way he was treated by his fellow *paisanos* at times certainly did not help matters. A few years later, he would be arrested yet again for making an illegal U-turn in South Los Angeles. The pressure and stress that he experienced was real and almost palpable to me as an intimate observer of his life. But it was only in the quiet morning moments when I sat with him in his truck that Manuel fully expressed all of these vulnerabilities.

Throughout my time with him, I was open with Manuel about my mishaps and awkward tendencies; there was no pretense between us. This way of being, I believe, allowed me to have more meaningful conversations with him. I often saw how he shut down in front of more imposing people—either customers or fellow *paisanos*. I knew that for him to open up to me, I had to be vulnerable and open up to him. However, with other vendors, like Daniel, this kind of behavior on my part would have further complicated our interactions.

Falling In

Though I spent a lot of time with individual men on their street corners or in trucks running errands, flirtation was not a major issue. I largely felt respect from them and quickly established that my romantic life would not be a topic of conversation. On street corners, male customers were often respectful because I was "protected" by the male vendor's presence. The vendor could easily be mistaken for my boyfriend or my boss, and as a result interactions with customers were never problematic. However, things were different when I worked with Carmen. Two young women working alone on a street corner inspired different interactions with customers. From the beginning, when Carmen began training me to prepare fruit salads, she set the stage for how I could use flirtation to make her more money. I was initially uncertain about the arrangement, and the first time I was "put on display" was awkward.

A young Filipino man approached us while I was being trained by Carmen to vend on my own. This man was a repeat customer and knew Carmen. As he walked up, Carmen was showing me how to hold the knife while supreming (a technique to remove the membrane from fruits) an orange and then a watermelon. She teased me and told the young man that I was her new worker in an effort to elicit patience from him while I prepared his fruit salad. Carmen then turned to the man and asked him, "Do you think she's pretty?" The man, who was standing next to me, proceeded to move two steps behind me. I glanced over my shoulder and caught him looking me up and down from behind. After his short inspection, he asked me how old I was. I told him I was in my early twenties, and he said I took good care of myself. He introduced himself and asked if I worked there often. Carmen told him I did. He said he would come back the following day and order more fruit from me. My initial reaction to his "inspection" was annoyance, but I remained quiet. I opted to ask Carmen more about the purpose of that flirtatious talk when he left. At the time, she said she was just having some fun with him.

As I spent more time with Carmen on the corner, I saw that she often flirted with male customers to get bigger tips or bigger orders. Afterward, we would laugh about the interactions. Once I understood that we could control the narrative and that these interactions allowed us to break up long, dull days of vending, I was fine with her using me as bait for customers. I played along and performed gendered heteronormativity to help her make money and to pass the time.

When I arrived on Carmen's street corner one afternoon, she had one customer. He was a short, middle-aged Latino man in a blue Dickies workman's uniform. He seemed familiar with Carmen given the content of their conversation. He asked for coconut water. Carmen hacked open one of her coconuts and overturned it into a plastic bag. She inserted a straw and quickly tied the ends of the bag around it. For this, she charged the man $1. Carmen teased the man and asked him to buy more fruit from her because she wasn't selling well that day and still had a lot of product left and the end of the workday was near.

She quickly incorporated me into the teasing. She made a fruit salad for me. She usually made one for me and gave it to me free of charge; I would sometimes bring her lunch or help her clean up at the end of the day, and this was her way of repaying me for the help. But the man did not know my fruit salad was free. Carmen told the man that he should be a "gentleman" and pay for my fruit. He looked at me, and I smiled sweetly to play along with Carmen's ploy. He said he would pay for my salad, and then he asked me if I had a boyfriend. I said no, and he proceeded to flirt with me. He asked me to go on a dinner date with him. I did not respond to his request and opted to stay quiet. I looked to Carmen to finish the interaction she started. Carmen jumped into the conversation and said I could not go to dinner with him because I did not know him. He then started talking to me through Carmen. "What does she want to know?" he asked. "I've been separated for a few years now. I live alone. I work six days a week. I make good money."

Carmen continued to joke with the man while acting as the broker. Other customers came and went, and the man started taking credit for the influx of customers. He said it was his presence that had brought them. Carmen countered by saying I was her lucky charm, not him, because every time I showed up the customers came. Eventually, the man asked Carmen to make him a fruit salad. He was going to pick up his things but would be back shortly to get the fruit. He paid $8 for everything before leaving ($4 for my fruit, $1 for the coconut water, and $3 for his small bag of fruit). After ten minutes, he returned to get his bag of fruit and to ask me again to go on a dinner date with him. I smiled, thanked him, and said no. Carmen then made some excuse about my shyness and told him to try again the following day.

Generally, vending with Carmen required more engagement with customers. She was talkative and had a bubbly personality. She often got into long conversations with customers. This helped her win over quite a few regulars. Conversely, most of the men I worked with limited their talk with customers and often dispatched them as quickly as possible. I often believed that Carmen and I were expected to perform both as vendors and as flirts by virtue of being women and because we worked in a public space.

Carmen began vending at a new location in the Pico-Union neighborhood of Los Angeles. This site, compared to her other corner in the Mid-City area, was bustling with people and traffic. One afternoon, I was having a conversation with Carmen when a Latino customer approached us. He had overheard part of our conversation in which I told Carmen something related to living alone. I was making the fruit salads while Carmen took a break and sat on a milk crate. The man came up and ordered fruit from me and quickly told me he would buy a bigger fruit salad if I gave him my phone number. In selling himself to me, he said he was a hard worker and that if I was his girlfriend I would never need to work or worry about money. I stayed quiet and looked away toward Carmen with wide eyes. Carmen did not engage and instead just giggled at what she was witnessing. She then began prodding me to say something to the man. "Tell him to buy a bigger salad," she said. I laughed and finished making his salad. After he left, I sat down on another milk crate with my back to the street. The Latino man, now idling in his truck at the intersection, honked his horn to get our attention. Carmen turned, and he asked her for my phone number. I glanced over my shoulder, and when I realized it was him, I turned quickly around again. Carmen teased me and said, "Just play along. It won't hurt you." We both laughed after he finally pulled away.

I knew that Carmen sometimes gave her phone number to male customers and sometimes carried on flirtations via text. I was more apprehensive about giving out my cell phone number. However, Carmen and I established that I would play along to get the tip, the sale, or the laugh. This worked for us and for the customers who wished to get a bit more from their interaction than just a fruit salad. With Carmen functioning as protective overseer, I fell into the flirtatious interactions. I performed for both Carmen and the customers, knowing that I could demur before the interaction went too far. Carmen would then have my back and explain away my unwillingness to follow through with digits or a date.

GETTING SHUT OUT

Due to my status as a researcher, I spent much of my time helping various *fruteros* (both vendor workers and independent vendors) on their street corners and later acting as a substitute worker when they needed to run errands or were sick. My role as a "prying eye" and low-status worker limited the interactions I had with the employers in the group, namely the García and the Martínez brothers. They were suspicious of my presence and never allowed me to interview or shadow them. Because the García brothers did not work as vendors on street corners, it was difficult to visit or observe them. The Martínez brothers did work as vendors for a brief period, but my interactions with them were limited to brief greetings at the end of the workday, when they would pick up the worker I was working with or visiting. By contrast, vendor workers and independent vendors who had formerly worked for the García and/or the Martínez brothers felt that my presence as a researcher made me enough of an outsider that they could speak to me openly about their grievances. I was thus able to hear stories and complaints that vendors might not have voiced among other Dos Mundos migrants or among the García or the Martínez brothers. ·

I did continuously attempt to hear the employers' side of the story and even attempted to interview the parents of the García brothers in Mexico. I was invited into their house and given a glass of cold Coca-Cola, but within ten minutes, a García brother in Los Angeles returned his mother's call and told her not to talk to me. Omar García, another son, who was visiting Dos Mundos at the time, later saw me in town and explained to me, "The thing is, our business is our business." I respected their decision and thought it might be useful for others in town to know that my requests for interviews could be denied. Although it was useful to come with referrals, I also felt that it might also make family members feel obligated to open their homes to me and speak to me.

During my stay in town, Doña Julieta, Manuel's grandmother, would walk me to the houses of the people I had to interview and often lingered; she witnessed me being denied an interview by the Garcías. Following that encounter, she would make mention of it in my subsequent interviews. The response of others in town was often, "Those Garcías have always been snobs," or, "That's what you get with those folks." Her tale of the García family's treatment of me revealed the resentment others held toward that family, or perhaps they created that narrative for me so that I would not feel offended. I was not, but getting shut out did make me increasingly curious about the reasons why. After this event, I explained to those I interviewed in Dos Mundos that they also had the option to opt out of our conversations or interviews at any point. No one who accepted to be interviewed ever took me up on that offer, but I cannot know if they felt compelled to speak to me.

LEAVING THE FIELD BUT NOT THE COMMUNITY

There has been no easy transition out of the "field" because of the various ways in which people stay in touch in this Internet age. I continue to live and work in Southern California, which means I continue to receive invitations to events in the *frutero* community. I was a part of the vendors' lives for so long, I met their families in Mexico, I celebrated birthdays, baptisms, and patron saint celebrations with them—and these connections are not easily broken or lost. I also have no desire to pull myself out completely from the vendors' lives. Over a decade after meeting them, I continue to stay in touch with a few vendors via text and social media platforms. I share in their joys and their grief when they give me updates. I am invited to and sometimes attend celebrations. The *fruteros* have always been welcoming of my presence at these events. It is my hope that my connection with this community continues long after this book is published. Whether and how researchers negotiate their exits from their field sites often receives little attention. Given the many ways in which we as researchers are and can be connected to people, in person and online, we should expect to remain accessible to those who offered so much to us.

Notes

1. INTRODUCTION

1. All names have been changed to protect the confidentiality of respondents. I have also changed the name of the town in the Mexican state of Puebla most of my respondents came from. I have changed respondents' names because I have an obligation to protect their anonymity from the wider public, insofar as I can. Respondents were told from the beginning that pseudonyms would be used to mask their identities from readers. This practice of "masking"—concealing or distorting identifying information about people, places, and organizations—is not without its critics and issues. As Colin Jerolmack and Alexandra K. Murphy (2019) write, it is increasingly difficult to maintain the promise of confidentiality to research subjects, given the increasing reach of the Internet and use of online social networks. Since I was known to work in some circles and not others, it is difficult to keep respondents anonymous to each other within the community. Furthermore, the information I collected from respondents was often well known in the *paisano* network. I have not changed characteristics of respondents' biographies. I have not created composite characters or altered historical events. My obligation to the reader compels me to show how the built environment, as seen in the enforcement of local and federal law, for example, shaped the structure and content of *paisano* networks. It is my hope that a future researcher will revisit the community of street vendors, writ large, to assess whether and how the legalization of street vending has reorganized the social

setting and ethnic community. In this way, as Jerolmack and Murphy note, the gatekeeping power of the researcher can be weakened, "making it easier for our subjects to tell their stories regardless of *our* consent" (2019, 808). However, I hope my central claim extends to other social settings and groups operating under comparable circumstances. For more on masking, see Jerolmack and Murphy 2019.

2. When the television series *Law and Order: Los Angeles* premiered in 2010, one of the season's first episodes featured an extra in the role of a fruit vendor working under a rainbow umbrella and vending in front of a police precinct. In this way, the show instantly tapped into the everyday streetscape of the city.

3. All conversations were conducted in Spanish. I am a native Spanish speaker, and the translations provided are my own. In some cases, especially when a turn of phrase is distinct, the original Spanish is included in the running text or endnotes. Early in my fieldwork, I carried a small notebook, and immediately after an interaction, I would jot down general notes and conversations. Sometimes, I would jot down small snippets of conversation that I remembered clearly. They were usually only part of longer extended conversations. These small snippets of talk often captured my interest, and I was able to remember them well enough to quote them verbatim (in Spanish) in my jottings. After some time in the field, I started carrying around a digital recorder as well. In fact, my mother sewed a special apron for me with a chest-level pocket where I could tuck my recorder so that I could record conversations while vending. Vendors knew that I carried the recorder and that I recorded constantly. Sometimes, when they felt they were telling me something important, they would stop talking to make sure my recorder was on before continuing. Quotes in the text capture conversations that were quickly jotted down verbatim after the interactions and conversations that were recorded.

4. The term *paisano* can also be translated as "countryman." In this text, and given how fruit vendors used the term, I translate it as "hometown associate." Vendors used the term *paisano/a* when referring to a person from the town of Dos Mundos or the state of Puebla. The term was not often employed when referring simply to other Mexicans in Los Angeles.

5. My use of the masculine pronoun is intentional. The majority of fruit vendors in this study are men. The occupation itself has a higher proportion of men than women; it is a gendered occupational niche, though it is not as exclusively male dominated as some other occupations, such as *jardinería* (landscape gardening). I often asked vendors—men and women alike—why this was so, and the gender talk often involved the job's need for a strong physicality (to load and unload pushcarts from pickup trucks), which made fruit vending "men's work" in their eyes. For an extended treatment of gender issues, see the methodological appendix. For more on gendered occupational niches among Mexican immigrant gardeners, see Ramirez 2011.

6. I use the terms "migrant" and "immigrant" interchangeably. Most vendors expressed a desire to return to Mexico, and their undocumented status made their prolonged presence in the United States uncertain (like migrants). However, Dos Mundos migrants often pushed back return dates and lengthened their stays while settling into homes and neighborhoods in ways that signaled more permanence (like immigrants).

7. For example, in the seminal work *Return to Aztlan*, American sociologist Douglas Massey and Mexican anthropologists Rafael Alarcón, Jorge Durand, and Humberto González extol the virtues of social networks: "Landless *jornaleros* [laborers] from a town such as Chamitlán may be poor in financial resources, but they are wealthy in social capital, which they can readily convert into jobs and earnings in the United States" (1987, 171). See Massey et al. 1987.

8. The term "ethnic cage" will likely remind some readers of Max Weber's iron cage (from Talcott Parsons's translation of *The Protestant Ethic*). For Weber, those in the iron cage were trapped in a role and pursuit without space for joy, passion, or spontaneity due to an excess of rationalization and specialization in the production process. Quoting Johann Wolfgang von Goethe, Weber believed this process created "specialists without spirit, sensualists without heart" (2001, 124). Yet Weber was not concerned only about limited autonomy in the production and work sphere. He feared that it could spill into the personal and home sphere as well. The *ranchera* song "La Jaula de Oro" showcases some of this constriction (i.e., financial gain without the possibility of enjoyment). The ethnic cage concept, like that of Weber's iron cage and the Tigres del Norte's golden cage, captures the conflict between increasing benefits in one sphere and decreasing satisfaction in another.

9. See also Mahler 1995.

10. Emir Estrada and Pierrette Hondagneu-Sotelo (2010) have written about the stigma experienced by the children of street vendors, who often work with their parents on the street. See also Estrada 2019.

11. In an essay written as a response to the creation of evaluative criteria within the National Science Foundation for qualitative studies, Howard S. Becker explains how researchers engaging in long-term field observation often do not know what ideas to investigate and test until research begins, an issue that does not render those studies less scientific or rigorous. Becker cites William Whyte's methodological appendix in the classic *Street Corner Society* to explain how Whyte did not and could not "have known what the final subject of his research was going to be or how to study it until he had been in the community for a few years" (2009, 549). My book presents another instance of research performed as an iterative process where, to paraphrase Michael Agar, you learn something, try to make sense of it, then go back and learn some more. For more, see Becker 2009; Agar 1996; and Whyte 1993.

12. New York City estimates of street vendors, which range from twelve thousand to twenty thousand, provided by the Street Vendor Project. The Street

Vendor Project is part of the Urban Justice Center, a nonprofit organization providing legal representation and advocacy for various marginalized groups of New Yorkers. For more, see Sluska and Basinski 2006. Los Angeles estimates provided by the Los Angeles Economic Roundtable; see Liu, Burns, and Flaming 2015.

13. Since I ended my fieldwork, Los Angeles has made some progress with regard to changing the antivending policy. After mobilization on the part of the Los Angeles Street Vendor Campaign, two city councilmembers put forth a resolution to decriminalize vending. The issue slowly moved from the local government to the state level. In January 2018, California senator Ricardo Lara introduced Senate Bill 946 (The Safe Sidewalk Vending Act) to decriminalize street vendors. For more, see the afterword.

14. The Los Angeles Municipal Code prohibited vending on city sidewalks, and vending in city parks was allowed only with a permit. Vending on sidewalks was considered a misdemeanor. Sidewalk vending pertains only to stationary and/or mobile carts situated on the sidewalk. Food trucks and pull trucks operating on the street or in parking spaces are governed by different municipal codes.

15. On June 21, 2013, the Los Angeles City Council adopted Article 1.2 of the Los Angeles Municipal Code, which established the ACE program (see Council File No. 10–0085). The ACE program was set up by the Los Angeles City Attorney and initially used for forty quality-of-life offenses, among them illegal vending, failure to keep a sidewalk clean, and loud noise. According to a Sidewalk Vending Fact Sheet issued by the City of Los Angeles, even with the ACE program, street vendors violating street vending laws could be arrested and/or issued a citation with a fine of up to $1,000, in addition to court-related fees (Los Angeles Economic Development Committee, n.d.). Activist attorney Cynthia Anderson-Baker has publicly criticized the ACE program for not providing due process and for lacking an appeals process.

16. For example, on August 27, 2009, Los Angeles became an activated jurisdiction of the Secure Communities (S-Comm) Program under the Department of Homeland Security (DHS). S-Comm is a federal information-sharing partnership between Immigration and Customs Enforcement (ICE) and the Federal Bureau of Investigation. When local law enforcement agencies arrest or book individuals, their fingerprints are sent to the FBI to check for a criminal record and then forwarded to ICE to check against immigration databases. ICE then determines if an individual is unlawfully in the United States, and if so, it prioritizes their removal based on their crime, criminal history, and other factors, such as repeat violations of immigration laws. Federal DHS officers make immigration enforcement decisions after individuals are arrested for criminal violations of local, state, or federal law, not for violations of immigration law. Programs like S-Comm impacted fruit vendors because they could be, and often were, arrested

for misdemeanors such as street vending, driving without a license, and driving under the influence. When fruit vendors were booked into Los Angeles County jails, their immigration status was checked. Because some of them had been apprehended by U.S. Border Patrol agents while attempting to cross into the United States or had been previously deported, whenever they were arrested for a misdemeanor offense, the arrest could set into motion proceedings that resulted in deportation.

17. Extensive research focuses on the devolution of immigration enforcement where local agents, such as police officers and sheriffs, are charged with the task of identifying and apprehending immigrants. See Armenta 2017; and Provine et al. 2016.

18. In his work on Korean-owned small businesses in New York, Dae Young Kim (1999) shows how the inability of Korean owners to pay coethnics low wages or assign them menial tasks resulted in these business owners employing Mexican and Ecuadorean workers instead of fellow Korean coethnics.

19. Although Alejandro Portes and Alex Stepick (1985) refer to the "informal" sector as a new and distinct part of the labor market made up of immigrant minorities working for subminimal and illegal wages, Jimy M. Sanders and Victor Nee see the "informal" labor market as an "extension of the enclave economy [that] provides an employment niche for both legal and illegal immigrants" (1987, 765n).

20. As sociologists Jimy M. Sanders and Victor Nee write, "Ethnic solidarity theorists focus on the institutions and social dynamics that facilitate the mobilization of ethnic resources for economic advancement" (1987, 746).

21. The names of hometowns, but not states, in Mexico have been changed to protect the confidentiality of respondents. None of the Mexican nationals from the state of Puebla identified as indigenous, nor did they speak any indigenous languages in addition to Spanish. Some of the Guatemalan workers I met later on during my fieldwork who were entering the job did identify as indigenous and spoke an indigenous language in addition to Spanish. As I was leaving the field, there was some ethnic succession that saw Mexican Poblanos hiring Guatemalan and Salvadoran workers. One such migrant from Guatemala, who only spoke K'iche' on arrival, would occasionally visit Carmen's corner for impromptu language lessons. Carmen and I would teach him Spanish words and he would teach us the K'iche' terms.

22. During my time in graduate school in Los Angeles, I never owned a car. This was undoubtedly a burden at times. However, a conversation with my father helped me make sense of this burden. When I asked my father, a former taxi driver, if he would help me buy a used car, he thoughtfully asked, "Do the *fruteros* have cars?" I replied that most of them did not, to which he responded, "Don't you want to understand how they live?" The deflection worked. My father was also tapping into a sentiment expressed by Erving Goffman (1989), who noted

that the core of participant observation entails "tuning your body up" by developing an ecological closeness to your subjects so that you are in a position to develop
empathy. To do so, you "subject yourself, your own body, your own personality
and your own social situation, to the set of contingencies that play upon a set of
individuals, so that you can physically and ecologically penetrate their circle of
response to their social situation, or their work situation, or their ethnic situation" (1989, 125).

23. In her study of West Indian social networks in New York, London, and the
West Indies, Vilna Francine Bashi (2007) develops a "hub-and-spoke" model of
transnational immigrant network organization, where veteran migrants function as "hubs" to the newcomer "spokes."

24. As Elliot Liebow noted in *Tally's Corner,* "Kinship ties are frequently
manufactured to explain, account for, or even to validate friend relationships,"
and sometimes, "pseudo-kinship is invoked in more casual terms, apparently to
sharpen and lend formal structure to a relationship which is generally vague"
(2003, 108, 112).

25. Information sheets approved by the UCLA Institutional Review Board
were distributed to all formally interviewed participants. Verbal consent was
sought and received from all respondents. I interviewed one group of vendors
that I later came to believe might have given me inaccurate or compromised
responses because of pressure from their employer (Nancy). I had first interviewed Nancy, one of the largest vendor employers in the business, who owned
multiple pushcarts and had several fruit vendors working under her, and financially compensated her for her time. She then offered her workers as potential
respondents and facilitated the interviews by making the workers available at
the commissary space. In this book, I did not use the content of these interviews
because, several weeks later, I heard that Nancy, knowing I was financially com-
pensating respondents, had compelled her workers to be interviewed by me and
was pocketing some or all of the compensation. I approached a few of these workers to verify the stories and was met with evasive answers. I offered these workers financial compensation again, in spaces and places where Nancy would not
find out, but the payments were rejected. I dropped these interviews from my
study and kept some distance from Nancy and her workers in an effort to not stir
up trouble for anyone.

26. The general area where my fieldwork took place included neighborhoods
west of the 110 Harbor Freeway, all the way to coastal Santa Monica; south of the
101 Hollywood Freeway; and north of the 105 Century Freeway.

27. I worked as a fruit vendor in two locations; one was an affluent, Mid-City
location, and the other was in a working-class neighborhood adjacent to downtown Los Angeles. The two neighborhoods are distinct. The Mid-City site was
located in front of a bank along a major thoroughfare. Mid-rise office buildings

line this major boulevard, and large, beautifully manicured homes are located in the adjacent residential areas. The majority of the customers were headed to or returning from the bank; other customers included office workers from the adjacent buildings and blue-collar workers who pulled off the main thoroughfare for fruit. Customers at this location were of mixed racial, ethnic, and class backgrounds, but the majority were Latino professionals. The second vending site was close to downtown Los Angeles and located in a large gas station lot. Four *fruteros* occupied this space, each about thirty feet from the next. Other street vendors, selling items such as roasted corn and hot dogs, worked adjacent corners. This location was near a busy public transportation node, and as a result, many pedestrians could be observed hurrying to or from buses and Metro links. The majority of customers were working-class Latinos buying fruit on their way to or from the public transportation nodes.

28. My six years of fieldwork resulted in hundreds of pages of field notes, which were coded into themes for analysis using a grounded theory approach.

2. BECOMING A *FRUTERO*

1. When prospective employers in Los Angeles helped Dos Mundos migrants come to Los Angeles—by paying for *coyotes* and promising work on arrival—they were initiating the migration process by creating opportunity and aiding in the selection process of who migrates. As Vilna Francine Bashi (2007) argues, this way of viewing international migration complicates push-pull and chain theories of migration. Bashi writes, "Migrants do not select themselves but rather are selected by others who facilitate the moving process on the basis of the character traits best adapted for survival in the new environment. . . . Migration in the network context occurs not when potential migrants decide to migrate and switch on their connections . . . but instead when people who have already migrated actually create opportunities and then choose a newcomer to take advantage of these opportunities" (2007, 3–5).

2. Many of the fruit vendors in this study mentioned this man by name, but I was unable to interview him personally because he was serving time for a domestic violence incident.

3. For more on immigrant niches, see Waldinger 1994.

4. For more on social closure, see Waldinger and Lichter 2003.

5. The meat processing industry offers a useful example of ethnic/racial displacement; over the course of decades, Latino immigrants have replaced African American workers in this industry. For more, see Fink 2003; and Ribas 2015.

6. These informal counts were based on street observation of major Los Angeles thoroughfares as well as an assessment of the locations of commissaries (i.e.,

pushcart storage warehouses) and the number of spaces available for pushcarts at each commissary. Commissaries have a certain number of spots for pushcarts, and at some locations, these are primarily filled by *fruteros*. This number was added to an estimate, provided by vendors, of non-commissary-based pushcarts.

7. All money, unless otherwise indicated, is in U.S. dollars.

8. For more on *tandas,* see chapter 4.

9. Cristian had first asked me if he could purchase a truck and put my name on the title. When I asked how the arrangement would work, he explained that he would pay a large portion of the truck's cost up front. When I told him I would not be a good choice, he asked Raúl. For Cristian, buying a truck was riddled with predatory practices. Cristian went to a used car dealership and was offered a loan with an interest rate of over 20 percent for a truck that had previously been in a wreck. In addition to the down payment, the dealer asked Cristian for proof of employment in the form of a letter from his employer. Cristian asked me if I could write a letter stating how long he had held a job and how much he got paid. When I asked him if he wanted me to write that he was a fruit vendor, he said no. Instead, I invented a company and listed him as a reliable longtime employee. However, I used actual information regarding time on the job and pay. I did not consider bending the truth in this way problematic, and my willingness to write the letter allowed Cristian to understand that I knew when policies or requests from the formal sector did not fit how workers in the informal sector operated (i.e., credit invisibility). Cristian took the letter, went to the dealership with Raúl, and bought himself his truck. He paid for it in full several months later. Researchers have given special attention to credit invisibility, or the lack of a credit score, among people who engage in behaviors that indicate credit worthiness. This invisibility leads to unequal financial lives and exists disproportionately among African American and Latino populations. For more, see Baradaran 2018; and Wherry, Seefeldt, and Alvarez 2019.

10. In Dos Mundos, Manuel had worked in the fields earning 50 Mexican pesos a day (roughly US$4.46 by 2005 exchange rates).

11. See the appendix for a discussion about my interaction with the two sets of brothers.

12. Legal violence is experienced by immigrants with tenuous legal statuses when they are criminalized at the federal, state, and local levels, which leads to exclusionary practices and generates violent effects in their everyday lives. See Menjívar and Abrego 2012.

13. The case of *padrones* provides one relevant historical example.

14. Because I had a driver's license, Carmen often asked me to drive her car when we ran errands together. It made Carmen feel at ease when I drove, even when my Los Angeles driving skills were lacking.

15. For an alternative case, see Kim 1999.

3. MANAGING RISK ON THE STREET

1. For one sheet of printed labels, Carmen was paying $20. When I found out she was paying someone to make labels for her, I asked if she wanted me to make them for her for free. She accepted.

2. Several years later, after I had finished my fieldwork, a fruit vendor did set up successfully in Westwood. On the few occasions I made it back to UCLA, I saw the pushcart, though I never approached to figure out if I knew the vendor stationed there.

3. Pierrette Hondagneu-Sotelo (1994) offered a similar argument about the enabling and constraining effects of social networks in her study of domestic workers, *Gendered Transitions*.

4. The trap of social networks is one major finding in Carol Stack's (1974) classic study, *All Our Kin*.

5. For example, a public memo dated September 28, 2006, issued by LAPD Senior Lead Officer Rashad Sharif to a West Los Angeles neighborhood association complaining of a street vendor problem, stated: "As long as there are people who continue to buy, there will probably be vendors who are willing to take a chance with the risk of being cited to make a living. We will never stop trying to combat the problem but it seems that when one vendor leaves the area, another one is there to take their place. . . . As a side note when other officers and myself do attempt to cite these individuals we have been yelled at and ridiculed by citizens who claim that we are harassing and racial profiling these vendors. There is support for these vendors by people who say that this is a victimless crime and who claim that these vendors are merely serving a community who wants, needs and welcomes there [*sic*] services."

6. Notable exceptions included LAPD sweeps that took place to secure the route of the presidential motorcade when the president of the United States made official visits to Los Angeles. Those sweeps often displaced vendors but did not result in citations or arrests.

7. For more on how residents in community groups define the deviance of street vendors to law enforcement, see Muñiz 2011.

8. For more on how race, crime, and punishment are also experienced as gendered phenomena, see Rios 2009.

9. Secure Communities is a federal information-sharing partnership between ICE and the FBI.

10. See also Howell, Perry, and Vile 2004; Rosenbaum et al. 2005; Seron, Pereira, and Kovath 2004; and Weitzer and Tuch 2004.

11. For more on policing brown bodies in public space, see Patel 2012; and McDowell and Wonders 2010.

12. Chio is a nickname for people named Rocío.

4. PERSONAL AND PROFESSIONAL ENTANGLEMENTS

1. As Charles Tilly writes, "People rely especially on those [interpersonal trust] networks when they are carrying on long-term, crucial enterprises such as procreation, child rearing, religious or political commitment, long distance trade, and, of course, migration. In those networks, members bet valued outcomes on the likelihood that other people will meet their responsibliities compentently" (2007, 5).

2. Anthropologist Clifford Geertz (1962) referred to *tandas* as "rotating credit associations" and noted that the essential component is that members have revolving access to a continuously reconstituted capital fund. The purpose of these *tandas* has been debated. Geertz considered them intermediate, or "middle rung," institutions of economic development that educated the peasants, urban proletariat, and peasant migrants turned city-dwellers who took part in them. He believed their participation in rotating credit associations would prepare them for participation in urban commercial structures and institutions. For more, see Geertz 1962.

3. The use of *tandas* by individuals to save and distribute money among a group of people is a widespread practice in Mexico. Anthropologist Oscar Lewis alluded to them in his seminal works without defining what they were. See Lewis 1959.

4. From an interview with Cristian conducted during a visit to Dos Mundos in 2011.

5. Elaine J. Hall (1993) examined the gendered scripts of waitresses who provided good service by being friendly, deferential, and flirtatious. For more on how gender frames social relations, see Ridgeway 2011.

6. Susan Brownmiller's critical examination of femininity is useful here to understand how the performance of a feminine ideal can be "a powerful esthetic based upon a recognition of powerlessness" (1984, 10). For more, see Brownmiller 1984.

7. I left the field in the summer of 2009. When I returned, I visited all the vendors individually to get caught up.

8. These HTAs began to grow in number during the 1990s. Los Angeles, in particular, is the region with the highest concentration of Mexican immigrants and Mexican HTAs in the United States. For more, see Zabin and Escala. 2002.

9. But see Bada 2014; and Theiss-Morse and Hibbing 2005.

10. For example, one stall sold products specifically for vendors who sold *esquites* (Mexican street corn in a cup). This stall sold corn, Styrofoam cups, plastic spoons, and chili powder.

5. ETHNIC TIES IN CRISIS

1. Manuel rented his room to a *paisano* while he was in Fresno and settled back in when he returned.

2. This story was pieced together from a conversation with Carmen on Saturday and follow-up questions I asked Doña Alicia.

3. As Shirley Ardener has noted, while the *tanda* may appear to be an equitable mechanism for saving, the advantages are not equal for all participants: "The first member to receive the fund becomes a debtor to all the other members and remains one until the last contribution has been made; the last member to receive it becomes a creditor to all other members throughout; while the other . . . members move in turn from being creditors to debtors" (1964, 201).

6. DOS MUNDOS TRANSFORMED

1. The "migration industry" concept has been traced back to Robert F. Harney (1977), who first coined the term "commerce of migration" in reference to the intermediaries who profited by offering services to migrants. Later, Robin Cohen (1997) introduced the concept of "migration industry," which included the lawyers, travel agents, recruiters, and brokers who maintained links in both sending and receiving countries. Stephen Castles and Mark J. Miller (2003), in their migration systems theory, also addressed the role of the migration industry. More recently, Rubén Hernández-León (2008) has expanded and argued for a comprehensive conceptualization of the migration industry. For more on the evolution of the concept, see Gammeltoft-Hansen and Nyberg 2013.

2. When I returned to Dos Mundos in 2017, money from migrants abroad, along with help from the local government, had helped fund a school bus that drove up and down the main road, taking local residents to the edge of town and back.

3. Manuel left Dos Mundos in 2005 to work in Fresno. I met him in 2009, when he was working in Los Angeles as a *frutero*. I visited Dos Mundos for the first time in 2011.

4. This conversation took place during my first visit to Dos Mundos, in 2011.

5. Immigration scholars who have documented the earning potential differentials between immigrant men and women in the United States have found that men do make more than women. However, despite this differential, scholars have found that financial remittances sent by women tend to be greater than those sent by men. For more, see Hagan 1994; and Abrego 2014.

6. Original: "Pues para que [Rosaura] se quedara conmigo porque él de por sí no la quiso llevar y después le decía, 'Oye, mándame dinero y me voy.' '¿Y a qué vienes?' le dice, '¿Qué crees que es tan fácil? Con escoba, ¿viene a barrer el dinero con escoba? Aquí se sufre,' dice."

7. Thirteen years later, in 2018, Manuel was still in Los Angeles and had not returned to Dos Mundos for even a short visit.

8. This number reflects the conversion rate in January 2005.

9. As Rubén Hernández-León noted, "[Migration industry actors] exist and thrive because of [their] distinctive capacity to span such [international] borders" (2008, 156).

10. Hernández-León defines the migration industry as "the ensemble of entrepreneurs who, motivated by the pursuit of financial gain, provide a variety of services facilitating human mobility across international borders" (2008, 156).

11. Target earner migration—along with cyclical migration, where workers enter and exit the country according to seasonal work availability—were far more common in the era before increased border enforcement. The tightening of security along the Mexico-U.S. border, which began in the 1990s, drastically changed large-scale migration patterns. In his work, Robert Courtney Smith (2006) divides migration from Puebla to New York over a span of sixty years (from the 1940s to the 2000s) into four phases. During the last phase, beginning in the late 1990s, more migrants crossed illegally and they were less likely to engage in circular migration due to tightened U.S. border controls and family reunification programs.

12. Original: "Pues gracias a esos días que se fue de aventura, me dejó una casa donde vivir."

13. Original: "Yo pienso que es difícil [estar en los Estados Unidos] porque como le digo que mi esposo me decía ahí, para que pidan de comer, ¿verdad? Como me platicaba, el entraba a restaurantes y él pedía de comer pero no le entendían. Entonces, dice, 'Yo nomás entraba allá y ellos ahí escogieron. Me daban lo que ellos escogían.' Dice, 'Pues yo no quería.' Pues claro que sí es difícil. Allí no conoce uno nada, no sabe uno leer nada de inglés ni nada. Sí, es . . . es triste para mí."

14. These numbers reflect the conversion rate in January 2005.

15. According to the June 2017 exchange rate.

7. CONCLUSION

1. Maya women's networks weakened as a result of the social isolation they experienced on the job as live-in domestics. However, Maya men working in a supermarket chain benefited from an extensive network of coworkers, large-scale hiring practices, and opportunities for promotion.

2. As Menjívar explains, "Obtaining and exchanging help entails a negotiated process of mobilization of resources, in which decisions to ask for and to provide help are contingent and fluid, not predetermined or fixed" (2000, 116).

3. Original: "Pues cuando a veces llegan a hacer juntas, igual, de todos modos—la gente como que cada quien como que se junta cada quien con los suyos. O sea, sí conviven pero . . ."

4. Original: "Ponle que dentro de nuestra comisión haya unos seis, unos siete que no quiera. Y los de ellos supongo que ellos, si son ocho; ponle, cuatro quieran regresar y los otros cuatro no. Entonces, en vez de que se vuelvan a unir o así, ellos pierden integrantes, nosotros perdemos integrantes. Se vuelven a unir y de todos modos quedan—igual quedan desunidos. Cuando pasó todo eso yo no fui, pero muchos lo tomaron muy personal. Como se dijeron varias cosas ahí. Entre ellos pelearon. O sea, verbalmente ¿verdad? Verbalmente, no físicamente, pero igual, yo pienso que se quedan con ese rencor."

AFTERWORD

1. After a series of working groups, organizers decided to focus on food vendors and shifted away from food truck and lunch truck operators, who had their own organization and had previously been successful in modifying ordinances that were restrictive to them. For more on lunch truck operators, see Eagly 2012.

2. The Southern California Library in South Los Angeles has a small archive dedicated to the records of the Asociación de Vendedores Ambulantes.

3. Research activist LeighAnna Hidalgo closely followed the street vendor organizers and helped collaboratively create a mixed-media story tool that offered a look at the struggles vendors faced. See www.streetvendorsforla.org. For more on *fotonovelas*, see Hidalgo 2015.

4. Between 2011 and 2016, I attended meetings and community forums hosted by the LASVC and interviewed organizers affiliated with that organization. I attended council meetings at Los Angeles City Hall and city-sponsored community meetings throughout the city and listened to testimonies provided by street vendors active with LASVC.

APPENDIX

1. Stefan Timmermans, my adviser, likely had some influence given his thinking and development of abductive analysis with my colleague Iddo Tavory. For more, see Timmermans and Tavory 2012.

2. In his work, Elliot Liebow addressed a comparable issue of studying parts as opposed to wholes. When Liebow set out to do his field work, the director of the project directed him to "Go out there and make like an anthropologist." In response to this, Liebow reflected, "'Out there' was not at all like the Indian village of Winisk on Hudson Bay in which I had done field work. I was not at all sure how one 'makes like an anthropologist' in this kind of 'out there.' Somewhat wistfully, perhaps, I thought how much neater things would be if anthropologists, as they had done in the early thirties, limited themselves to the study of

'wholes,' a tribe, a village, or some other social unit with distinct boundaries and small enough to be encompassed in its entirety by direct observation" (2003, 153).

3. I left the field during the summer of 2009 because my father passed away and I returned to Texas to spend time with my mother. When I returned to my fieldwork in Los Angeles, I spent several months reorienting myself with the community. By that time, Carmen and Manuel had begun their work collaboration.

References

Abrego, Leisy. 2014. *Sacrificing Families: Navigating Laws, Labor, and Love across Borders*. Stanford: Stanford University Press.

Agar, Michael H. 1996. *The Professional Stranger: An Informal Introduction to Ethnography*. San Diego: Academic Press.

Alvarez, Robert, Jr.. 1990. "Mexican Entrepreneurs and Markets in the City of Los Angeles: A Case of an Immigrant Enclave." *Urban Anthropology* 19(1–2):99–124.

Ardener, Shirley. 1964. "The Comparative Study of Rotating Credit Associations." *Journal of the Royal Anthropological Institute* 94:201–29.

Armenta, Amada. 2017. *Protect, Serve, and Deport: The Rise of Policing as Immigrant Enforcement*. Oakland: University of California Press.

Bada, Xóchitl. 2014. *Mexican Hometown Associations in Chicagoacán: From Local to Transnational Civic Engagement*. New Brunswick, NJ: Rutgers University Press.

Bailey, Thomas, and Roger Waldinger. 1991. "Primary, Secondary, and Enclave Labor Markets: A Training Systems Approach." *American Sociological Review* 56(4):432–45.

Baradaran, Mehrsa. 2018. *How the Other Half Banks: Exclusion, Exploitaition, and Threat to Democracy*. Cambridge: Harvard University Press.

Bashi, Vilna Francine. 2007. *Survival of the Knitted: Immigrant Social Networks in a Stratified World*. Stanford: Stanford University Press.

Becker, Howard S. 2009. "How to Find Out How to Do Qualitative Research." *International Journal of Communication* 3:545–53.

Browning, Harley L., and Nestor Rodriguez. 1985. "The Migration of Mexican *Indocumentados* as a Settlement Process: Implications for Work." In *Hispanics in the U.S. Economy,* edited by George J. Borjas and Marta Tienda, 277–97. New York: Academic Press.

Brownmiller, Susan. 1984. *Femininity.* New York: Open Road Media.

Castles, Stephen, and Mark J. Miller. 2003. *The Age of Migration: International Population Movements in the Modern World.* New York: Guilford Press.

Chauvin, Sébastien, and Blanca Garcés-Mascareñas. 2012. "Beyond Informal Citizenship: The New Moral Economy of Migrant Illegality." *International Political Sociology* 6(3):241–59.

Cohen, Jeffrey H. 2005. "Remittance Outcomes and Migration: Theoretical Contests, Real Opportunities." *Studies in Comparative International Development* 40(1):88–112.

Cohen, Robin. 1997. *Global Diasporas: An Introduction.* London: University College London Press.

Coutin, Susan Bibler. 2003. *Legalizing Moves: Salvadoran Immigrants' Struggle for U.S. Residency.* Ann Arbor: University of Michigan Press.

Cranford, Cynthia J. 2005. "Networks of Exploitation: Immigrant Labor and the Restructuring of the Los Angeles Janitorial Industry." *Social Problems* 52(3):379–97.

Del Real, Deisy. 2019. "Toxic Ties: The Reproduction of Legal Violence within Mixed-Status Intimate Partners, Relatives, and Friends." *International Migration Review* 53(2):548–70.

Dennis, Mike. 2014. Phone interview conducted by the author. January 30, 2014, Los Angeles.

Du Bois, W. E. B. 1899. *The Philadelphia Negro.* New York: Lippincott.

Duneier, Mitchell. 2000. *Sidewalk.* New York: Farrar, Straus and Giroux.

Duquette-Rury, Lauren, and Xóchitl Bada. 2013. "Continuity and Change in Mexican Migrant Hometown Associations: Evidence from New Survey Research." *Migraciones Internacionales* 7(1):65–99.

Eagly, Ingrid V. 2012. "Criminal Clinics in the Pursuit of Immigrant Rights: Lessons from the Loncheros." *UC Irvine Law Review* 2(1):91–124.

Estrada, Emir. 2019. *Kids at Work: Latinx Families Selling Food on the Streets of Los Angeles.* New York: New York University Press.

Estrada, Emir, and Pierrette Hondagneu-Sotelo. 2010. "Intersectional Dignities: Latino Immigrant Street Vendor Youth in Los Angeles." *Journal of Contemporary Ethnography* 40(1):102–31.

Fink, Leon. 2003. *The Maya of Morganton: Work and Community in the Nuevo New South.* Chapel Hill: University of North California Press.

Fitzgerald, David. 2004. "Beyond 'Transnationalism': Mexican Hometown Politics at an American Labour Union." *Ethnic and Racial Studies* 27(2):228–47.

———. 2006. "Towards a Theoretical Ethnography of Migration." *Qualitative Sociology* 29(1):1–24.

Galison, Peter. 1987. *How Experiments End*. Chicago: University of Chicago Press.

Gammeltoft-Hansen, Thomas, and Ninna Nyberg, eds. 2013. *The Migration Industry and the Commercialization of International Migration*. London: Routledge.

Geertz, Clifford. 1962. "The Rotating Credit Association: A 'Middle Rung' in Development." *Economic Development and Cultural Change* 10(3):241–63.

Glick, Peter, and Susan T. Fiske. 2001. "An Ambivalent Alliance: Hostile and Benevolent Sexism as Complementary Justifications for Gender Inequality." *American Psychologist* 56(2):109–18.

Goffman, Erving. 1959. *The Presentation of Self in Everyday Life*. New York: Anchor Press.

———. 1989. "On Fieldwork." *Journal of Contemporary Ethnography* 18(2):123–32.

Gold, Steve. 1994. "Patterns of Economic Cooperation among Israeli Immigrants in Los Angeles." *International Migration Review* 28(1):114–35.

Granovetter, Mark S. 1973. "The Strength of Weak Ties." *American Journal of Sociology* 78(6):1360–80.

Hagan, Jacqueline Maria. 1994. *Deciding to Be Legal: A Maya Community in Houston*. Philadelphia: Temple University Press.

———. 1998. "Social Networks, Gender, and Immigrant Incorporation: Resources and Constraints." *American Sociological Review* 63(1):55–67.

Hall, Elaine J. 1993. "Smiling, Deferring, and Flirting: Doing Gender by Giving 'Good Service.'" *Work and Occupations* 20(4):452–71.

Hamilton, Nora, and Norma Stoltz Chinchilla. 2001. *Seeking Community in a Global City: Guatemalans and Salvadorans in Los Angeles*. Philadelphia: Temple University Press.

Harney, Robert F. 1977. "The Commerce of Migration." *Canadian Ethnic Studies* 9(1):42–53.

Hernandez, Mike. 2008. Personal interview conducted by the author. March 25, 2008, Los Angeles.

Hernández-León, Rubén. 2005. "The Migration Industry in the Mexico-U.S. Migratory System." California Center for Population Research On-Line Working Paper Series, no. CPR-049–05, University of California, Los Angeles.

———. 2008. *Metropolitan Migrants: The Migration of Urban Mexicans to the United States*. Berkeley: University of California Press.

Hidalgo, LeighAnna. 2015. "Augmented Fotonovelas: Creating New Media as Pedagogical and Social Justice Tools." *Qualitative Inquiry* 21(3): 300–14.

Hondagneu-Sotelo, Pierrette. 1994. *Gendered Transitions: Mexican Experiences of Immigration.* Berkeley: University of California Press.

Howell, Susan E., Huey L. Perry, and Matthew Vile. 2004. "Black Cities/White Cities: Evaluating the Police." *Political Behavior* 26(1):45–68.

INEGI. 2010. "México en cifras: Información nacional, por entidad federativa y municipios." Instituto Nacional de Información Estadística y Geográfica. www.inegi.org.mx/app/areasgeograficas/?ag=21.

Jacobs, Jane. 1961. *The Death and Life of Great American Cities.* New York: Vintage.

Jerolmack, Colin, and Alexandra K. Murphy. 2019. "The Ethical Dilemmas and Social Scientific Trade-Offs of Masking in Ethnography." *Sociological Methods & Research* 48(4):801–27.

Jiménez, Tomás R. 2008. "Mexican Immigrant Replenishment and the Continuing Significance of Ethnicity and Race." *American Journal of Sociology* 113(6):1527–67.

Jones, Richard C. 1988. "Micro Source Regions of Mexican Undocumented Migration." *National Geographic Research* 4(1):11–22.

Kandel, William, and Douglas Massey. 2002. "The Culture of Mexican Migration: A Theoretical and Empirical Analysis." *Social Forces* 80(3):981–1004.

Kettles, Gregg W. 2004. "Regulating Vending in the Sidewalk Commons." *Temple Law Review* 77(1):1–46.

——— 2006. "Formal versus Informal Allocation of Land in a Commons: The Case of MacArthur Park Sidewalk Vendors." *Southern California Interdisciplinary Law Journal* 16(1):49–96.

———. 2007. "Legal Responses to Sidewalk Vending: The Case of Los Angeles, California." In *Street Entrepreneurs: People, Place, and Politics in Local and Global Perspective,* edited by John Cross and Alfonso Morales, 58–78. New York: Routledge.

Kim, Dae Young. 1999. "Beyond Co-Ethnic Solidarity: Mexican and Ecuadorean Employment in Korean-Owned Businesses in New York City." *Ethnic and Racial Studies* 22(3):581–605.

Kubal, Agnieszka. 2013. "Conceptualizing Semi-Legality in Migration Research." *Law & Society Review* 47(3):555–87.

Latour, Bruno, and Steve Woolgar. 1986. *Laboratory of Life: The Construction of Scientific Facts.* Princeton, NJ: Princeton University Press.

Lewis, Oscar. 1959. *Five Families: Mexican Case Studies in the Culture of Poverty.* New York: Basic Books.

Liebow, Elliot. 2003. *Tally's Corner: A Study of Negro Streetcorner Men.* Oxford: Rowman and Littlefield.

Light, Ivan. 2006. *Deflecting Immigration: Networks, Markets, and Regulation in Los Angeles.* New York: Russell Sage Foundation.

Light, Ivan, and Carolyn Rosenstein. 1995. *Race, Ethnicity, and Entrepreneurship in Urban America.* New York: Aldine de Gruyter.

Liu, Yvonne Yen, Patrick Burns, and Daniel Flaming. 2015. "Sidewalk Stimulus: Economic and Geographic Impact of Los Angeles Street Vendors." Los Angeles: Economic Roundtable.

Los Angeles Economic Development Committee. n.d. "Sidewalk Vending Community Meetings and Related Materials." Accessed December 10, 2018. http://sidewalkvending.lacity.org.

Mahler, Sarah J. 1995. *American Dreaming: Immigrant Life on the Margins.* Princeton, NJ: Princeton University Press.

Massey, Douglas, Rafael Alarcón, Jorge Durand, and Humberto González. 1987. *Return to Aztlan: The Social Process of International Migration from Western Mexico.* Berkeley: University of California Press.

Massey, Douglas, Jorge Durand, and Nolan Malone. 2002. *Beyond Smoke and Mirrors: Mexican Immigration in an Era of Economic Integration.* New York: Russell Sage Foundation.

Massey, Douglas, and Kristin E. Espinosa. 1997. "What's Driving Mexico-U.S. Migration: A Theoretical, Empirical, and Policy Analysis." *American Journal of Sociology* 102(4):939–99.

McDowell, Meghan G., and Nancy A. Wonders. 2010. "Keeping Migrants in Their Place: Technologies of Control and Racialized Public Space in Arizona." *Social Justice* 36(2):54–72.

Menjívar, Cecilia. 1997. "Immigrant Kinship Networks and the Impact of the Receiving Context: Salvadorans in San Francisco in the Early 1990s." *Social Problems* 44(1):104–23.

———. 2000. *Fragmented Ties: Salvadoran Immigrant Networks in America.* Berkeley: University of California Press.

———. 2006. "Liminal Legality: Salvadoran and Guatemalan Immigrants' Lives in the United States." *American Journal of Sociology* 111(4):999–1037.

Menjívar, Cecilia, and Leisy J. Abrego. 2012. "Legal Violence: Immigration Law and the Lives of Central American Immigrants." *American Journal of Sociology* 117(5):1380–421.

Mines, Richard, and Ricardo Anzaldua Montoya. 1982. *New Migrants vs. Old Migrants: Alternative Labor Market Structures in the California Citrus Industry.* La Jolla: Center for U.S.-Mexican Studies, UCSD.

Mohajer, Shaya Tayefe. 2018. "Baghdad on the Border." *Curbed,* October 24, 2018. www.curbed.com/a/texas-california/san-diego-immigration-iraqi-california.

Moya, Jose C. 2005. "Immigrants and Associations: A Global and Historical Perspective." *Journal of Ethnic and Migration Studies* 31(5):833–64.

Muñiz, Ana. 2011. "Disorderly Community Partners and Broken Windows Policing." *Ethnography* 13(3):330–51.

Orozco, Manuel. 2002. "Latino Hometown Associations as Agents of Development in Latin America." In *Sending Money Home: Hispanic Remittances and Community Development,* edited by Rodolfo O. de la Garza and Briant Lindsay Lowell, 85–99. Lanham: Rowman and Littlefield.

———. 2003. "Hometown Associations and their Present and Future Partnerships: New Development Opportunities?" In *Inter-American Dialogue,* edited by U.S. Agency for International Development. Washington, DC.

Orozco, Manuel, and Michelle Lapointe. 2004. "Mexican Hometown Associations and Development Opportunities." *Journal of International Affairs* 57(2):1–21.

Patel, Tina Girishbhai. 2012. "Surveillance, Suspicion and Stigma: Brown Bodies in a Terror-Panic Climate." *Surveillance & Society* 10(3/4): 215–34.

Peck, Gunther. 2000. *Reinventing Free Labor: Padrones and Immigrant Workers in the North American West 1880–1930.* Cambridge: Cambridge University Press.

Petrissans, Catherine M. 2018. "Ethnic Identity Formation among Basque-American Adolescents." *BOGAL Basque Studies Consortium Journal* 6(1):1–17.

Portes, Alejandro. 1981. "Modes of Structural Incorporation and Present Theories of Labor Immigration." In *Global Trends in Migration,* edited by M. M. Kritz, Charles B. Keely, and S. M. Tomasi, 279–97. New York: Center for Migration Studies.

Portes, Alejandro, and Robert L. Bach. 1985. *Latin Journey: Cuban and Mexican Immigrants in the United States.* Berkeley: University of California Press.

Portes, Alejandro, and Julia Sensenbrenner. 1993. "Embeddedness and Immigration: Notes on the Social Determinants of Economic Action." *American Journal of Sociology* 98(6):1320–50.

Portes, Alejandro, and Alex Stepick. 1985. "Unwelcome Immigrants: The Labor Market Experiences of 1980 (Mariel) Cuban and Haitian Refugees in South Florida." *American Sociological Review* 50:493–514.

Provine, Doris Marie, Monica W. Varsanyi, Paul G. Lewis, and Scott H. Decker. 2016. *Policing Immigrants: Local Law Enforcement on the Front Lines.* Chicago: University of Chicago Press.

Ramirez, Hernan. 2011. "Masculinity in the Workplace: The Case of Mexican Immigrant Gardeners." *Men and Masculinities* 14(1):97–116.

Rath, Jan, and Robert Kloosterman. 2000. "Outsiders' Business: A Critical Review of Research on Immigrant Entrepreneurship." *International Migration Review* 34(3):657–81.

Reyes, Emily Alpert. 2018. "After Years of Debate, L.A. Legalizes Sidewalk Vending: 'This Means Freedom.'" *Los Angeles Times,* November 28, 2018.

Ribas, Vanesa. 2015. *On the Line: Slaughterhouse Lives and the Making of the New South.* Oakland: University of California Press.

Ridgeway, Cecilia L. 2011. *Framed by Gender: How Gender Inequality Persists in the Modern World.* New York: Oxford University Press.

Rios, Victor M. 2009. "The Consequences of the Criminal Justice Pipeline on Black and Latino Masculinity." *Annals of the American Academy of Political and Social Science* 623(1):150–62.

Rodriguez, Javier. 1995. "Community Essay: 'Not a Single Vendor Has a License'; Los Angeles' Effort to Set Up a Permanent Legal Vending District along the Lines of Olvera Street Is Too Small in Size and Vision." *Los Angeles Times,* November 18, 1995.

Rodriguez, Nestor. 2004. "'Workers Wanted': Employer Recruitment of Immigrant Labor." *Work and Occupations* 31(4):453–73.

Romero, Sandra. 2006. Personal interview conducted by the author. August 2, 2006, Los Angeles.

Rosenbaum, Dennis P., Amie M. Schuck, Sandra K. Costello, Darnell F. Hawkins, and Marianne K. Ring. 2005. "Attitudes towards the Police: The Effects of Direct and Vicarious Experience." *Police Quarterly* 8(3): 343–65.

Sanders, Jimy M., and Victor Nee. 1987. "The Limits of Ethnic Solidarity in the Enclave Economy." *American Sociological Review* 52(6):745–73.

Sassen, Saskia. 1990. "Economic Restructuring and the American City." *Annual Review of Sociology* 16(1):465–90.

———. 1993. *The Global City: New York, London, Tokyo.* Princeton, NJ: Princeton University Press.

Saucedo, Leticia M. 2006. "The Employer Preference for the Subservient Worker and the Making of the Brown Collar Workplace." *Ohio State Law Journal* 67(5):961–1022.

Seron, Carroll, Joseph Pereira, and Jean Kovath. 2004. "Judging Police Misconduct: 'Street-Level' versus Professional Policing." *Law & Society Review* 38(4):665–710.

Sluska, Sara, and Sean Basinski. 2006. "Peddling Uphill: A Report on the Conditions of Street Vendors in New York City." Street Vendor Project. www.scribd.com/document/18948529/Peddling-Uphill.

Smith, Robert C. 1996. "Mexicans in New York: Membership and Incorporation in a New Immigrant Community." In *Latinos in New York,* edited by S. Baver and G. Haslip Viera, 57–103. South Bend: University of Notre Dame Press.

———. 2006. *Mexican New York: Transnational Lives of New Immigrants.* Berkeley: University of California Press.

Southern California Library Archives. 2001. "Asociación de Vendedores Ambulantes (Street Vendors Association) Records, 1986–1995." Los Angeles, CA: Southern California Library.

Stack, Carol B. 1974. *All Our Kin: Strategies for Survival in a Black Community*. New York: Harper Collins.

Theiss-Morse, Elizabeth, and John R. Hibbing. 2005. "Citizenship and Civic Engagement." *Annual Review of Political Science* 8:227–49.

Tilly, Charles. 2007. "Trust Networks in Transnational Migration." *Sociological Forum* 22(1):3–24.

Timmermans, Stefan, and Iddo Tavory. 2012. "Theory Construction in Qualitative Research: From Grounded Theory to Abductive Analysis." *Sociological Theory* 30(3):167–86.

Waldinger, Roger. 1994. "The Making of an Immigrant Niche." *International Migration Review* 28(1):3–30.

Waldinger, Roger, and Michael I. Lichter. 2003. *How the Other Half Works: Immigration and the Social Organization of Labor*. Berkeley: University of California Press.

Weber, Max. 2001. *The Protestant Ethic and the Spirit of Capitalism*. London: Routledge Classics.

Weitzer, Ronald, and Steven A. Tuch. 2004. "Race and Perceptions of Police Misconduct." *Social Problems* 51(3):305–25.

Wherry, Frederick F., Kristin S. Seefeldt, and Anthony S. Alvarez. 2019. *Credit Where It's Due: Rethinking Financial Citizenship*. New York City: Russell Sage Foundation.

Whyte, William Foote. 1993. *Street Corner Society: The Social Structure of an Italian Slum*. Chicago: University of Chicago Press.

Zabin, Carol, and Luis Escala. 2002. "From Civic Association to Political Participation: Mexican Hometown Associations and Mexican Immigrant Political Empowerment in Los Angeles." *Frontera Norte* 14(27):7–42.

Zhou, Min. 1992. *Chinatown: The Socioeconomic Potential of an Urban Enclave*. Philadelphia: Temple University Press.

———. 2004. "Revisiting Ethnic Entrepreneurship: Convergencies, Controversies, and Conceptual Advancements." *International Migration Review* 38(3):1040–74.

Index

access: to customers and infrastructure in risk management, 55–57; to *fruteros* in fieldwork, 16–17, 155, 156; to storage for pushcarts, 86–87; to *tandas*, 81, 178n2; to work spaces, in fieldwork, 154, 160
adaptability, 136, 175n1
adventure, as motivation for migration, 30, 42–43, 117, 129, 131, 133
agency, human, 138, 154–55
agricultural work, 115, 117
Agustina (mother of Cristian), 129–30
alerts, in risk management, 61–64, 77
Alicia (*frutera*), 101–2, 103–5, 106–7, 108–9, 111–12
alliance-building, 18, 56, 58–61, 65–72, 77
Alvarez, Robert Jr., 21
Ambulatory Vendors, Association for (AVA), 146–47
anonymity of respondents, 169–70n1
antivending ordinances, 7, 8–9, 46–47, 66–67, 77–78, 146–50, 172nn13–14. *See also* ordinances and policies, local
aprons as symbolic hygiene, 73, 74
Ardener, Shirley, 179n3
arrests: in crackdowns, 8–9, 56–57, 63–65; in deportation, 172–73n16; of Jesús, 63–65, 74; managing risk of, 66–67, 77–78; of Manuel, 18, 40–41, 98, 99, 101, 104–5,

111–13, 162–63; in marginalization, 18; risk of, 22–23, 55
Attorney Administrative Citation Enforcement (ACE) Program, 9, 172n15
autonomy, 29–30, 45

Bach, Robert L., 49
bail, 22–23, 61, 105–6, 108
Bashi, Vilna Francine, 175n1
Becker, Howard S., 171n11
border crossings: of Carmen, 27–28; of Cristian, 30–33, 130; employers in, 44–45; of Gonzalo, 42–43, 134–35; of Jesús, 36; of Manuel, 39–40
boundaries: employers traversing, 37–38; interactional, 155, 159–60
Brown, Jerry, 149

Camilo (father of Jesús), 126–28
capital, socioeconomic, 5, 44–45, 49–50, 124–25, 138, 171n7
Carmen (*frutera*): baptism celebration for children of, 143–45; flirtation in interactions with customers, 163–65; in LAPD/LACDPH crackdown, 53–55; location-based altercation of, 60–61; in Manuel's crisis, 103–11; occupational trajectory of, 25, 26–30; remittances to Cristian's

191

Founded in 1893,
UNIVERSITY OF CALIFORNIA PRESS
publishes bold, progressive books and journals
on topics in the arts, humanities, social sciences,
and natural sciences—with a focus on social
justice issues—that inspire thought and action
among readers worldwide.

The UC PRESS FOUNDATION
raises funds to uphold the press's vital role
as an independent, nonprofit publisher, and
receives philanthropic support from a wide
range of individuals and institutions—and from
committed readers like you. To learn more, visit
ucpress.edu/supportus.